LIFE WISDOM FROM A SMOOTH JESUS
AND A CLUMSY COLLEGE PASTOR

Smyth & Helwys Publishing, Inc.
6316 Peake Road
Macon, Georgia 31210-3960
1-800-747-3016
©2023 by Skyler Daniel
All rights reserved.

100% of the author's royalties are donated directly to Project Ruth in Bucharest, Romania, a Christian mission that serves the Roma community through education and humanitarian aid. More info can be found at facebook.com/projectruthromania or instagram.com/projectruth.

Library of Congress Cataloging-in-Publication Data

Names: Daniel, Skyler, author.
Title: Practical life wisdom from a smooth Jesus and a clumsy college pastor / by Skyler Daniel.
Description: Macon, GA : Smyth & Helwys, 2023. | Includes indexes.
Identifiers: LCCN 2022051537 | ISBN 9781641734141 (paperback)
Subjects: LCSH: Christian youth--Prayers and devotions. | Conduct of life--Christianity. | Spiritual life--Anecdotes. | Devotional calendars. | Jesus Christ--Example.
Classification: LCC BV4850 .D36 2023 | DDC 242/.63--dc23/eng/20230127
LC record available at https://lccn.loc.gov/2022051537

Disclaimer of Liability: With respect to statements of opinion or fact available in this work of nonfiction, Smyth & Helwys Publishing Inc. nor any of its employees, makes any warranty, express or implied, or assumes any legal liability or responsibility for the accuracy or completeness of any information disclosed, or represents that its use would not infringe privately-owned rights.

Advance Praise for
Life Wisdom from a Smooth Jesus and a Clumsy College Pastor

Skyler Daniel is one of the bright young ascending leaders who gives me hope for the mission of God in North America. He is able to do evangelistic work among college students (and many others), not by resorting to trite formulas or hackneyed cliches, but by making the gospel intelligible and compelling in post-Christendom contexts. I hope this is the first of many books from Skyler.

—*John P. Chandler*
Founder of uptick.org and author of Uptick: A Blueprint for Finding and Forming the Next Generation of Pioneering Kingdom Leaders

Rev. Daniel speaks from the heart in *Life Wisdom* and delivers simple lessons to reflect on each day. His messages, ranging from as little as thirty seconds to no more than five minutes, show us how our own everyday actions can affect—improve—the lives of many when those actions come from a deep connection to Christ. And although his writings are ostensibly aimed at a generation of people in their twenties, *Life Wisdom* is not just for the young! Rev. Daniel's reflections bring inspiration to readers of all ages. His heartfelt messages of hope, spiritual resilience and compassion offer reader-friendly and practical Christian guidance during unsettling times. This book is a wonderful bedside companion for all.

—*Dr. Tiffany Franks*
President, Averett University
Danville, Virginia

Studies have consistently shown students' faith engagement during the transition from high school to college is spotty at best. Skyler Daniel's wit and relatability come through his devotionals. His words are practical and point to Christ's grace and love. Every college student should have a copy!

—*Rev. Andy Jung, DMin*
Senior Director of Church Engagement
Fuller Youth Institute

Our choices in young adulthood determine the course of our lives—yet we are often ill-prepared for these important decisions. Skyler writes with a unique combination of grace and wit, connecting daily experience with spiritual truth. This book is a wonderful guide for young adults who are finding their way in a wide world.

—Andrew Garnett
Pastor, Hampton Baptist Church
Hampton, Virginia

For a young generation weary of insincere and inapplicable religious platitudes, *Life Wisdom* provides authentic meditations on real life from one who genuinely desires for students to embody real faith. Through each reflection, Skyler Daniel combines the wisdom of Holy Scripture with his own personal faithful and sometimes fumbling efforts to follow Jesus. *Life Wisdom* offers the kind of essential support every college student needs in their journey with Jesus; it offers a thoughtful and caring friend to travel with them.

—Welford Orrock
Kairos Collegiate/Young Adult Coordinator,
Baptist General Association of Virginia (BGAV)

In *Life Wisdom from a Smooth Jesus and a Clumsy College Pastor*, Skyler Daniel provides a collection of devotionals designed for today's college student. They can be read in just a few minutes, but they have the power to help students connect with Jesus, follow his wisdom, and be transformed. Every page offers good news for students who will take up and read.

—Ralph K. Hawkins, PhD
Author of Discovering Exodus *and*
Ancient Wisdom for the Good Life
Averett University

LIFE WISDOM
FROM A SMOOTH JESUS
- AND -
A CLUMSY COLLEGE PASTOR

SKYLER DANIEL

For Dad

*If only I could show you
trails across this valley,
good things God is doing in my little church,
a granddaughter's living room piano concert,
a grandson who loves Luke Skywalker with the green lightsaber,
and of course,
even something
like this.*

Acknowledgments

I want to thank Bruce Wilson, my former pastor, for helping me find a place to land in the dizzying world of modern ministry, showing me a way to bring Jesus Christ into the center of our common human life. This book simply would not have happened were it not for Bruce's guiding spiritual wisdom in the years leading up to its production.

Averett University, Lesley Villarose, and Dr. Tiffany Franks, too, deserve credit for this book. They provided its incubator, giving me the professional freedom in my years as their chaplain to write to our disparate and diverse community of students, trying to point them back to Jesus in the many pressures of college life.

Contents

Introduction 1

January

    high wires 3
    the broken guitar 4
    Jesus and Mujica 5
    picking up hope 7
    sparrows and androids 8
    heavy laden 9
    the helper 10
    houses 11
    find joy 12
    "help the poor," part 1 13
    "help the poor," part 2 15
    "help the poor," part 3 16
    "help the poor," part 4 17
    "help the poor," part 5 18
    Jesus math 19

February

    underground 21
    respect 22
    oxygen 24
    forgotten people 25
    sex 26
    birth pains 27
    exorcism 28
    friends 29
    blame 30
    choice 31

Lazarus is dead: spiritual resilience, part 1 32
Jesus is weeping: spiritual resilience, part 2 32
responsible: spiritual resilience, part 3 33
control: spiritual resilience, part 4 34
options: spiritual resilience, part 5 34

March

let it go: spiritual resilience, part 6 37
consume 38
screaming 39
beware! 40
tie down clouds 41
the plastic bottle 42
books 43
church 44
my unbelief 45
songs about justice 46
peasants and gods 48
dry 49
Palm Sundays 50
that guy 51
upon your lips 53

April

stunned 55
eyeballs 56
crosses 58
rivers and caves 58
think of it 60
pressure 61
rise again 62
influencers 63
sparrows 65
trying 65
rat park 66
dopamine 67
flowers 68
he withdrew 69
the goose 70

May

- ancestors 73
- wedding invitations 74
- 352 quintillion 75
- surprised by goodness 76
- pronouns 78
- sledgehammers 79
- slanderous lies 80
- a helper 81
- rise 83
- back to here 84
- boxes and stars 85
- ready. set. fail. 87
- beloved 88
- silence 89
- Saturdays and Sundays 90

June

- religion 93
- spilling salt 94
- terrible and horrible and awful 95
- patience 96
- sunshine and shadows 97
- faith and heart 99
- Roger 100
- the beginning of murder 101
- the devil 102
- holes in the sky 104
- salt 105
- spilled milk 106
- keep fishing 107
- air is grace 109
- treasures 110

July

- Skyler's fence 111
- enough 112
- foreigners 113

what is normal 115
dress well 117
crazy uncles.. 118
more freedom 119
empty crosses 120
belonging.. 121
threshold... 123
resurrected life 124
biscuits 125
tables 127
a deserted place 128
blind guides 129

August
birds 131
college culture... 132
Zebedee 133
in you 134
never lose heart 135
broken grace 137
seasons.. 138
character... 139
gentle... 140
pages.. 141
responsibility 143
tomorrow.. 144
unmeasured 145
friends and missions... 147
possibility 148

September
worry 151
above 151
prayer and compassion.. 153
family 154
the dark 155
ugly demon.. 157
had to 159
loneliness 160

arrived 161
return to you.. 162
the logic of Jesus 163
the truth: part 1 of seeing clearly in unclear times 165
sell everything: part 2 of seeing clearly in unclear times................ 166
hopeful: part 3 of seeing clearly in unclear times.......................... 168
on the ground... 169

October

drowned rats.. 173
breath 174
broken pieces... 175
cathedrals and castles 176
broken treadmill 177
the perfectionist... 178
alone in my room 179
solicitors 181
pouring ointment 183
the performer... 184
debts.. 186
scary things.. 188
vulnerable Jesus... 189
rest... 191
pale blue dot.. 192

November

thrones 195
stillness: part 1 of centering prayer... 196
lamentation: part 2 of centering prayer 197
confession: part 3 of centering prayer.. 199
gratitude: part 4 of centering prayer 200
trust: part 5 of centering prayer.. 202
surrender: part 6 of centering prayer 203
save thanksgiving... 204
boring.. 205
red pills.. 207
good people 208
how to get to heaven.. 210
deep... 211

people 212
loneliness 213

December

home and family 215
free time 216
expensive blenders 218
the origins of peace 219
boat ride 220
soccer games 221
plosions 223
van rides to Disney 224
judgment 225
heartbreak 226
the first Christmas 227
gifts 228
how to be happy 229
the observer 230
habits 232

Scripture Index 235
Topic Index 239

Introduction

My first week at college, I parked my kind-of-fancy new mountain bike in the bike rack outside my dormitory, O'Bannon Hall. I had an expensive, thief-proof bike lock, impossible to cut through, that I looped through the front wheel and the rack. (That was about five seconds faster than me running the lock through the bike frame.) The next morning, a lot of bikes were missing. A smart thief knew that scores of naive eighteen-year-olds had just arrived with new bikes. There was my front wheel, securely locked to the rack. The rest of my bike had easily been released from the front wheel and was gone. Oops.

The late teens through early twenties is a time when virtually all people will make some unfortunate life decisions. It's not that we're trying to be dumb. (OK, some of us are trying.) It's just that until we're about twenty-five, we have to deal with an underdeveloped prefrontal cortex and an overdeveloped limbic system. Plus, we have little actual experience adulting. We likely have little money and lots of heartbreak, and life is filled with lots of wanting and less having. Even while these years often have plenty of excitement, they are mostly messy and hard.

Jesus can make it better. I promise. Just take a few minutes a day, literally less than five minutes, to connect with the story of Jesus and follow his sage wisdom. Your relationships and your inner life can run a little smoother. You can be a more positive, life-giving person in your world. You can be connected with God. Jesus is truly helpful. Jesus indeed saves.

This book is not about how to get to heaven or hell after you die. (There are plenty of other great books about that.) This is about how Jesus can make your twenties a little less hellish and can use you to usher God's kingdom into your own heart and into the suffering world around you. This is a spiritual but practical book. Every page offers a little good news for your life.

Keep this book by your bed. You'll see that there are fifteen devotionals for each month, acknowledging that most of us will probably do well to read one every other day. Also, call your mom sometimes. (Or your dad, or whoever was so crazy for you they bought you this book.) Jesus's practical life wisdom and his good people can help you sort it all out as you go.

In Christ,
Skyler

January

high wires

> *"Peace I leave with you; my peace I give to you. I do not give to you as the world gives. Do not let your hearts be troubled, and do not let them be afraid."* —John 14:27 (NIV)

I know. Things are hard and crazy right now. You've been here, what, a week? Already you're freaking out about a class, your health feels frayed, you've totally embarrassed yourself, you're caught up in some drama, or you feel like you don't belong here.

Life is such a balancing act on such a very high wire. How in the world can we manage each class, each relationship, each dollar we possess (and we don't possess many)? How can we stay on top of all this?

Here are two questions: What gives you peace in life? What takes it away?

Folks who walk high wires and slack lines don't succeed with aggression and frenzy and reaction. They take deep breaths. They focus. They get ahead of the problem. It is an art of peace.

What gives you peace in life? What takes it away?

Managing the storm is not an issue of changing your external circumstances, not about how popular or good-looking you are, not about how athletic or intelligent you are. The key to overcoming the storm lies inside of you.

What gives you peace in life? What takes it away?

I know religious folks can sometimes be more stressful than peaceful, with lots of impossibly high standards, constant judgment, and angry preachers. But Jesus and many of his followers are not like this. The peace he offers you right now will save your sanity and get you through this. Jesus really does save.

Jesus doesn't give peace like our world gives. Jesus offers unconditional and limitless love. Jesus offers the promise of God's presence through the storm. Jesus offers his brothers and sisters other people who embody his teachings of acceptance, inclusion, welcome, forgiveness, and support.

Will you find those people of peace? Will you reconnect yourself to Jesus and his message? Will you pull yourself away from the things and people and ideas that take away your peace?

Do not give up. Do not be afraid. Do not be troubled. Peace can be yours, and with a little help from Jesus and his followers, you can do whatever you have to do.

broken guitar

The Word became flesh and made his dwelling among us. We have seen his glory, the glory of the one and only Son, who came from the Father, full of grace and truth.—John 1:14

My family moved to a new place right before I began high school. By January of that year, I was still working on building friendships and our family was still church shopping. My mom told me I had to go on a weekend youth retreat with her friend's church. I didn't know the kids and only consented to go if I could bring along my beautiful new acoustic guitar, which I had received for Christmas that year. It was the most extravagant gift I had ever received.

As it turned out, I got along terribly with that youth group, which talked dirty and drank secretly on the church trip. I was in my hotel room strumming my guitar and propped it up at the foot of the bed to step out for a second. My hyperactive sixth grade roommate, Nick, was flying around our room. He rolled down my bed and knocked the guitar before he landed right on it and snapped it in half.

I stormed out of the room and went for a walk, praying that God would reveal his glory and fix my guitar. I believed with all my heart God would do it. I would tell the world what an awesome God I worshipped. I went back to my room. When I returned, my guitar was still just as broken. It was then, that I slowly began to see God for who God really was.

"The Word of God took on flesh." It's hard to believe that God could take on something as corruptible and finite as flesh. I wanted my God to be impenetrable, unmoving, and all powerful. I wanted my God to be a conquering hero who could mow down all my problems. I was less interested in a God who would take on my flesh, who would take on my problems into the folds of his own vulnerable skin.

The problem with gods who make our problems go away is that they are the gods of spiritual immaturity. They blast away mountains and raise up valleys in front of us, and our characters, our spirits, and our hearts are never refined and shaped and molded further into the image of Jesus. As long as we have no challenges, we can remain spiritual infants.

God had bigger plans for me on the day my most extravagant gift was destroyed—plans not to say *yes* to my prayers and give me a "flesh-free" life, one devoid of suffering. I began to see the one true God . . . the God who takes on my flesh, the God who is always with me in the catastrophes of a normal human life. In other words, the God of the Bible was here, not to fix my life, but to have a relationship within it.

Seeing God as God is, the God who takes on flesh instead of the God who fixes all my circumstances, helps me become a person who is more interested in being present to people who are suffering and hurting, more interested in empathizing with hurting people, than being someone trying to fix their problems.

Today, may you believe in a God who takes on your vulnerable skin and makes his dwelling in the imperfect, messy life you are living. When disaster strikes, may you pray for God to be with you and to give you strength, instead of making all the messes go away. And when the people around you suffer, may you take on their flesh and make your dwelling alongside them, just like you see Jesus doing.

Jesus and Mujica

> *[Jesus said,]* "*Whoever wishes to be great among you must be your servant, and whoever wishes to be first among you must be your slave; just as the Son of Man came not to be served but to serve, and to give his life a ransom for many.*" —Matthew 28:27-28

I want to tell you about Jose Mujica. Mujica lived on a small chrysanthemum farm with his wife and three-legged dog, Manuela. He happily lived off of $1,200 a year and drove a 1987 Volkswagen valued at $1,800, and when he got sick, he waited in the long line of the local public hospital used by the poor.

He was also the president of the country Uruguay.

You see, Jose and his wife were supposed to live in a presidential palace, manned by a host of personal maids, butlers, and staff. He was supposed to ride around in a limousine with bodyguards and live off his presidential salary of $12,000 a year. He was supposed to receive the highest standard of health care in his country at a private hospital.

But Mujica, the leader of his country, understood that "whoever wishes to be great among you must be your servant." Do you?

Our minds constantly ponder the ways we are better than others. I am better because . . .

I'm a better student.
I'm a better athlete or musician.
I'm a better Christian.

The stories we play in our heads manifest in our actions, our lives, and our relationships even without us realizing it. Our culture idolizes people like Kobe Bryant and Taylor Swift and Chance the Rapper and preachers in expensive suits and private jets and anything else that promises prosperity to faithful followers.

But Jesus said, "whoever wishes to be first among you must be your slave."

Who among you has a poster of Mother Teresa or Jose Mujica? Who among you carries a photograph of Pope Francis dining with the homeless or Jesus washing Peter's feet?

Jesus laid down his life and showed the world a radically different model of leadership and living life. Instead of focusing on himself and always trying to win, Jesus focused on everyone else and he let them win. He let them crucify him on a cross, trusting that God would vindicate and resurrect his life and honor.

Jesus set his attention on healing others and setting them free from their demons. He got on his hands and knees and washed the grime from his followers' feet.

Jesus, the Son of God, the King of kings, the Creator of the universe, the Lord of all did not come to be served but to serve others.

I want my life to look like that, and I'm not so sure it does. I want to expend my resources on others rather than myself. I want to esteem others and not myself. I want to be strong enough to appreciate others when they are better than me at something. I want to serve others from the deepest parts of my mind and heart to the outer expressions of my actions. And I want to help the poor, to assist needy kids with their homework and bring food to hungry people and relief to hurricane survivors.

I want to be like Jesus and Mujica—joyful, content, thankful, at peace, and a servant to all.

picking up hope

> [Jesus said,] "You are the light of the world.... Let your light shine before people, so they can see the good things you do and praise your Father who is in heaven." —Matthew 5:14a, 16

If you visit the memorial to the 1995 Oklahoma City bombing, you will find twin bronze gates. One of the gates is inscribed with "9:01," memorializing the final, preceding moment of peace. At 9:02 AM, the bomb exploded, killing 168 people and devastating our national conscience. The opposing twin gate is inscribed with "9:03."

The memorial's designing artist said that "9:03" was the moment that the healing began.

All eyes were on Jesus, and he was considered a great teacher—possibly even one whom thousands could follow into battle to victory over the Romans. Yet he repositioned that positive attention to look at the crowd of oppressed Jewish peasants listening to him—"you are the light of the world," he said. They were overwhelmed by the despair of their oppression and the success of evil powers in the world. They were poor and powerless. They wanted to follow the light of another. Yet Jesus radically transformed how they, and we, discover hope in dark times.

To follow Jesus is to hear these words spoken over you: "Let your light shine before people." You must hear these words when the darkness around you is great. When you despair because evil is in the world. When you despair because life is hard. When you despair because people disappoint you, betray you, hurt you. When "9:02" falls upon you, you must hear these words again: "Let your light shine before people." We earnestly want the world to be filled with light and goodness, but Jesus insists that we hold fast to the one thing we can control—the light that we receive from God and choose to shine in this world.

This is how we pick up hope when it has fallen away. We remember Jesus's words about our identity. We let our light shine for others to see goodness and even see God. We let the hope and healing begin with us.

sparrows and androids

"Even the very hairs of your head are all numbered." —Matthew 10:30

You push your cart up to the conveyor belt and unload your items.
She scans your food.
You stop texting.
You swipe your plastic card.
You grab your stuff.
"Thank you. Have a nice day."
"Yes, you too, thank you."
Done.

Rewind. Somewhere between the cell phone, the plastic card, and the employee in the green apron, between the cash register, the conveyor belt, and the profusion of polyethylene bags, there is a human. She has a name.

Much like the machines surrounding her, she has a capitalistic purpose: assist you with an efficient, accurate, and cordial checkout at the grocery store. Make you happy. Feed your ego. She was trained to do what the machines were designed to do.

But she was not designed like the machines. She was formed in the womb, threaded together like a masterful quilt, mathematically perfect, scientifically phenomenal, and artfully magnificent—not by humans but by God—and guess what? God didn't design her to be your ego-satisfying button presser.

According to Jesus, the woman at the register is of limitless value, interesting, and important . . . even mysterious. She was carefully formed by God as a human being before she became your corporate android at the checkout counter. She has deep concerns, hopes, dreams, feelings.

Don't treat people like machines. Put your phone down and ask them how they're doing. Maybe even address them by the name on their name tag. Ask them about their shift. Make a joke. Make eye contact. Be grateful for the person giving you one of your favorite things . . . food. Smile.

Jesus said that the very hairs on our heads are numbered and that we have more value than all the sparrows in the field. Each encounter with a person is a gift, and when we treat people like they are valuable, we are living like Jesus lived. We are living in a different kind of kingdom—one founded on love and faith instead of determination to please the self.

heavy laden

"Come to me, all you who labor and are heavy laden, and I will give you rest. Take my yoke upon you and learn from me, for I am gentle and lowly in heart, and you will find rest for your souls." —Matthew 11:28-29

"I hate myself." Have you ever said those words? Perhaps the better question is, how many times have you said those words? Or how many times today? Perhaps, for you, it is a common refrain.

It is true that we live in a cruel world, but I sometimes wonder if it's not our own heads that make it so vicious. An individual makes one critical or cruel remark to us, and we repeat the line a thousand times, debating its truth, twisting its knife, descending . . . descending . . . descending.

It is exhausting to hate ourselves. The truth is that we can never measure up to our own demands and the impossible standards that our society (and even our religion) impose on us. We are our own cruel masters. And those who manage to convince themselves that they are indeed valuable because they are prettier, or smarter, or holier—their delusion is shallow, frail, and hurtful to those around them.

The solution is not to finally attain perfection or to rest in shallow self-esteem that constantly makes excuses and convinces ourselves that indeed, "I am truly pretty, smart, righteous." No. Jesus teaches us how to remove this terrible weight on our shoulders: through compassion.

"I am gentle and lowly in heart." Be gentle with others. Be humble with others. Be gentle with yourself. Be humble with yourself.

You are not perfect. She is prettier than you or smarter than you, and he is more talented than you or funnier than you. That's OK. Jesus was gentle with the imperfect people around him, and he showed us how to treat ourselves and those around us. Living with this compassionate love is the truly good, rewarding life. Be like Jesus to the imperfect people around and within you, and surround yourself with the kinds of people who follow his teaching to be gentle, lowly, and compassionate.

In that place, with those people, you can lay down the heavy burden of self-hatred.

the helper

After he had dismissed them, he went up on a mountainside by himself to pray. —Matthew 14:23

When I think of some of my deepest desires in life, they include to be the best husband, dad, friend, minister, and neighbor I can possibly be. And therein lies an even deeper longing: to have the greatest marriage, the happiest family, and spaces of deep, spiritual healing and salvation in my ministry and daily life.

But this deep longing in my heart leaves me wide open to temptation, pain, and struggle. The truth is that such love and care are often not reciprocated. Or it seems that I'm more interested in helping people than they are in helping themselves. Or I quietly sacrifice my own well-being to help while secretly feeling resentful. Or I make mistakes and my relationships aren't perfect, and so I feel disappointed and not good enough. I also have this helper ego: I yearn to be appreciated, adored, and owed for all the "wonderful" things I have done for others. When I more deeply examine this helper attitude of mine, I begin to wonder who I'm really "helping" after all.

Perhaps you have experienced some of these feelings.

Jesus was no doubt a helper. He was constantly pressed by crowds to heal them, liberate them, and teach them, and the Bible says that usually, he did. Once, he was walking through Jericho when a blind man cried out for help. Everyone pressed Jesus to keep walking, but he insisted that he would help this man. Jesus was a helper.

But the Gospels periodically record Jesus escaping the crowds to be alone and pray. For Jesus, prayer was centering and restorative, an invitation to draw God into every dark corner of the heart and the world, to move hard things from isolation to connection. Prayer meant resting in vulnerable, intimate trust with a weary mind and heart. Jesus begged his disciples to pray alongside him in a garden when he felt afraid and anxious, because prayer was about connection with God but also about connection with others.

Jesus valued his self and his well-being, so sometimes he told the crowds "no" and said "yes" to connecting with his deeper self, with God, and with his closest friends in prayer. There he could experience rest in trust. The result was that Jesus was not desperate for attention and adoration. Jesus was not burned out and used up. He was balanced. What are other ways for helpers to find restoration? Meditation, walking, reading, music, exercise, play, and laughter are some suggestions. Dismiss the crowds and make space for what you need when you need it.

Many often point to Jesus's crucifixion as a model for how we should let others bulldoze us and take advantage of us as we offer unending help. But the New Testament teaches that Jesus's sacrifice was to be the sacrifice to end all sacrifices, the sacrifice to put an end to and save us from sacrifice, to set us free so we can finally be OK with knowing we can disappoint people when we need to. It is true that self-sacrifice is unavoidably called for in times of great crisis, but the call, good news, and vision of the gospel is for sacrifice to be rare. Jesus wants to save helpers. May you follow him to the mountainside and rest with him.

houses

But the Pharisees and the teachers of the law who belonged to their sect complained to his disciples, "Why do you eat and drink with tax collectors and sinners?" Jesus answered them, "It is not the healthy who need a doctor, but the sick." —Luke 5:30-31

In fall 2015, my wife and I bought our first home. We love it. It's right in the city and has a sizable fenced-in backyard, a screened-in porch, and even more space than we wanted. When we were new to town and house shopping, lots of folks we knew felt obligated to warn us of certain streets and sections of town to avoid: "That street is shady," or "Don't even think about that neighborhood." Then there were the looks of mortified terror when describing potential homes on potential streets. We had just moved from the poorest neighborhood of Bucharest, Romania, where most folks live on two dollars a day. I suppose we were less phased by some things than other people.

The operating assumption of house shopping in our culture is basically that if you live in particular areas, you risk being robbed, being attacked, having noisy or weird neighbors, and being surrounded by ugly houses and yards. I think the risks are usually exaggerated a bit, but there is certainly some truth in it too. It is definitely desirable to have decent neighbors and be zoned for good schools!

I wonder, where would Jesus buy a house? Step down the rabbit hole with me.

Where would Jesus sit in the dining hall? With whom would Jesus pursue friendship?

Sometimes I wonder, if Jesus were around today, would he intentionally make all the wrong decisions? Rent an apartment on the wrong street? Befriend the weirdo down the hall? Eat dinner at the local homeless shelter? Go to church with the poor? Laugh with the "trailer park trash" and play with the kids in the housing project and show grace to the girl whose reputation is pretty bad?

I think Jesus would spend all his time with all the wrong people in all the wrong places. I think he would do that because that is what he did. He was mocked and criticized for eating with traitor tax collectors and scandalous sinners, and it led him down a path of being executed between two criminals.

Today, I pray that we wake up. To follow Jesus is to become a doctor for the sick, not the healthy. May we pursue friendship outside our comfort zones. May we step off that ladder towards the proverbial but empty "top." May we buy houses on "shady" streets and enjoy the company of annoying people. May we see the image of God in surprising people and discover beauty in surprising places. May we stir others to wonder, what do they have that I do not?

find joy

"But I say to you, love your enemies and pray for those who harass you." —Matthew 5:44

"You don't have to like certain people; the Bible just says you've gotta love them."

I first heard that twenty years ago at church, and I'm still trying to figure out what the speaker and everyone who repeated the same words later meant. How can you love someone if you don't like them? I'm not so sure I would feel very loved if my spouse, my parent, or my child told me, "I don't like you." And what if God didn't "like" me?

Jesus is famous for teaching us to love our enemies. The way he uses it, "love" comes from the Greek word *agapao*. It's a spiritual, unconditional kind of love. One commentator defined *agapao* like this: "finding one's joy in anything." So we might translate Jesus's words, "But I say to you, find joy in your enemies." Find joy in my enemies?

I try to think of the person I "hate" the most. Maybe someone who has hurt me in the past or in the present. Maybe the people I don't know but certainly distrust. Maybe someone with wildly different opinions. Or maybe just an acquaintance whom I find extremely annoying, obnoxious, and socially inept. "Find joy in your enemies."

Jesus challenges me to find at least one thing I like about that person. And another thing about him or her for which I am grateful. And something we share in common. Jesus challenges me to pray for my enemy . . . that God would bless them and help them find peace. Maybe Jesus challenges me to hold fast to my convictions and boundaries that keep me safe from people who use me but also to hold that in tension with liking something about them. Can I find some joy in the individuals God uniquely created them to be?

I recall that God made everybody, and God doesn't make junk. Everyone has at least a little goodness in them, some Divine spark, something to offer the world. I have at least one thing in common with each of the seven billion people on this planet. Will I have eyes to see that? After all, anytime I "find joy" in someone, that means I have found more joy. I am happier and more at peace. The more enemies I find joy in, the more joy I will find.

Do you want more joy in your life? Start by looking for it in your enemies.

"help the poor," part 1

Sometimes I wonder, what is the best way to help the poor? Give them jobs? Give them stuff? Save their soul? Let's take five days to look at five ways Jesus helped the poor so that we can help them too.

> *"The Spirit of the Lord is upon me, because he has anointed me to bring good news to the poor. He has sent me to proclaim release to the captives and recovery of sight to the blind, to let the oppressed go free, to proclaim the year of the Lord's favor."* —Luke 4:18-19

Jesus himself was a poor and powerless carpenter who lived among and ministered to poor peasants his whole life. Consider how Jesus spoke to the emotional world of the poor and oppressed.

Fear is the fuel of oppression, violence, crime, and poverty. But courage to face the enemies within us and stand up to the enemies around us unlocks the gate to push past psychological barriers that hold the poor down. So Jesus taught things like this: "The very hairs of your head are all numbered. Fear not, therefore; you are of more value than many sparrows" (Matt 10:30-31).

Anxiety distorts our ability to think clearly and make good, positive decisions for ourselves and our community. So Jesus reduced anxiety by teaching things like this: "Look at the birds of the air, for they neither sow nor reap, and yet your Father provides for them" (Matt 6:26).

Despair and low self-esteem keep the poor chained in a narrow and limited world. So Jesus constantly referred to God in heaven as "your Father." He emphasized that each of us is a beloved child of God. We are worthy, and we each have hope for the best possible life.

Deception of the rich, the law, and of one another can become a way of survival in the minds of the poor. But deception reduces dignity and increases a sense of shame, and shame leads to exploitation. So Jesus cleared a new path and said, "Let your yes be yes and your no be no" (Matt 5:37), teaching that God sees everything and that all will one day be disclosed. The poor can overcome when they make the hard choice to live with honesty, sincerity, and integrity.

Hatred of oneself, neighbor, and enemy is a source of self-destruction, especially when you are poor. Jesus proclaimed that we are all tremendously valuable and loved, and we cannot hate ourselves or others—even our enemies—if we are to thrive. The poor can overcome when they keep choosing love.

Part of Jesus's good news for the poor rests in his teachings, all of which are rooted in the idea that God is a God of unconditional love and grace. We are to share that love: "You are the light of the world" (Matt 5:14). Jesus provided the emotional tools to equip the poor and oppressed to rise up, stand strong, push back, and discover true freedom in this life for themselves and their communities. These teachings empower us all because in some way, all of us are poor.

How can I help the poor? I can learn from Jesus alongside the poor.

This devotional is a frail summary of the brilliant (and short) 1939 book, *Jesus and the Disinherited*, by Howard Thurman. It is one of my all-time favorites.

"help the poor," part 2

The Word was God . . . the Word became flesh and made his home among us. —John 1:1, 14

It took a couple of centuries to settle on it, but the Christian tradition eventually agreed that the man called Jesus of Nazareth was God's Son—indeed, God-in-the-flesh. God was alive in Jesus, experiencing a human life. He was vulnerable to cuts and bruises and heartache just like us. Perhaps most compelling, when God took on our flesh, God did not take on the flesh of a great king, emperor, or warrior. Instead, God took on the flesh of a simple carpenter in a poor and oppressed region. God made his home among the poor and powerless. God had an infinite array of choices for how to help the poor of the earth, and this is how God chose to do it. God left the comfort of heaven to live and die side by side with us. How do you help the poor? Usually we ask how much money or time we donate, but let me ask you a new question: Where do you live?

I once heard of a church lady who kept dropping off food for poor families in a trailer park. One day it occurred to that her that her ministry was inauthentic. She realized she was simply dropping off donations and then driving away from all their problems. But the residents there didn't have that choice. That was their world. So the woman sold her house and moved into the trailer park. She took on the residents' flesh, lived their life. By "becoming one of them," she earned their trust and was able to make a much more meaningful, life-changing impact in the lives of the poor.

Many people on the front lines of poverty work agree: a good way to combat poverty is "gentrification with justice." That is, create "mixed-income" neighborhoods that have the goal of improving the community and all the neighbors' lives. One house is owned by a pharmacist. The one next door is rented by a lady living on disability. Mixed-income neighborhoods desegregate the rich from the poor. Through those more intimate relationships, we can see each other as brothers and sisters in life and trust one another better. Upper-income folks can connect the poor with better jobs and life opportunities and perhaps expand their vision for the future. Meanwhile, folks with lower incomes often provide amazing help to their richer neighbors as well. Everyone wins.

There are smaller ways you can "make your home" among the poor and change the world. Don't be afraid to buy groceries among them. Or to go to school among them. Or to ride public transportation with them. Or to go to church with them. Don't be afraid to be friends with the poor. Don't ever think you are too good to take on the flesh of the poor. Even God didn't think God was too good to be associated with the poor. Any way you can desegregate yourself, take on the flesh, and make your home among the poor is a way to be more like Christ and change the world for the better.

To dig deeper, read Shane Claiborne's *Irresistible Revolution* and Robert Lupton's *Charity Detox*.

"help the poor," part 3

And wherever he went—into villages, towns, or countryside—they placed the sick in the marketplaces. They begged him to let them touch even the edge of his cloak, and all who touched it were healed.
—Mark 6:56

When I was a college student, I spent every Saturday morning leading a ministry called "Crossover." We drove around and shared groceries and prayers with poor families across the railroad tracks. I became enmeshed into this poor neighborhood and met many great friends there.

I realized that American poverty has a symbiotic relationship with poor health. Many of the poor are disabled or elderly. Many of them have survived immense emotional trauma. Things have happened to them to make them unable to work and thrive. But many of them also smoke and drink too much, eat terrible (cheap and convenient) food, and live in homes rundown with unhealthy molds and pests. I have spent much time with poor Americans, but I have rarely seen poor Americans in pristine health.

So let's think about Jesus.

It's hard to find a page in the Gospels where Jesus does not provide physical healing (health care) to someone. Caring for health is absolutely central to Jesus's ministry. We religious people easily gloss over this, focusing on how miraculous it was or looking for some sort of deeper, spiritual meaning behind Jesus's health care. The deeper meaning is certainly important, but we must remember that by restoring human health, Jesus restored lepers, the blind, and the paralyzed back into the heart of the community where they could celebrate life and earn their own bread.

Health-care work helps the poor. Health-care work is "Jesus work."

If you are a nurse or doctor or medical researcher, you are doing Jesus work. If you are a personal trainer, a volleyball coach, or an athletic trainer, you are doing Jesus work. If you work in public policy to make health care more affordable and accessible to the poor, you are doing Jesus work. Strong bodies empower us to rise above the threat of poverty. Anything you do that heals bodies from the plagues of illness, disease, injury, paralysis, and poor nutrition follows the great example of one of Jesus's core priorities.

Health-care work helps the poor. Health-care work is Jesus work.

Let us each become more like Jesus, doing fundraisers for medical research, supporting free health clinics, and encouraging community gardens. Let us each become more like Jesus in pressuring our leaders to make health care more affordable for all. We can prevent and reduce poverty by restoring human health just like Jesus did on every page of the Gospels.

"help the poor," part 4

[Jesus] was moved with compassion for them. —Matthew 9:36

Have you ever known or seen someone who is poor but felt like they weren't trying to get their life together? Maybe you didn't see them looking for jobs or you were frustrated because they couldn't seem to afford groceries or rent but could afford alcohol and cigarettes. We see some of these things and think poverty is that person's fault or government welfare's fault. Blame is a low-hanging fruit when we witness the poor choices of poor people.

Let me offer you this word: *splagchnizomai* (splag - niz - o - my).

Translated "moved to compassion," this Greek word is like a verb version of the word for "inner parts" or "organs." It's like your insides are moved, which is generally considered an unpleasant experience. When we suffer with another person, we call it empathy (suffering into) or compassion (suffering alongside), and the Gospels often describe Jesus experiencing *splagchnizomai*.

Consider the idea that the harmful actions of individuals come from a place of shame and pain. The life choices of addiction, dishonesty, compulsion, violence, and anger are unhealthy and isolating ways of avoiding, numbing, or discharging inner shame and pain. Such choices could be seen as "armor" or "coping mechanisms." This analysis is not an excuse; it's a way to make space for *splagchnizomai*.

When you see a person who has despaired or lost control, who is hurting others to avoid their own pain on the inside, you are seeing ugly weeds from seeds of inner trauma and torment. So be like Jesus. *Splagchnizomai*. Empathize. Be moved with compassion. See the pain and shame beneath those damaging behaviors, and identify the places in your heart where you have felt the same pain.

"You're afraid to apply for a job at Hardee's because you're forty-five and you don't want to admit this is the best you can do? I sense that same, painful sense of shame when I look at the car I drive." *Splagchnizomai.* Me too.

This is how Jesus helped the poor. He didn't judge, stereotype, blame, or try to fix. He showed *splagchnizomai.* He saw the pain beneath the person's behaviors, and he met them there to sit in the darkness with them, to suffer with them, to connect with them in that place of sin, oppression, possession, and disabled health. He let his inner parts lurch forward in agony, feeling their pain, and as he suffered with the poor, as he hung on a cross alongside the poor, the poor were no longer alone in their pain. They could finally see hope for abundant life.

The poor (or any of us) cannot confront the demons within and around until someone sits in the darkness with them, until someone hangs on a cross alongside them, until someone says "me too," until someone's insides splinter open with empathy and compassion.

"help the poor," part 5

> *They . . . threw their cloaks on the donkey and put Jesus on it. As he went along, people spread their cloaks on the road . . . . "Blessed is the coming kingdom of our father David!"* —Matthew 21:7-9

Did you know that there is no such thing as a "poor country"? True, many places have poor people. But all the world is rich in natural and strategic resources for the global market. Instead, one of the strongest causes of poverty in places rich in resources is political corruption. This is true at the local level in the US too. A poor community likely has weak or corrupted leadership. A strong community, or a community that is starting to get better, likely has servant-hearted, hardworking community leaders.

This reminds me of donkeys.

Jesus rode into Jerusalem on a donkey—a symbol of peaceful kingship in his day. The crowds greeted him with the words, "Blessed is the coming kingdom of our father David!" Jesus rode that donkey as Passover Week began—a week when Jews remembered the time God liberated them from the all-powerful Egyptian Empire and anticipated the same liberation from Rome. Ultimately, the Roman Empire executed Jesus as the "King of the

Jews," the guy who was always talking about "God's kingdom." And they executed him using crucifixion, a method reserved for enemies of the state. The Romans viewed Jesus as a threat to their political power, so they killed him.

Religious people don't talk about this very much, but Jesus was politically subversive. Jesus's life and message resisted the very idea of an empire in which a distant, powerful, rich few selfishly exploit and impoverish the many. Jesus's life was a threat to bad politics.

What about you? Is your life a threat to bad politics? Politics are complicated, but what if Jesus people committed themselves to the practice of staying informed and voting in elections? The truth is, one of the best ways you can help the poor in your city is to get good leaders in place who build stronger communities, who facilitate economic opportunities and justice for all.

The image of Jesus riding a donkey suggests that there should only be one king—King Jesus. We dethrone kings—corrupt men and women—only by embracing this gift of Jesus's life, this great gift of democracy. How did Jesus help the poor? He said that he, not anyone else, is king. How do I help the poor? I embrace that gift. I vote and work for change.

Jesus math

"At the beginning of creation, 'God made them male and female.' 'Because of this, a man should leave his father and mother and be joined together with his wife, and the two will be one flesh.' So they are no longer two but one flesh." —Mark 10:6-8

Wearing a white dress against a faded brick wall, with vintage string lights lighting the scene, she looked at the man in the suit. "Before I met you, I was happy. But you have given me so much more happiness." They kissed. The pastor pronounced them husband and wife. They ran off together. And now? They have two adorable kids. A house with a picket fence. A dog.

I'll never forget those words, which one of my best friends from college said to her groom on the day of their wedding. These two friends of mine have endured lots of issues—personal problems and marriage problems that they have had to work through (as do most married people). But what my friend said on their wedding day has made a big difference in the resilience of their union: "I was happy before I met you."

Romantic movies, pop songs, and all the images on social media give us this message all the time: the best romance stories are the ones where two unhappy people find each other and finally discover happiness in their togetherness. "You complete me." "I wasn't truly alive until I met you."

And then the Bible gives us Jesus's weird math: "Two become one."

Jesus's view of marriage is that two whole, complete people become permanently combined into one unit. But the emphasis is on the number two. In Jesus's view of marriage, you cannot have two half people, two "incomplete" people, two people who are unfulfilled and miserable until they meet "the one." For Jesus, two individuals who are both happy, complete, whole, and confident create an equation for one successful marriage.

This is crucial for those who are married and those who want to be married. Marriage provides partnership, love, stability, possibly children—so many wonderful things! But your spouse cannot make you happy. No one can make you happy. Happiness is a choice within you. And if you cannot find it before marriage, if you are looking for it from a spouse, you are destined to be miserable and to cause misery.

I strongly recommend that my single friends focus on their relationship with God to find contentment, peace, and joy as a single person. God is near and God is love before, during, and even after marriage. I strongly recommend that my married friends focus on their relationship with God to find contentment, peace, and joy, both with and also without their spouse. They will be free to enjoy and serve their spouse rather than becoming embittered with what they are "missing out on" and whatever the spouse lacks.

The best marriages are produced with Jesus's math: two whole, complete, happy individuals loving and serving one another, their world, God.

February

underground

"I assure you that unless a grain of wheat falls into the earth and dies, it can only be a single seed. But if it dies, it bears much fruit."
—John 12:24

Faith sees best in the dark. —Søren Kierkegaard

I graduated college in 2009, at the rock bottom of the great recession. With my aim to start seminary the next year, absolutely no one was interested in hiring me for just a year—or at all. I finally got a job as a sales associate for JC Penney in their home section, where they sell toasters and lamps. That was a truly terrible job. No one ever bought stuff in that section of the store. I might sell five things an hour. I mostly just stood around watching the clock tick. I had spent four years working on a college degree, studying theology and literature and psychology—exploring the deepest and most perplexing questions of the human condition and the universe. And now I was staring at blenders for eight hours at a time.

Sometimes life forces things on us that we would prefer not to be forced on us, and so Jesus tells us about a seed.

In the fields and forests of the world, seeds regularly fall to the soil. Hopefully, they find a way to bury in, to cover themselves in the soil's darkness. There, they drink in the nutrients and water. They split and break open. They "die," and new life is formed. In a similar way, we are sometimes forced underground into a place where we cannot see, and in the painful cracking open of our tough outer shells and the subsequent pouring forth of our vulnerable, inner selves, we discover change and something new and beautiful and life giving for the world. This is what theologian Joseph Sittler called "the germinating darkness." It is where life stops being about "me" and starts being about "we." A seed that is never buried in the darkness will never bear fruit that feeds the world.

All of us are undergoing tremendous challenges right now. Unfair things are being forced on us and taken away from us. But these are precisely the circumstances we need to stretch and grow and create something new. This is how we bear much fruit. Unlike with seeds, it is not an automatic process. Each of us must make the choice to interpret our circumstances through faith and hope and gratitude. It is on us to ask, "What can God teach me about myself through this?" Jesus shows us that behind all the mess, we can find something beautiful. There is hope, even here underground. How are you going to translate this challenging time into a gift that makes you stronger and more life giving?

respect

> *As they went, they entered a village of the Samaritans . . . but they did not receive him . . . . And when his disciples James and John saw this, they said, "Lord, do you want us to command fire to come down from heaven and consume them?" But he turned and rebuked them, and said, "The Son of Man did not come to destroy men's lives but to save them." So they went to another village.* —Luke 9:52b-56

The Jews (an ethnic, religious, geographical group of people) were convinced that the Samaritans (another ethnic, religious, geographical group of people) needed to receive Jesus into their village. They were so convinced that they believed they had a right to blow them up when they rejected Jesus.

This may sound extreme, but I'm not sure you and I are all that different. We think we know what is best . . . not only for ourselves but for other people too.

For instance, I am a white guy. I can't change my race, and I should never feel bad or guilty about it. But the truth is, I grew up in a Southern culture that has a sad, racist history that still rears its ugly head. Relatives told me racist things. In most of my movies, shows, and comic books, the heroes were white, and the characters supporting that hero were Black. That's the world I was born into.

Like Jesus's Jewish disciples, I was raised with subtle, subconscious cues I hardly noticed that elevated my distrust of my Black neighbors along with my own self-assurance. Like Jesus's Jewish disciples, those cues made me more disposed to believing that I was right and they were wrong, that I could value our well-being more than theirs, that without even noticing I was doing it, I could shrug off violence against Black people by people who looked like me.

But what did Jesus do? What *would* Jesus do?

Jesus, who was a Jew, offered to come to the Samaritans to help them. When they said no, Jesus condemned violence and respectfully went on to another village. Jesus sought a relationship with and respectfully listened to people who were different from him.

He heard their side of the story and respected their experience. This is what Jesus would do. No violence. No anger. No power. No insisting he is right. Just a simple act of respect: "they went on to another village."

I am a white Southerner. That is not bad (its great!), and it's not my fault. But now I must actively resist any prejudice wired into me by that upbringing. It is my responsibility to hold myself in check. To see the many real-life, normal people of color. To listen more to friends of color and to read books by authors of color. I am Christian, so I am listening more to atheists and other religious perspectives—not to change my faith but to check my respect. I am a man, so I am trying to listen to women more (don't tell my wife!). What is their experience and perspective?

Like Jesus, I want to respect others' experiences and opinions. How can I say I love someone if I am unwilling to openly listen and learn from them? How can I say I love someone if they tell me my words or actions are upsetting and offensive but I insist on ignoring them? How can there be love where respect is absent?

I think Jesus was brave when he went on to another village. He gave them their space and thus their dignity. I think he was holding true to his dictum to save lives instead of destroy. Let us save lives, starting with our own. Let us begin with humble respect for those who are different from ourselves. With that respect, let us listen to their voices, learn their stories, hear their history, and come out better on the other end.

In the eyes of God, after all, we are all equal.

oxygen

"My soul is overwhelmed with sorrow to the point of death."
—Mark 14:34

Tired. That would be a pretty good word to describe our lives. Permission is denied when our feet cry out to stop, impossibly pulled in ten opposing directions. The lions encircle us. The creditors call us. It feels like everyone is taking and no one is giving.

We wonder, where is the oxygen? When will my head break above the surface of the waters for a deep breath and the warm sun on my face?

I wonder if part of the problem is that we're not very good at reading Jesus's story. Everyone knows what happens in the end: he resurrects from the dead and then floats up into heaven, and everyone is happy. Being taught that Jesus was God, we read the story imagining Jesus with a bulletproof vest, a glowing halo, and a wise sage look on his face, even on the cross.

That is the wrong way to read the story.

Jesus was also fully human, and his suffering was not special. It was common. It was human. On the cross, Jesus wondered where the oxygen was, just like you and I do. You can't heal something you're not willing to touch, so Jesus was touching our pain and feeling it to the fullest.

If you are overwhelmed with sorrow to the point of death, or you just feel the pressure of a big exam or paying the bills, know that Jesus is with you and he feels your pain. You are not alone.

And yes, you cannot read your whole story right now. But resurrection can await you too. Your head can break the surface of the waters and your mouth can open wide and you can gasp in the fresh air. The sun can rise and warm your face. The trick is this: do not despair—and keep believing. Today is Friday, and Sunday is coming. Your faith will make you well because Jesus is with you in the water, and he will be with you at the surface.

Today, keep breathing, stepping, speaking, loving. Soon, just like Jesus, you will find your oxygen.

forgotten people

"He was led like a sheep to the slaughter, and as a lamb before its shearer is silent, so he did not open his mouth. In his humiliation he was deprived of justice. Who can speak of his descendants? For his life was taken from the earth." . . . Starting with that passage, Philip proclaimed the good news about Jesus. —Acts 8:32-33, 35

I need to tell you about my neighbor Dianna. Dianna lived in the apartment next to us and we rarely spoke. Still, she opened up to me one day and bravely shared her story. She had been a stay-at-home wife and mother for many years. One day, her husband announced that he was in love with someone else and was leaving her. He used his wealth to hire expensive lawyers and convince the judge he had no money to share and to lavish gifts upon their daughter and persuade her that he was the victim. Dianna was kicked to the curb and lost most everything. Having not worked in years and with the recession, she couldn't get much of a job. In her story, there was a lot of heartbreak and injustice—like a thin layer of ice underneath a refrigerator of one man's selfishness and betrayal. Her heart and her life and her story had been shattered and left cold.

She began crying and said, "Sometimes I feel like God has forgotten me."

Sometimes shepherds we should be able to trust kindly lead our throats to knives in slaughter pens. Our hearts are so hurt that we can barely speak a word of protest. Sometimes the people we love and depend on the most let us down, disappoint us, and betray us. We can be dealt injustice by our church down the street, an officer who pulls us over, our teacher at school, or someone we thought we loved. In our humiliation, we are deprived of justice.

Jesus didn't do anything wrong. He followed all the rules. He was responsible and compassionate. Still, his best friend betrayed him and everyone else bailed on him in crisis. Religious and government leaders caved to the mob, torturing and executing a man whom they refused to accept was innocent.

In the New Testament, this is the starting point of sharing the good news: God's promise of resurrection in the face of the world's injustice. The good news Philip shared two thousand years ago started with wide-open eyes to our broken world that is unjust in the most horrendous ways. It is filled with good but sinful people who build sinful institutions and sinful systems, and so things quickly get off track, all the time. If you will receive it, God promises to resurrect us in the face of every injustice in our story.

Our world will use the excuse of our age or race or gender or faith or poverty or physical abilities to push us over and take what it wants. But God has not forgotten anyone. God doesn't turn God's face away from any rugged cross or cruel divorce or tilted courtroom or shantytown in the waysides of this world, this world that celebrates and sings but all too often whimpers and weeps and screams.

Remembering the unfair and unjust things you see in the world and perhaps in your own life, hear these final words from Mother Julian of Norwich from six centuries ago: "All shall be well, and all shall be well, and all manner of thing shall be well."

May trusting that good news give us the repose to become agents of the Lord's peace and compassion in our own journey. It has done so now for twenty centuries of those who heard and received it.

sex

> *For love is as strong as death,*
> *passionate love unrelenting as the grave.*
> *Its darts are darts of fire—*
> *divine flame!*
> *Rushing waters can't quench love;*
> *rivers can't wash it away.* —Song of Solomon 8:6-7

Should I save sex for marriage?

You will not find the following words explicitly in your Bible: "Thou shalt save sex for marriage." But let me make a thirty-second case for saving sex for marriage.

There is incredibly raw power in sexuality. That is why advertising relies on it so much, why pornography is a $98 billion industry, why sex trafficking is such a huge problem. Sex is utterly basic to the human experience. It is powerful. With such power, sex can be amazing or incredibly hurtful. That is why the civilized human race has always been careful to place tight parameters around sex.

Here are some other things that are powerful: dynamite, bulldozers, race cars, jets. Properly channeled, powerful things can do incredible good for human life. We can use dynamite to blast pathways for new roads. We can use jets to transport us across hundreds of miles to see loved ones. We can use bulldozers to build hospitals. We can watch three hours of left turns in NASCAR. When powerful things have no constraints or safeguards, though, bad things tend to happen. The dynamite explodes in someone's hand. The jet crashes into the mountain. The bulldozer backs over a car. The race car screams through a neighborhood and runs over all the cats.

For this reason, the Jewish-Christian tradition has safeguarded the powerful combustion of sex into the container of marriage for thousands of years. Marriage is an ancient, time-tested way for us to channel all that power and energy into one person, one bond, one story. It's a beautiful thing to figure it all out with this one person, wrapped in the arms of graceful, patient, communicative, covenant love. In a culture hellbent on consuming and pursuing pleasure, people get used, forgotten, and abused by the dangerous power of unrestrained sexuality.

When sex has little constraint, vulnerable people are hurt the worst and powerful people get away with the most, so it is a matter of justice and mercy to corral the explosive energy into one singular, lifelong bond. I know all of this can become ethically complicated with questions around various "what if" scenarios. I'm not trying to establish legalistic laws but instead to focus on values. I'll let you buy your pastor a cup of coffee and hash it out more. But take this idea with you: powerful things make a mess of things when they don't have strong safeguards. May you save the powerful energy of sex for the strong container of covenant marriage.

birth pains

> *"A woman giving birth to a child has pain because her time has come; but when her baby is born she forgets the anguish because of her joy that a child is born into the world. So with you: Now is your time of grief; but I will see you again and you will rejoice, and no one will take away your joy."* —John 16:21-22

My wife gave birth without using any pain meds. It was crazy. (Yes, she did this on purpose.) For nine months she endured sickness, a changing body, exhaustion, hunger, worry, and more. Then the day came with all its drama and suffering and work, and with me watching my wife do this incredible thing . . . and our baby girl was born. It was, and ever more has become, an absolute joy to have our daughter and fall in love with her over and over again each day. And now we have a son too. (Love ya, son!)

Life is difficult. We are all on a journey, making mistakes that we regret, enduring the pain of hurtful people. We are trying to keep our heads above water in a world that is too expensive to live in, too competitive to feel beautiful or valued in, and too hurtful to love others in.

Jesus was not blind to our suffering. But he offers meaning and purpose to it. This time—what you are going through right now—is part of the writing of a great story. You are not the villain or the hero of that story. You are its author. So write a new story during this difficult time. Write that you were a champion in it. Write that you clung to Jesus in it. Write that when things were tough, you kept your head up and remained faithful.

With Jesus, the sickness, exhaustion, and worry are all leading to the birth of something great. Someday you will look back at this time with a sense of release and victory and love. This anguish you are experiencing will soon recede and be forgotten as your story unfolds and something beautiful is born. "Now is your time of grief . . . but you will rejoice."

exorcism

> *"Love your enemies, bless those who curse you, do good to those who hate you, and pray for those who mistreat you and persecute you."*
> —Matthew 5:44

I was walking through the house when an embarrassing memory from earlier in the day flashed through my mind. Before I could even think, I was muttering to myself, "You're so freaking stupid." Indeed, there is a me who does things that are stupid—things that are compulsive and hurtful to others—and this me is like a curse in my life. Why do I keep messing up?

A long time ago, I embraced our world's wisdom on addressing thorny issues and thorny people. You quash them. You raise your voice and make threats. You do what you must to make them feel afraid, small, and stupid so that they submit to your will and everything can finally be good and at peace. You can feel brave, big, and smart if you just isolate that person or that part of yourself.

This inner critic, this accuser, this demon of self-loathing is hatred. It is hating the things we do, and, if we're honest, it is hating parts of ourselves. So here is a lesson on hatred: we are held by the thing we hate. Hatred is a chain. It holds us to the thing we hate. It connects us to it. Hating something is like saying, "Don't think about a pink elephant." (Now you are thinking about a pink elephant; you are caught in the trap.)

It is often said, "God hates the sin but loves the sinner." This is as unbiblical as it is unhelpful. Hating our sin keeps us connected to it—pulled right back into its snare. We wallow in shame over our weak moments and the parts within us that flounder. This hatred, criticism, and shame creates more problems than it solves.

Jesus taught a much better way. Bless the things that curse. Be nice and polite to your demons: "Thank you for all you've done to try to help me feel better and feel safer and solve my problems. But I have found something better. I've been shown a better way. I will choose a different path this time." Be kind and gentle to the addiction, the shame, the demon inside. Forgive the enemy. Bless and do not curse. Yes, thank the demon for its kind offer while you graciously show it the door.

Here is another lesson on loving your enemies that is probably much harder to hear. You can only show love to your mom or your kid or your neighbor or that scoundrel politician to the extent that you show love to your extra twenty pounds or your stinging regret. The people in our lives and the battles we fight within us are just different boats in the same canal lock, and our hearts control the water level. Together, it all sinks or floats. The journey towards blessing our inner demons is the same as the journey towards blessing our outer enemies. It is the same journey as loving our most precious loved ones well.

We universally bless or curse, universally are kind or critical, universally are forgiving or bitter. So what kind of heart will we cultivate?

When the shame rises up within me, I will aim to forgive it with a smile. Who knew that even exorcisms must be done with such gentleness? May we turn away from hate. May we finally be free.

friends

> *"Therefore everyone who hears these words of mine and puts them into practice is like a wise man who built his house on the rock. The rain came down, the streams rose, and the winds blew and beat against that house; yet it did not fall, because it had its foundation on the rock."*
> —Luke 6:47-48

When I was in college, I got reeled into a feeding ministry. On Friday nights we would go out or play ball, run around town, and watch Chuck Norris reruns. Early the next day, we would drag ourselves out of bed and across the railroad tracks to the poorest neighborhood in the city. We would visit families in their homes, bring groceries, and pray with them. I did this every Saturday for the better part of four years. The other students I worked with became some of my best friends. One of them became my wife. And this leads me to challenge you with a question: On what kind of foundation are your friendships built?

That's a weird question. Let's try again: When you're with your friends, what kind of stuff do you do and say?

Relationships can be built around all kinds of things: being roommates or teammates in a sport, having a passion for music, or having similar majors or careers. But friendships can also be built on crazy party stories or constant drama. Conversations can be full of good humor and light fun and shoulder-to-shoulder work and, yes, talks about the things that matter most in life. But they can also be full of gossip or cutting people down or objectifying women. When you're with your friends, what kind of stuff do you do and say?

Jesus was clear: storms will come in your life. When those storms arise, building your relationships on the foundation of practicing Jesus's teachings of vulnerable, self-giving love and faith will make all the difference. Choose your friends wisely, and choose what you do and say together wisely too. Together, may you do things that serve your world and build up your character and ground you in your faith and draw you closer to Jesus. Friends build foundations for our lives, so choose and cultivate them well.

blame

> [The Pharisees said,] "Teacher, this woman was caught the act of adultery!" [Jesus said,] "Let the one without sin cast the first stone."
> —John 8:4, 7

We're familiar with pointing fingers.

We live in a divided, hostile world. Turn on any news media and you'll inevitably find a few talking heads telling you whom you should fear and whom you should blame. Get a roommate and you will inevitably be tempted to blame them when you can't find your car keys. Get married and you will inevitably be tempted to blame your spouse when a bill is unpaid, a light is left on, or the sky decides to rain. It just feels better to blame someone else.

But Jesus wasn't merely critical of playing the blame game for complex social problems or mysteriously missing car keys. Jesus nixed the idea of condemning one another altogether. Often when we are accused, our default response is something like this: "Well, maybe I did this, but it's only because you did that, and that is way worse than what I did." We try to "out-accuse" one another.

Jesus, though, ignored that whole system. Assigning blame in order to consign distrust or retribution rarely solves actual problems. Instead of asking whom to blame and condemn, try this: forgive the alleged wrongdoer, and think long and hard about how you contributed to the problem. How did your actions or inactions help make this mess? How do you need to change yourself? I guess sometimes this can look like saying, "Hey, I need to draw some better boundaries here." But usually, our best bet is to focus on our own responsibility.

Drop the rock. Put your finger down. Look in the mirror because real change begins with you.

choice

"See, I have set before you an open door which no one can shut." — Revelation 3:8

Choice. That can seem like an inconvenient word. Sometimes it is easier to concede to the pressures around us, to go with the flow, to throw up our hands in surrender. Regardless of what we know to be right, true, or wise, we begin to act in ways that we know are wrong while a voice in our head preys on our fears and says, "I don't have a choice in this situation anyway." We blame our bad choices on the powerful forces behind and around us.

This week you may find yourself in a new place with new people and new ideas. Slowly, as you face decisions that you intuitively know could be harmful or shallow and confront behaviors that you secretly understand cheapen your relationship with others and with God, you let go of the choice you have as you dissolve into the crowd around you.

Today, remember that you have a choice to remain true to who you are and true to who God has called you to be. The door is always open. You are not a helpless victim of the crowd around you or the events of your past. No one and nothing can shut the door to true, abundant life. Jesus promises to hold it open for you. You always have a choice of who you want to become and what you want to do.

Perhaps today you will choose to close the doors that cheapen life and walk through the one that you intuitively know brings God's abundant life—the one that is still always open.

Lazarus is dead: spiritual resilience, part 1

"So then he told them in plain language, 'Lazarus is dead.'"
—John 11:14

Young adulthood can be crazy and overwhelming. You're probably working a lot while trying to juggle three, four, five . . . what seems like a million classes. There are so many things to worry about between school, sports, work, and your important relationships.

In the midst of all the crazy, sometimes we fail to stop and say it out loud when we are in a time of difficulty, great stress, or even trauma. Sometimes it's hard to stop and say, "This relationship is not working." Sometimes it takes a lot of courage to admit that the family in which you were raised had dysfunction, and you need to figure out how you can do better. It takes great bravery to admit that you made a terrible mistake and that you are at fault. Accepting loss, recognizing rejection, articulating dysfunction, admitting how hard things are . . . these are some of the biggest challenges we humans face, and all too often we fail to face them as we bury ourselves in life-destroying denial.

When Jesus's friend Lazarus died, his shocked friends couldn't believe it. "He is sleeping," they said. So in Jesus's own distress, he gathered the courage to tell them "in plain language" the painful truth they had to face. He didn't beat around the bush or soften the blow. He didn't just think it in his head. He said it out loud. He said to them what had happened.

What do you need to say to yourself or say to others in plain language? The healing and resilience begin there.

Jesus is weeping: spiritual resilience, part 2

Jesus wept. —John 11:35

Growing up in Tennessee and Kentucky as a young boy meant I was only allowed to express one emotion that would be considered permissible or "cool." You can likely guess what that emotion was. Anger.

For most of my life, the only emotional response I willingly chose was anger. In response to defeat and struggle and unfairness and getting dished on, if I was angry I felt more in control and stronger. Perhaps others would be scared of me instead of looking down on my humiliation in pity. If I raised my voice, screamed profanity, slammed my fist, hit someone, threatened someone, maybe I could convince others and even myself that somehow I was still in control of the situation and would come out on top. But Jesus wept.

If you think about it, Jesus is the ultimate example of what a man should be. The guy built houses for a living and probably had a beard and spit and scratched and had some killer biceps. But in the storm of a friend's death, even knowing it would work out in the end, Jesus wept.

If the only emotion you allow yourself to express is anger, you will destroy yourself and those around you. If you are humiliated, sad, embarrassed, anxious, stressed, or lonely, say it out loud. Try to use words like that instead of just "I feel bad" or "I'm frustrated." With precise words, express feelings to yourself, to God, to others. Weep if you need to. Such expressions are a critical component of resilience and healing in the storms of life.

responsible: spiritual resilience, part 3

"Lazarus is dead. . . . But let us go to him." —John 11:14, 15

Things go wrong in life. And when things go haywire, the fascinating truth about humans is that our default is to maximize the fault of others and minimize our own fault. It's because of my girlfriend's attitude. It's because my teacher sucks at teaching. It's because my teammates didn't do their part. Our first inclination and most powerful impulse is to convince ourselves and those around us that we are not to blame.

Jesus, who is regarded as "sinless," took a different approach. His good friend Lazarus died. It was a terrible thing. Twice in John 11, friends accuse Jesus, saying if he had come earlier he could have saved Lazarus. But Jesus never defended himself. He admitted and accepted his responsibility for not saving Lazarus's life.

In the storms of life, we must confess what we are responsible for. "Yes, it's true that he did this, but the truth is that I am responsible for that." The truth is, you are always responsible for your thoughts, feelings, and behavior, and rarely are you completely blameless when things fall apart. If someone insults you and you retaliate with hard words, you are still responsible for those words. You cannot blame your mom or dad or spouse or roommate for your words or actions. Similarly, you must have the courage to confess what you are not responsible for: your parents' divorce, the death of a loved one, the behavior of others.

What are you responsible for? When the storms come for us, we must answer that question before we can raise dead things back to life.

control: spiritual resilience, part 4

"I am the resurrection and the life. The one who believes in me will live, even though they die." —John 11:25

In one of the most emotional chapters of the New Testament, Jesus's beloved friend Lazarus dies. As he and his friends try to cope with their loss, doubt, accusation, grief, and hysteria set in. Jesus weeps with his friends. He is not above the suffering. But at one point, Jesus pauses and recognizes the control he has in this situation.

Notice how Jesus begins with an "I am" statement: "I am the resurrection and the life," he says. That's his sphere of control. Then he acknowledges the disciples' sphere of control: "The one who believes in me will live." Jesus could not control whether they believed in him or not, but if they did, he had the power to raise the dead, and he says so out loud.

When the storms come, we need the maturity to recognize where we do and do not have control in the situation. We can easily torture ourselves trying to control things and people when we have no control, while forgetting the things we can control. You can't make someone love you. You can't bring someone back from the dead. You can't control the past. There are things in life you simply have absolutely no control over, but there are a lot of things you can and should control and work on. When the storm comes, think long and hard about that question: "What am I in control of in this situation?"

options: spiritual resilience, part 5

"Lazarus, come out!" —John 11:43

When I was seven years old, my three siblings, my mother, and myself were in a boat. It blew up. It was an old ski boat, and the engine exploded. The boat caught on fire. Mom started screaming her head off. My little sister and I leapt into the safety of the water. My older brother and sister stood there, staring dumbfounded at the engine fire. Finally, Mom grabbed a fire extinguisher and put out the flame. But I will never forget what my five-year-old sister grabbed as she jumped in the water: a can of root beer.

When a five-year-old girl is fleeing for her life, why does she forsake her entire family but grab her root beer? The short answer is that our parents never let us drink sodas, so it was a precious opportunity. But the fact is, when chaos and trauma and tragedy storm into our lives, we don't have a sufficiently clear mind to determine our best choice. We think we have a clear mind, but we don't. So if we want to be like Jesus and bring "resurrection power" into our storms—to enact positive change—we need to follow three simple steps.

1. Talk about our options with someone we trust.
2. Write a list of every possible reaction we could choose in this situation—positive and negative.
3. Circle the most Christ-like and wise option, and then do it.

After you have plainly stated what has happened, expressed your feelings, and clarified your responsibility and sphere of control in the storm, you can figure out your options, choose the most Christ-like one, and do it. Have a friend hold you accountable. You may not be able to fix everything in your situation, but you can fix something. You can roll a stone away. You can call something out of the grave and give it new life. God has given you the power to push back the storm, even if it's just a little bit.

March

let it go: spiritual resilience, part 6

"Loose him, and let him go." —John 11:44

After Jesus experienced the tragic death of his friend Lazarus, he was able to resurrect him from the grave and give Lazarus a second shot at life. Jesus had the power to push back the storm.

When the dead man began going about his day again, Jesus could have become anxious about what else might happen to Lazarus or what Lazarus might do with his new life. Jesus certainly could have demanded gratitude or worship. Jesus could have continued to pursue more control of the situation.

When the storms hit our lives, we make choices about what to do, and we do it. But there are usually endless snares waiting just outside our doorstep. We can become afraid of executing action, even when we're relatively confident it will bring healing and positive transformation. Why? We're afraid it won't be enough. We're afraid there will still be some unpatched holes. But we must have the courage to do what we can and let go of the rest.

Lazarus could have walked off and become the biggest jerk with his second life. Jesus didn't puppet Lazarus or insist to him, "You owe me your life." "Loose him," Jesus said, "and let him go." In the storm, do what you need to do, and then let go of the rest and live in the love that God has shown you. You can't control people. Do what you can, let them go, and choose love. You'll never have the perfect personality, body, or talent. Do what you can, let it go, and choose love. You can't singlehandedly choose every professor, coworker, boss, or even the family you were born into. Do what you can, let it go, and choose love.

In a life of faith, we can receive only glimpses of resurrection and salvation. Storms will always swirl about us, so, for now, do what you can, let it go, and choose love.

consume

> *Then Jesus was led up by the Spirit into the wilderness . . . and when he had fasted forty days and forty nights, afterward he was hungry.*
> —Matthew 4:1-2

We cannot imagine a life restrained from consuming. We wake up and the consumption begins. We are constantly scrolling through media on our phones or playing mindless games on them. Constantly, televisions are on, our music is on. Constantly, we are drinking something, eating something, talking with someone. Constantly, we are working and playing. It seems we cannot tolerate a moment of boredom. We cannot be content to pause and observe the way the giant tree gently sways in the breeze and yet does not crack. We cannot stop and observe the people around us in the room or notice the person eating alone each day. We cannot stop anxiously checking our phones, hoping for the next ping. We gorge ourselves at meals and keep a steady stream of snacks in the evenings and we somehow cannot pause to give thanks. Maybe we judge people who are addicted to drugs and alcohol, but the truth is, we have our own addictions. We cannot stop consuming.

When Jesus was thirty years old, he began to teach and heal people. But he started his ministry by heading into the desert for forty days and going without food. Think about what it would be like to go out into a desert, with no other people, no technology, no entertainment, and above all, no food. Nothing to consume. What would you do all day? What would you do all day every day if you had nothing to consume?

Jesus saw this choice—this choice to go forty days without consuming—as an essential foundation to begin his work to change the entire world. It's called "fasting," a spiritual discipline where someone intentionally chooses to refrain from consuming in order to grow closer to God and remember that life is more than food and phones and games and screens and whatever else one's habits demand.

For centuries, spiritual people have practiced fasting for forty days during this time of year. They have chosen something—like meat, coffee, sugar, or (more recently) social media—from which to fast. It serves as a reminder that life is bigger than that thing, love is bigger than that thing,

God is bigger than that thing. It frees us from the handicaps we impose on ourselves, the false narrative that "I need" that thing, whatever it is.

What do you need to take a break from? What do you need less of so that you can have more love, more God, more peace in your life?

May you be like Jesus. May you find your wilderness. May you fast from the consumption, and may you find purpose and peace in the journey.

screaming

> *"Lord, do you not care that my sister has left me to serve alone? Therefore tell her to help me." "Martha, you are worried and troubled about many things. But one thing is needed, and Mary has chosen that good part, which will not be taken away from her."* —Luke 10:40-41

Have you ever screamed at a car key? I have. I was walking along and the thing fell out of my hand to the ground. I was in a hurry, so I quickly leaned down to a minimum level to efficiently snatch it back up without stopping. The key was delicately balanced between two fingers as I launched my body back up into full stride, and sure enough, the key once again flew out of my hand to the ground. Frustrated that I had just wasted more time, I once again tried to pick it up with maximum efficiency, and for a third time the key flew from my hand.

So I screamed at the car key.

I sheepishly looked around to see who had witnessed my primal behavior. I slowly picked up the key and carefully placed it in my pocket.

But I don't think I was mad at the car key for wasting two whole seconds of my life. I think I was screaming because I was a senior in college and had 900 pages to read a week, over 100 pages of research papers to write, a part-time job, a soon-to-be fiancée, and car trouble. I was worried and troubled about many things. The car key just picked the wrong day to mess with me.

Martha came to Jesus because she was doing hard work in the kitchen while her lazy sister was laughing at all of Jesus's corny jokes in the living room. It wasn't fair.

But Jesus saw right through Martha's words to what she was going through. She had a lot of anxiety weighing down her heart, and her pent-up aggression spilled over onto Mary. Jesus knew that buried within her, Martha loved her sister as well as he did. Jesus knew that Martha would normally be happy that others could enjoy a moment of laughter and repose. But Martha was projecting her anxiety into petty arguments about fairness and labor. She couldn't see past these concerns to understand the importance of the moment.

Perhaps you find yourself judging others, bitter at people you love, screaming at car keys on the ground or people in your home. Often (usually), keys and sisters are not the ones to blame for your anger. It is the things you are carrying around inside of you. Maybe today you can choose to take responsibility for your own feelings and hand over your worry and trouble and resentment to God in prayer. There's a lot of peace and freedom in doing that.

beware!

> *"Beware of the scribes, who like to walk around in long robes, and to be greeted with respect in the marketplaces, and to have the best seats in the synagogues and places of honor at banquets! They devour widows' houses and for the sake of appearance say long prayers."*
> —Mark 12:38-40

Once when I was in Washington, DC, I met a sort of celebrity—a popular religious author and activist. The guy was full of himself. I couldn't have a coherent conversation with him because when anything came out of my mouth, his mind twisted it into a delusional congratulations directed at him. I later found out that years before he had left his wife for his younger secretary and that he had a reputation for his vanity.

Jesus saw the way his community revered popular men—the way they overvalued the words and attention of these men who were vain and ambitious. The disease is no doubt a million times worse in our culture today, and the wisdom of Jesus calls out to us: "Beware!"

Focusing on celebrities moves our attention from the people and things that matter and takes us to a delusional version of a distant person who does not love us or know us and cannot authentically speak into our lives. Focusing on the drama and problems and controversial Twitter storms of celebrities keeps us from looking inward and doing the brave work of improving ourselves and our communities. Their celebrity lives are usually overly glamorized but often inwardly shallow and empty. Whether it is athletes, actors, socialites, performance artists, or even religious figures—beware of them and the attention you give them.

Instead, focus on the people you love. Focus on yourself. Focus on your community. Instead of listening to the "cool" pastor in some distant city, listen to the pastor down the street who knows your name and can speak into your life. If you need more drama, pay attention to how you can become better at loving others. Work on that. Talk that out with friends. Do you need a role model? What about your mom or uncle or teacher or pastor?

Beware! Beware! Beware! Beware of cheapening the deep, transformative life; the wild adventure; the abundance of love you are offered right here in your community among family and your friends, apart from our celebrity culture. This is a call to remember the boring, mundane, not-so-sexy world in which you live—to love it and to discover its enduring wonder and greatness.

tie down clouds

"For I have set you an example, that you also should do as I have done to you." —John 13:15

It has been a difficult week around the block. As a minister on my campus and beyond, I've had some difficult conversations. I've had to say words that challenge my own notions of hope and "good news." What do you say to the immigrant facing deportation to a dangerous country? What do you say to the girl being abandoned by her parents because she told them she is gay? What do you say to the kid whose home was ransacked? "I'm sure it'll all work out?" No. You don't say that. Because if you promise things you cannot guarantee, then you do not have integrity, and if you minimize someone's pain that you did not experience, you lack compassion.

Jesus lived in hopeless times. The people around him were mostly poor and oppressed. Political and religious leaders were bad. Life was hard and unfair. But Jesus had few words of guaranteed hope. Mostly, his words were directed at teaching people how to live with each other. He called people out on their religious hypocrisy or selfishness. He talked a lot about loving the unloved, the enemy, and the unlovable. And then there were his actions. The Gospels record Jesus healing people of their sickness, setting people free by casting out evil spirits, and walking. Lots and lots of walking. He saw a lot of folks getting crucified by religion and government. He said, "I'll be crucified with them" (Mark 8:31).

I cannot fix your broken car, your growing cancer, or the broken people around you. I cannot even promise that you will get the thing you are hoping for or that it will all work out in the end. I don't know these things because not only am I not an auto mechanic but I am also not God.

But take heart: I can love you just as you are, no strings attached, no matter what others say or do. I can reach out and touch you; walk with you; heal a little hurt; cast out a bitter mood. When you suffer, I can suffer with you. I guess we can all do these things.

Some of us are reeling, wondering how we can make sense of the world in which we find ourselves. We are trying to tie down clouds, wishing we could save our hurting world or just the friend down the hall. Those are things we cannot do. But choosing to be like Jesus is something we can do.

the plastic bottle

And when blind Bartimaeus heard that it was Jesus of Nazareth, he began to cry out and say, "Jesus, Son of David, have mercy on me!" Then many warned him to be quiet . . . but Jesus stood still and commanded him to be called. . . . "Go your way, your faith has made you well." —Mark 10:47-49, 52

I swerve up to the industrial green containers, pop my trunk, swing my body from the car, and begin to pull the stuff out. It is trash. Or what most consider trash. Glass and plastic bottles, aluminum cans, and all kinds of paper. In just a few minutes, I take a trunk completely full of the stuff and leave it behind me. Its destiny is a local plant, where it will be fashioned into new materials and products. My old bottle will give a local person a job, melting it down and turning into a new item. It will benefit others.

Read the Gospels. Jesus doesn't throw away things or people. In his culture, a blind man had no worth. He didn't work or raise a family. He stood outside the city gates and begged. So in this story, the blind man begs, and everyone else walks by. They "warned him to be quiet." But the story says that "Jesus stood still." When everyone kept moving, he stood still. When everyone assumed that Bartimaeus's life didn't matter, Jesus saw past those assumptions and saw his value and importance. It's like the plastic bottle we drink out of one time and throw away. We don't see its value, so instead of taking the time to redeem it to ultimately benefit others, we toss it, and it will sit in a landfill until the end of time . . . wasted.

Look around you. Who is being looked over or walked by because they are not popular enough, pretty enough, smart enough, or whatever enough? Who is your culture "warning to be quiet," and who does your culture mistrust and fear? Our challenge is to be more like Jesus and see the potential value in surprising places. With your love and faith, heal those who are broken: the poor, the disabled, the elderly, the ridiculed and outcast.

I recycle my trash as a spiritual discipline. It fills me with purpose and reminds me every single day that it is always better, more Jesus-like, to redeem a thing, a life, a community, than to dismiss and throw it away. Our culture dismisses the value of people just like it does trash. Jesus never did. May you follow in his footsteps and work to redeem others and yourself through the incredible power of faith and love.

books

> *They said to him, "Rabbi" (which translated means "Teacher").*
> —John 1:38

Warren Buffet, one of the richest men in the world who started with nothing, said that in the beginning of his career, he read between 600 and 1000 pages per day, and after that he continued to devote 80 percent of each day to reading. Self-made billionaire Bill Gates reads one book a week. Self-made billionaire Mark Cuban reads at least three hours a day. In elementary school, self-made billionaire Elon Musk was reading ten hours a day. President Barak Obama read for at least an hour a day, every single day, while serving his terms. (Oh, you think you're too busy to read?)

And then there is Jesus, the "rabbi." In Jesus's time and place, a rabbi was a local teacher who, from the early age of five, had been carefully and fully immersed in literature and Scripture. They were challenged not only to memorize and regurgitate but to think critically, to interpret, and, most importantly, to act and behave as a leader in the faith and the community—the natural conclusion of their life of learning.

According to rabbinic customs, Jesus became an authoritative teacher at age thirty. After twenty-five years of reading, studying, and listening all day every day, Jesus finally spoke and began something absolutely incredible. He invested the first thirty years of his life into himself. He then changed the whole world in just three years.

How much are you investing into yourself? How much time are you investing in reading and study each day? Do your habits reflect those of the most successful, high-impact people in our world, and those of Jesus? Or do you prefer watching television, scrolling through social media, playing video games, or partying mindlessly for hours?

Perhaps you do not aspire towards greatness in life. Perhaps you are content to cruise through, entertain yourself, live easy and happy, and make little or no impact.

But if you are not content with mediocrity, you must make the sacrifices. You must read voraciously, and you must invest in yourself continually. You must give up the constantly entertained and leisured lifestyle for one that not only works incredibly hard but keeps seeking wisdom. You must read a broad spectrum of ideas, thinkers, subjects, and stories. Finally, you must live into the wisdom you receive.

Like Jesus, may you commit your whole life to learning, and through that, may your life change our world.

church

> *". . . that they all may be one, as you, Father, are in me, and I in you; that they also may be one in us . . . that the world may be made perfect in one."* —John 17:21-22

"Get married." That's what he needed to do, he told me. He was alone and miserable. His self-esteem was terrible, and he felt like there was no point to life. "But" he insisted, "once I find my soulmate . . . ."

Are you lonely? Jesus, an unmarried man until his death, saw past the dysfunctional view that romantic partners solve all our internal woes. Jesus offered no advice or programs to help his followers find soulmates. Instead, he lived and tried to teach us how to build a different kind of community that consisted of people who were imperfect, grouchy, overweight, short, or whatever else you can think of (you know, people like you and me.) He prayed "that they may be one." Jesus knew that before we try to fix our lives with a spouse, we need a community of imperfect people guided by unconditional love and individual responsibility. Jesus understood that what we need before (and even more than) a soulmate are friends and family that unconditionally accept us while also consistently challenging us to become our best selves. That community, that family of faith, will empower us. We will become more connected and confident people, ready for the deep challenges of the path towards marriage and the many trials we will face in life.

For this reason, Jesus gave us the church. This was not a brick building or an awesome worship concert or good preaching. Church meant a family of faith that unconditionally cared for one another and inspired others to become more like Jesus. This is described in chapter 2 of the biblical book of Acts.

Are you rooted in a family of faith, a church? A place where you are known and cared for and connected and inspired?

my unbelief

The sun rose as Jacob passed Penuel, limping because of his thigh.
—Genesis 32:31

The father of the child cried out and said with tears, "Lord I believe; help my unbelief!" —Mark 9:24

Have you ever wanted to believe in God, but you found it hard to do?

I remember lying on the floor of my dorm room one night of my freshman year of college, staring at the ceiling, having no idea what to do with myself. My mind was racked by impenetrable questions about the historical truth of the Bible, about why God let terrible things happen, and about how the world came to be. Further, I was surrounded by a lot of phony Christianity. That didn't help. Now this young man who wanted to grow up and be a preacher found himself lying on the floor with nothing to say. If I tried to pray, I felt like a fool, like someone stupidly talking to the white concrete wall in front of me. I was like a heartbroken father, watching someone or something he loved suffer and die.

A long time ago and across the distant horizon, there was a man who had been broken by the cruel hammer of life. His son, his precious and beloved son, was suffering and in constant danger. He could not speak, and he endured seizures. His body would become rigid, he would foam at the mouth, and he would lose control. The dad was desperate. Then he heard that a traveling healer had come to his village.

He found Jesus and begged him for compassion, but he had to be honest with him. He couldn't truly believe that Jesus would be able to heal the child. He only partly believed. I have known some earnest believers. This dad wasn't one of those people. He was more like a young man on a cold dormitory floor, wanting to believe but finding himself not entirely able.

I endured my doubts for two years. Then a friend of a friend came and visited from another town. She said that for her, faith is about the word "surrender." It's about spreading wide your arms and letting go of control and mastery and certainty—about letting yourself be carried by the thing that is bigger than you. Faith is saying, "I am small, I know so little, and I choose to trust there is something that is beyond all of us." Faith and surrender look like a dad who would risk wasting his breath on God, who would risk giving his time and attention to Jesus, who would spread wide his arms and let go of control and mastery and certainty because he knows that he at least has to try.

All the great saints of old tell stories of entire seasons of prayers that felt pointless, of dark nights of the soul. They share stories, sometimes agonizing stories, of doubt. We, like them, keep putting one foot in front of the other. We live with honesty and integrity. Jesus says that God is patient and compassionate and gentle, even with heartbroken fathers, even with people who struggle to believe. We are safe to keep looking and trying and surrendering.

I remember the way that faith crawled back inside me when I heard that word "surrender." It took a long time. Today, my faith walks like Jacob after Penuel, limping like a man who has struggled and overcome but has not walked away unscathed. If you struggle to believe, you must pray the prayer of the father: "Help my unbelief!" It turns out that believers who limp some are usually nicer people anyway. Let's come together, not as perfect and polished people but people who struggle, who doubt, who limp when they walk. There is a lot of grace and glory in that.

songs about justice

> *"How can I inherit eternal life?" [the rich man asked.] . . . [Jesus told him,] "Go and sell everything you have and give it to the poor."*
> —Mark 10:17, 21

Have you ever felt like the people around you were a little too self-absorbed? A little too selfish? Or maybe you've recognized this about yourself.

Today I analyzed one of the most popular worship songs being sung around the country. I noticed that it uses the pronouns "I" or "me" twenty-one times, while it refers to God seventeen times. The worship song talks about me and what God can do for me more than it talks about God.

Maybe there's a problem here.

Recently, an evangelical Bible professor looked at the top twenty-five most popular worship songs and compared them to Psalms, the hymnal of the Bible from which Jesus sang his entire life. The psalms are about God's faithfulness, but they are also about God's deliverance for the poor and oppressed, about justice for the widow and refugee, and they hammer God with hard questions about why God allows such great suffering and injustice in the world.

But the professor found that the most popular songs being sung in the church today told a different story. "Justice" was mentioned just once in passing. There were zero references to the poor or to poverty, zero questions tuned into why God would allow life to be so unfair and cruel. The worship in the church at large is so thematically different from the worship of the Bible that it's almost as if they represent two different religions.

One day, a very spiritual man asked Jesus, "How can I go to heaven when I die?" It's like he was saying, "What is the prayer I can pray? What is the thing I can do to straighten things out between me and God for some good fire insurance?" Absorbed with his own, individual self, he asked the same central religious question of most Americans today. Jesus's answer, however, is hardly the one we usually hear.

"Sell everything you have and give it to the poor."

That's how Jesus answers the question of how to inherit eternal life. It's the only time Jesus is ever asked this question, and unlike the Apostle Paul, he does not say anything about confessing that he is Lord or inviting him into one's heart. Jesus says nothing about the man's relationship with God. Instead, Jesus says that this religion thing, this faith thing, this salvation thing is all about how we treat the vulnerable people around us. And he says we have to give our whole lives to it—to helping the poor, to demanding justice for those who have been pushed over, to caring for those who need it, to paying attention to those who have been overlooked. (See also Matthew 25:31-46.) That is how we inherit eternal life in the literal and precise words of Jesus. We have to sing an entirely different song than the ones we are probably currently singing.

The question you must ponder today is this: what is your faith about? Is it about you or about other people? What are you doing for the elderly who are all alone and forgotten? What are you doing for the lost kids in foster care? What are you doing for the families mourning sons lost to violence? For the daughters damaged by sexual assault? For the falsely accused and imprisoned? For the immigrant and the homeless and the hungry and the kids living in broken homes? If you want to experience a life of purpose and peace, you have to give your life to loving the vulnerable people in our world. It's that simple, and it's that big and that challenging and that adventurous. With your whole life, may you sing songs about justice.

peasants and gods

And Jesus came down with them and stood on a level place with the crowd. —Luke 6:17

Each of us, I think, is born with a desire to stand over others. We want the world to look up to us as the "best" athlete or musician or whatever. We want to be smarter, sexier, grittier, holier, or just the most popular famous person, standing tall above the crowds. Our different personalities, gifts, and journeys manifest that desire in different ways, but it is the same impulse lurking beneath: we want to stand above others in order to garner their respect and admiration. There's a lot of security in that feeling.

All the gods of history have acted the same way. They have remained in heaven and sent down instructions. They have sent their lightning bolts and locusts when the ant-humans below disobeyed. They have demanded fear, groveling, and sacrifice while calling themselves compassionate and merciful. Jesus was different.

Jesus claimed to be God's Son but came down and stood on a "level place" with all the Jewish peasants around him and with all of us. He experienced our scary, painful, life things with us . . . like being a little kid and having less money than others and even dying a cruel death. When he taught, he did not teach from a throne or decorated stage or television set. He was right there with us, touching common folks and talking with them rather than at them. What an inspiring vision of God, and what an inspiring model of leadership!

In doing so, Jesus not only elevated all of us who struggle with loving and respecting ourselves. He also brought down the old myth that some people should stand over other people.

If Jesus stood on a level place with others, surely I should too. The deep impulse of my heart is to justify how I'm better, how my school or church or race or country or minor league baseball team is better. To imitate Jesus is to resist that impulse. It's hard to do, but I have to stop knocking down others in my mind and certainly in my words and actions. I have to choose to view everyone around me—no matter how immoral or idiotic I feel they might be in that moment—as someone who is standing in the level place with me. To be like Jesus is to stand on a level place with those around me.

dry

"Father, forgive them, because they do not understand what they are doing." —Luke 23:34

"I cannot believe what she just said!"

Someone says something so incredibly untrue, so incredibly unfair, so incredibly dumb, that we are left reeling and incredulous. We fight with our family or significant others, and people make unfounded accusations at us and have an inaccurate memory of recent events. We see an unfiltered social media post, endure an arrogant teacher, or know exactly what "that tone" means from someone. People ratchet our emotions with their careless, nearly unbelievable words.

On the cross, Jesus, who saw himself as God's son, Israel's messiah, and a teacher of peace and love, was ridiculed and mocked based on untrue things. He was abandoned by his best friends—those to whom he had given three years of his life. In a legal court, the evidence was twisted and faked in order to condemn him to a slow, painful, slave's death. It was one unbelievable betrayal and falsity after another, and it cost him everything.

Jesus's response when he was affected by such ridiculous behavior was forgiveness. His forgiveness was based on one thing: "they do not understand." Jesus forgave everyone because he knew that they simply did not understand what they were doing. If they could see the full impact of their actions, they would not do them.

The people hurting you are normal and, yes, sinful human beings of limited life experience and emotional intelligence just like you and me. We all are usually but unknowingly guided by our unresolved anxieties, fears, and ignorance. (We'd like to think that isn't true, but it is.)

Forgiveness is a state of the heart. It means understanding that everyone should ultimately be held responsible for their actions, but it refuses to let anger, hurt, and bitterness lay hold and destroy one's own heart and right actions. Forgiveness sets us free to love people despite their offenses because we have clarity about the human condition.

I want to be saved from the chaos. I don't want to hate, disrespect, distrust, and resent people who are different from me or who have let me down. All around me, I see people sinking in a sea of all these things, sometimes without even realizing it. In view of everything I endure and hear every day, I want something to cling to that will keep me dry above the waves. I want to soak up the sun of this beautiful life I get to live and enjoy people rather than despise them. I want something that will give me less enemies and more friends.

When I look at the cross and Jesus's very good words, I think that maybe I have finally found it.

Palm Sundays

> *When he came near the place where the road goes down the Mount of Olives, the whole crowd of disciples began joyfully to praise God in loud voices for all the miracles they had seen . . . . Some of the Pharisees in the crowd said to Jesus, "Teacher, rebuke your disciples!" "I tell you," he replied, "if they keep quiet, the stones will cry out."*
> —Luke 19:37, 39-40

What would you do and how would you feel if everything was going awesome today, but you knew you would be murdered in less than a week? That's a pretty intense question, but think about it. Would you be able to enjoy yourself? Could you be happy and find peace? If someone close to you was having a bad day, do you think you could find compassion in your heart and be a healing presence for them?

I think of all the summer evening shifts I had to wash dishes at KFC when I was in high school. I kind of hated that job. And all day, I was kind of a mess. I was obsessed with trying to get in as much fun and relaxation as I could before I clocked into that kitchen. I think about those times I gushed over how cute my three-year-old son was or how sweet my six-year-old daughter was. Sometimes a nasty little demon would grab my head and say, "Before you know it, those kids won't even want to talk to you." I think about folks in their eighties. I bet they sometimes think, "Wow. My time of healthy living is limited." In short, it is hard to fully enjoy our good moments when we remember the bad moments that will surely follow them.

I think about these kinds of things when I think about Jesus's "palm" Sunday. Just a few days later he would be arrested and then tortured to death. And he knew it was coming. He absolutely knew that his messianic entrance into Jerusalem would ensure his doom.

The Pharisees refused to accept the goodness of the moment. They tried to quiet the voices celebrating his entrance. If I were Jesus, knowing how the week would play out, I probably would have caved to them. I probably would have said, "Guys, they're right. Really, these good vibes will be tragically over very soon. Honestly, it's not even worth celebrating."

Instead, Jesus endorsed the integrity of the moment. He was resolute about it. "If they keep quiet, the stones will cry out." Tomorrow could bring whatever it wanted—he was going to affirm and celebrate the goodness of today, of right now. He would not silence the voices celebrating. He knew this welcome would only last a day, but he celebrated it even still.

I'm trying to learn from Jesus about being present in the good times. I have been trying to pray a new prayer, a Palm Sunday kind of prayer. It goes like this: "Thank you, God, for this fleeting moment." That's all. It's a prayer to say as I go throughout my day. I am trying to pray this prayer in mundane moments of entering common rooms and when I feel the sweet weather of a short season. I'm trying to pray this prayer when I hear my little kids laughing and when I notice how lovely my wife is.

Like Jesus, I cannot stop the hands of time or hold on to my happiest days. I cannot hold on to the Sundays when it feels like everyone around me is waving branches and saying I'm great. I know that one day I will die, and just like Jesus Christ himself, I cannot prevent that. But like Jesus, I can bat away the sharp claws of tomorrow. I can reprimand the voices of dissent and anxiety in my head. I can celebrate each fragile moment of my ever-fleeting life.

Thank you, God, for this fleeting moment.
Thank you, God, for this fleeting moment.
Thank you, God, for this fleeting moment.
Peace in heaven and glory in the highest.

that guy

Jesus, knowing that the Father had given all things into his hands, and that he had come from God and was going to God, rose from supper and laid aside his garments, took a towel and girded himself. After that, he poured water into a basin and began to wash the disciples' feet, and to wipe them with the towel with which he was girded.
—John 13:3-5

Since I was one of four kids, my mom bought all our clothes at Walmart and JC Penney. This wasn't considered very cool. Everyone at school paid attention to the particular brand of pants or shirts and the latest trends that everyone was or was not wearing. In the seventh grade, I started wearing a white tee shirt to school every single day. That was my thing. I was "that guy" who wore a plain white tee every time you saw him. It made me unique within the parameters of my cheap wardrobe. I was hoping this could make me cool, but probably everyone thought it was weird and dorky.

I have always had a sort of anti-conformist streak. I wanted to set myself apart from the main crowd with the music I listened to, the clothes I wore, and the hobbies I played. I was hyper-skeptical of the values and belief systems of the people around me and questioned everything. All of those things helped me feel unique and special, and all of this made me feel more important than all the "normal" people around me.

Do you ever strive to feel special and stand out in the crowd?

The night before his crucifixion, Jesus laid aside his garments, wrapped himself in a towel, and, as if he were some kind of slave, scrubbed the filth from the feet of his twelve students.

There are many examples in the Gospels of Jesus eschewing attention, telling people that only God is good or that they shouldn't tell others what he had done for them. Jesus was a normal, middle-class carpenter who pursued a religious education to become a traveling religious teacher and healer and prophet. As special as Jesus was, he didn't seem particularly interested in folks calling him that.

Instead, John says that Jesus knew. He knew! Jesus was able to set aside whatever garments he wore and then get on the floor to wash the feet of those beneath him because of something he knew. John says he knew that God had put everything into his hands, that he came from God and was returning to God. Jesus knew that about himself, so he was free to give all the attention to others.

The same is true about your life. If you will have the faith to see it, God is putting into your hands divine and special work to do here on earth. You came from God and will one day return to God. You are made from stardust and dirt and the breath of God, and your destiny is to rest forever with the angels. These are the kinds of true things you can rest in. You can remember these things and cease from your striving. You don't have to fight to feel special and earn attention. Seeing God's truth about your identity sets you free to focus on lifting up others and serving them instead.

May you pray this foot-washing prayer with me today:

God, you have put works of love and faith in my hands to do.
You created me with excellence and with love.
My destiny is to return to you.

In the way of Jesus, help me lift up others and make them feel loved in every human encounter I have today.
Amen.

upon your lips

And hanging upon the cross, Jesus said, "Of course this would happen to me." —Nowhere in the Bible

In my life, I feel like I've had this mysterious force following me, always ensuring that anytime I buy something expensive or nice, it will shortly be broken, lost, or stolen. I was given a guitar for Christmas at age fifteen. Three weeks later, someone accidentally broke its head off. I was given nice new Nike shoes for track season. The first day at practice, someone stole them. "Of course this would happen to me," I thought.

Misfortune befalls each of us, but we often have a way of convincing ourselves that we are somehow special or unique to that human experience. The verse "quoted" above is made up, but even if you don't read the Bible that much, it's hard to imagine Jesus being sarcastic and cynical in his time of immeasurable suffering. So when misfortune befell Jesus, how did he respond? What were the actual words on Jesus's cracked lips?

"Father," he said, "forgive them, because they don't understand what they are doing" (Luke 23:34). He focused on love, forgiveness, and understanding.

"Today you will be with me in paradise" (Luke 23:43) Jesus shared incredible hope with a fellow sufferer.

"Behold your son: behold your mother" (John 19:26-27). Jesus looked beyond his suffering to care for Peter and his own mother.

"My God, my God, why have you forsaken me?" (Mark 15:34). Jesus expressed his feeling of doubt and pain directly to God in passionate prayer.

"I thirst" (John 19:28). Jesus shared his needs with others and permitted them a small way of relieving his pain.

"It is finished" (John 19:30). Jesus found purpose and meaning and finality in his life and even his suffering. He saw it accomplishing something in the world.

"Father, into your hands I commit my spirit" (Luke 23:46). Jesus surrendered all his anguish and his whole self in total trust and surrender to God.

Jesus was not cynical when he was crucified. He instead focused on love for others and connecting with God and others in his pain. Even if the cards seem particularly stacked against you in life, you are not alone in the experience of trials and pain. Cynicism will not heal you or empower you to overcome the mountains before you. So if your partner dumps you and your car gets broken into and you get a nasty paper cut all in the same week, may you brave your crucifixion like Jesus: focus on connecting with God and others. Let love and prayer be the words on your lips.

April

stunned

Then they went in and did not find the body of the Lord Jesus.
—Luke 24:3

My pastor and I took our youth group on a weekend youth retreat in March. Late one night after the worshiping and partying, we settled into our hotel room and turned on March Madness. The iron-clad, nearly undefeated, probably number-one team in the entire nation, the University of Virginia, was ready to pummel into the ground the scrawny, 16 seed UMBC, which had barely squeaked into the tournament.

The high-energy frenzy that characterizes the NCAA tournament plowed on, and progressively, we realized this game would not be a pound fest. It was going to be epic sports history. The Retrievers were hitting every single shot, even the threes. Their defense was insurmountable. Slowly, the Cavaliers lost the neck-to-neck pace as the Retrievers ran away with the scoreboard. In the final minutes, jubilee airlifted their feet and the UVA boys started to get sick.

Stunned. The impossible was happening before our eyes. Something everyone said would never, ever happen. A 16 seed beat the 1 seed by twenty points. David beat Goliath. The no-names beat the name. Millions of people's brackets were royally messed up.

It reminds me of that time Jesus stopped being dead.

It is an extravagant claim, because waking up from a barbaric, crucified death three days later and bursting forth from a stone tomb is impossible. It defies innumerable laws of biology and physics. You and I live in a data-driven, empirical, Newtonian-physics kind of world. Things are supposed to make sense, be predictable and even certain. Meanwhile, no one can prove or disprove the resurrection of Jesus 2,000 years ago. We can only accept it by faith. But I like what accepting that empty tomb by faith does to me.

I like that it opens me up to possibility in the impossible. That it helps me believe the Retrievers of the world can beat the Cavaliers. That sometimes cancer loses the fight. That sometimes the shredded marriage can piece itself back together. That sometimes the prodigal kid will come home against all odds. Or even weird things, like the night my car took me for two hours through the mountains with no gas to get me safely home as I desperately prayed. Or when my father-in-law, alone in his hotel room, just happened to be checked on by a colleague minutes after his catastrophic heart attack, saving his life.

Usually, miracles do not happen. Usually, impossible things remain impossible. Usually, 16-seeds are crushed by 1-seeds. Usually, dead men stay dead. But sometimes we are stunned. The impossible happens.

For the most part, we need to live in a realistic, predictable, grounded world. We need to be informed by things like science and math. But being a student of Jesus means being open to empty tombs and bracket upsets and answered prayers. This is your invitation to faith. Open yourself up to the mystery, the possibility, the humility of knowing that at any moment you could be like the Cavaliers or the disciples that first Easter morning—stunned by a universe infinitely larger than your greatest expectations could have ever anticipated. Maybe Jesus is alive. Maybe anything is possible.

eyeballs

> *"But I tell you that anyone who looks at a woman lustfully has already committed adultery with her in his heart. If your right eye causes you to stumble, gouge it out and throw it away. It is better for you to lose one part of your body than for your whole body to be thrown into hell."*
> —Matthew 5:28-29

The summer I was nineteen years old, I lived in the Colorado Rockies with my brother and cousin, working construction and playing in the mountains. On July 4th weekend, we drove fifteen hours nonstop to stay with friends in San Diego, California. San Diego was an awesome place to visit—a whole different world. We hung out on the beach and learned how to surf. But for us three Tennessee boys, what stuck out most was probably all the girls. Wow . . . beautiful women were all over the place! I remember driving back to Colorado, plotting how I might transfer to a college in

Southern California. But I knew better. If I did that, I would never get anything done. I figured if I wanted a future, I probably needed to steer clear of San Diego.

Jesus lived in a world where women didn't show their skin, privacy hardly existed, and no one had ever seen a magazine, television, or the internet. Somehow, he and the people around him still struggled with the same inner tensions we battle today. Spouses cheated on one another. Women got pregnant before weddings. Men assaulted women.

But unlike nearly all the other men of history, Jesus never, absolutely never in any way, shape, or form, held women responsible for the things men did to them. Scour your Gospels and look for Jesus's diatribe against female attire, female drinking, or even female prostitutes. He says absolutely nothing about any of it. The only thing he had to say was directed to men: "Adultery begins in the heart. If your eyes are causing you to sin, pluck them out." In the great wisdom of Jesus, it doesn't matter what someone else wears or does; each of us is responsible for our own thoughts and actions.

Religious men judge women, gripe about Hollywood and pop music, and try to keep their own wives and daughters in line and covered up. This is anti-gospel. In a world full of sexual addiction and violence, battered and worn-down wives, and girls questioning their own intrinsic value, Jesus has very good news. Women are people; they are much more than their bodies. And Jesus calls us all to take responsibility for our own thoughts and actions. Jesus insists that men, not women, always be held accountable for sinful violence against women. Why? Because Jesus knew that this is where the healing begins—when we stop blaming and shaming and begin to take charge of our own selves.

When Jesus tells us that in order to avoid lust we must look inward, he is saying that our sexual brokenness is a symptom of our inner spiritual and emotional brokenness. That our compulsive behaviors are ultimately a way of avoiding some hard truths about our own story. When we stop using our compulsive behaviors as a crutch and look at the broken things within us, it will feel like gouging out an eyeball. It will hurt so bad. But it will be worth it. Freedom for ourselves and safety for all women is most certainly worth it. And God's warm compassion walks with us every hard step of that inward journey.

crosses

Those crucified with him also heaped insults on him. —Mark 15:32

Jesus was not the first faithful Jew who died on a Roman cross outside Jerusalem—nor would he be the last. In 4 BCE, Emperor Varus crucified 2,000 Jews there, and in 70 CE, Emperor Titus crucified 500 Jews every day. The Jews awaited a day when a Messiah would come to rescue them from Roman rule, and there would be no more crucified Jews decorating their roads to the temple. It would seem ironic if their Messiah were to end up hanging on a cross himself, victim to the very thing he was supposed to overcome.

We live in a world with its own crosses, don't we? There are at least 20 million slaves in our world, over 60 million war refugees, and 2.8 billion people living on less than $2 a day. There are crosses of cancer and addiction and mental illness, crosses of broken hearts and big mistakes and mosquito bites in otherwise perfect moments. We too desire some kind of Messiah, be it a president or a drug or, yes, a god, to deliver us from this crucified world.

And yet God sent God's Son to die with our world, to be crucified with our world. That may not be the easy solution or quick fix we wanted. It may not be the god those Jews or anyone else wanted, but it offers us something more important than we ever would have imagined for ourselves. When Jesus hung on the cross between his fellow Jews, he was both fully God and fully human. This means that God experienced all the pain, rejection, and humiliation of crucifixion. It means that God was a crucified God. This means that when you suffer, God suffers with you. When you hurt, God is equally hurt. When your heart is broken, God's heart is broken too. It means that we are never alone, even in our most excruciating and lonely moments.

God cannot forget you or forsake you because God is hanging on the cross with you. God suffers with all those in our world who endure their own crosses. God is with us in this journey, and God will see us through to resurrection.

rivers and caves

Now Thomas (also known as Didymus), one of the Twelve, was not with the disciples when Jesus came. So the other disciples told him, "We have seen the Lord!" But he said to them, "Unless I see the nail marks in his hands and put my finger where the nails were, and put my hand into his side, I will not believe." A week later his disciples were in the house again, and Thomas was with them. Though the doors were locked, Jesus came and stood among them and said, "Peace be with you!" —John 20:24-26

My first summer in college, I worked at a Christian camp for inner-city kids in Missouri. Almost all my campers and half of my fellow counselors were Black. It was the first time in my life that I lived in a diverse community. On a free night, a few other counselors and I traveled into town for a Walmart run. Walking across the parking lot with five big Black guys, I noticed a few things. A woman, almost to the entrance and seeing us, stopped dead in her tracks and pulled out her remote car key to lock her car door. Shoppers threw us a lot of nervous glances. Little things like that kept happening the whole time we were there. These young men were born with dark skin, and that made them scary to the white people around them.

At that same Christian camp, another counselor who wanted to live with integrity confessed his sin to the camp director. A month before camp had started, he had spent the night with a girl. The director demoted him from camp counselor to maintenance for the whole summer. He felt that he should hold the young man down to that mistake from the past.

The name Thomas, or Didymus, means "twin." One of the twelve disciples was born a twin, and that moment, fair or not, would forever shape his name and identity. Can you imagine running around with everyone calling out, "Hey, Twin!" your whole life? Still, Christian history was even less generous to this man. Due to his momentary lapse of faith, we would forever dub him "Doubting Thomas." Centuries of Christians have summarized his identity with his worst, ephemeral mistake. Here is a man who has only been known by the accident of his birth and the accident of his doubt.

But in the midst of this, Jesus came to him and said, "Peace be with you." Thomas was more than his name and more than his brief moment of doubt. He was a complex man with a complex story, and the resurrected Jesus freely looked past his birth and doubt and offered him peace.

This is good news if you have ever felt like someone put you in a box or wouldn't let your worst mistake go. Something inside us screams, "There is more to me than what you assume!" There is more than our skin color, more than our upbringing, more than our financial struggles, more than our sins. Deep in our souls, we sense that God has made us endlessly complex and mysterious. God has made us like rivers, constantly changing and becoming new. God has made each of us to be deep caves full of treasure, waiting to be explored by the people in our lives.

In a world content to label us and move on, Jesus says these words to us: "Peace be with you." The resurrected Jesus makes no assumptions about us based on the color of our skin, our gender, our job, our dress, our income, where we come from, or who our parents are. Jesus says we are more than our worst mistakes and more than our past. Receiving this good news, we are free to welcome and own our life story and to write how it ends. We are free to become actual individuals, blaze our own trails, and open our hearts to pursue God's dream for our lives instead of living in other people's boxes.

But remember this too: a resurrected life imitates this resurrected Jesus. We must confess our own subtle tendencies to simplify others based on their mistakes and surface-level marks, and we must strive to resist that impulse. Let us say to each person along the way, "Peace be with you," and let our curiosity replace the gravity of judgment within us. Resurrection feels like that—like curiosity driving out judgment.

think of it

> *There was a woman who was bent over and could in no way raise herself up . . . . "Ought not this woman whom Satan has bound—think of it—for eighteen years, be loosed from this bond?"* —Luke 13:11, 16

My car broke down five times this morning. Five times! It kept overheating. And then I would sit there and just let the car think about things for a few minutes before cranking the engine again and driving to the next stoplight. At first, I couldn't figure out what the problem was. The car made sounds I hadn't heard before. When I lifted the hood, things seemed fairly normal—no smoke, good fluids, normal gauges, etc. After driving further, I realized "This thing smells hot," so I investigated again. Unlike before, I opened my coolant reservoir. Sure enough, from the outside the reservoir looked full, but inside it was bone dry and needed attention.

Jesus met a woman who had been bent over for eighteen years. The folks around Jesus felt like she was fine and wanted him to wait until after the Sabbath to heal her, but Jesus insisted on looking deep into the pain that plagued her. Jesus challenged those around him: "Think of it!" He wanted them to be sensitive to the woman's pain, compassionate and empathetic. The "straight-walkers" were privileged to be able to stand freely and comfortably, so it was easy for them not to and truly and thoroughly put themselves in her shoes and consider her suffering, not to worry about peeling back the coolant cap. But Jesus was sensitive to and curious about her pain, and he refused to "drive on." He challenged others to be sensitive too.

The unwritten rules in our culture dictate that we keep driving the car. It may be OK to open the hood, but only for a quick glance. "Don'g dig deep. Mind your own business. Let them suck it up and keep moving." Every day we pass by people who are ready to explode from a lack of care. They are waiting for Jesus-like people to stop and listen to their story, to think about it, and to help heal them in the way they need.

pressure

> *Then Jesus went with his disciples to a place called Gethsemane, and . . . going a little farther, he fell with his face to the ground and prayed, "My Father, if it is possible, may this cup be taken from me. Yet not as I will, but as You will."* —Matthew 26:36, 39

The infamous "Garden of Gethsemane"—it's the place where Jesus went, knowing he was about to be betrayed, arrested, tortured, crucified. The word "Gethsemane" means "oil press," as it was essentially a small olive tree garden, presumably with a press for making olive oil. In this space, Jesus was squeezed into a situation in which he preferred not to be. In this space, he had to face up to something he wanted to avoid.

This is what happens in life. At some point, you must have a difficult conversation with a friend that you've been putting off. At some point, you must take the big exam you've been hoping would simply disappear. At some point, you must face financial hardship or choose to face the way you've treated others. We all have our Gethsemanes . . . difficult places we must choose to enter in order to do the right or best thing.

How did Jesus have the courage to enter that place of pressure? He relied on two things: friends and prayer.

The story says that Jesus brought his eleven closest friends with him into the garden. He asked them to pray with him. Jesus knew that there was no reason to willingly face such difficulty alone. If you're about to enter a place of high pressure and difficulty, have you talked to trusted friends about it? Can they come with you?

Second, Jesus prayed. "God, make this situation go away." That was his first prayer, and it's OK for you to pray that too. It's OK to get off your chest how much you hate to do this. But Jesus followed by saying, "Yet not as I will, but as you will." In prayer, Jesus remembered the higher purpose and higher calling, and he saw that it was worth whatever pain he would suffer in the following twenty-four hours. Meditating on the greater purpose in prayer gives us strength and courage to take the long view and do what is right.

In the end, we come out of the olive press broken and shaped into something new. We leave our calloused shells behind and pour out love and grace for all those around us and all those in our future. With friends surrounding us and prayer beneath us, we do incredible things for our God, our world, and ourselves.

rise again

"Peter, do you love me? Feed my sheep." —John 21:15-17

It burned every square inch of my insides, and I could feel the hot embarrassment flushing my head, stiffening my limbs, clenching my jaw. I kept a straight face while the mother of one of the dedicated students in my youth group told me (very nicely) that my messages at youth had come across as demanding and judgmental. As a youth pastor who worked hard to create a safe, inclusive atmosphere for youth to grow and be shown God's love, it was the worst thing a parent could say to me. Despite my good intentions, I had betrayed my own values and possibly hurt a young person.

Peter, the guy who had sworn he would never be "that guy" and deny Jesus, had failed and done precisely that—not one but three times before Jesus's crucifixion. After dying and rising again, Jesus gave Peter the opportunity to say "I love you" three times. Three times, Jesus trusted Peter to "feed the sheep," to take care of Jesus's other followers. For each of those embarrassing failures, Jesus gave Peter one affirmation and an opportunity to do right.

I imagine Jesus's words to Peter directed towards me. I failed. What I wanted to do was quit. To stop "putting myself out there" and exposing my best efforts. To stop putting myself in a position where I might be criticized. I didn't want to be embarrassed again. I didn't want to fail again.

But failure is not an option; it's a guarantee. Every one of us who are trying will fail repeatedly, often, in the past, and in the future. It is unavoidable. We will say stupid things that embarrass us. We will blow it in relationships. We will upset good friends. We will walk out of the bathroom with toilet paper stuck to our foot and food in our teeth. We will do selfish, immoral things that betray our spiritual values. None of us escapes this monster named Failure. People who do not become comfortable living with that monster are the same ones who insist on always being right and become the most defensive when they are criticized. They never learn from their failures.

Jesus is looking right at you. Like Peter, he hears you saying, "I love you." He is trusting you once again to get back on your feet. Rise up. Do the right thing. Live life. Love fully. Put yourself out there. Hold your chin up. Be vulnerable. Take responsibility for your failure and don't deny it, but don't let it destroy you. Try again.

Yes, you messed up (again). But do not wallow in self-pity or hide from this brutal world. Get back up and rise above the fog where all those afraid of failure hide. When you look up, you will carry each of your mistakes to the stars you see in the night sky. They will make you stronger and brighter for this world that is hurting all around you.

influencers

"Why do you call me good? No one is good but God alone. You know the commandments." —Jesus, Mark 10:18

I want to tell you about a man who lived about 2,000 years ago. He lived in a land far from here, near the Mediterranean Sea. He was descended from a king and, at his birth, almost killed by a king. He was called High Priest, Savior, King of kings, and the Prince of Peace. He had twelve faithful followers, but in the end he was killed, betrayed by a friend. After his death, he ascended into heaven and was vindicated and called the Son of God. I'm talking, of course, about a man whose initials are J. C. I'm talking, of course, about Julius Caesar.

There is a long line of people with big assurances about what they can do for my life and for my world. They have lots of followers who buy into those promises. They offer hacks and easy answers and cheap fixes. Like Caesar, they warn me of whom to distrust so I will only listen to them, and like Caesar, they have little actual interest in serving the most vulnerable and marginalized people. Their focus is helping and protecting me.

This is true of cable news with their talking heads, and it is true of social media with its quotable memes, and it was true in the palace halls of ancient Rome. The long line of dictators takes many shapes in many places in many ages.

Then there is Jesus Christ. A lot of people thought he was God's Son, the Lord of the Universe, and the Great Teacher. But Jesus refused even to let someone call him "good." In the four Gospels, Jesus is asked 183 questions, but he only directly answers 10 of them. Instead, he replies with stories or with questions of his own. This good teacher asked his followers 307 questions, 30 times the rate of the straightforward answers he offered. Thinking hard is something our screen-addicted, entertainment-obsessed minds usually don't want to do. But when Jesus asked his followers questions and refused even to be called "good," he forced them to do more careful thinking.

And then what did Jesus tell the rich man who called him "Good Teacher" and asked how to live eternally? "You know the commandments," Jesus said. Jesus went on to quote six of the Ten Commandments—only the ones about loving others. The man wanted his problems to magically go away, but all Jesus would talk about was caring for other people. The Jews expected a messiah who would wipe out the Romans. Jesus wouldn't do that for them. He just said, "Think hard and love deep." This is the great disappointment in the real Jesus. We want him to fix everything for us, and he won't do it. He just lovingly guides us to think hard and love deep. If we get past our disappointment and understand the benefits of a Savior like Jesus, his kind of life will transform us and our community from the inside out.

So much of American religion has become all about protecting and helping "me." So much of American religion has become entertainment driven, mindless, and thoughtless. This is Caesar religion, not Jesus religion. Look and see how all the influencers on your screen and around you offer lots of opinions but few stories, lots of answers but few questions, lots of self-help but no challenge to care for others. Think hard and love deep. Jesus offered something so fresh and different. What kind of influencer will you find and choose to be in this world?

sparrows

"So don't be afraid; you are of more value than many sparrows."
—Matthew 10:31

Religious folks talk a lot about what we deserve. "We deserve to go to hell!" "We're not worthy of God's mercy!" "We are unworthy!" It can all become a bit, well, depressing. Human beings are altogether sinful, incapable, and ultimately deserve all the bad stuff that comes their way and none of the good.

But Jesus has something different to say—good news instead of bad. "You are of more value than many sparrows," he assures us. You have value. Worth. Goodness. The ancient Hebrew Scriptures Jesus read describe how God created humankind and then called them "exceedingly good." Jesus shared the love of a God who is proud of and delighted with all the crazy humans God created. You are of more value to God than all the sparrows in the air. You were made with the good stuff.

The painful and destructive and sinful and shallow decisions you make are simply that: decisions. Choices. Something from which you can turn away because it doesn't reflect how you were made.

Today you might choose to live in anger and accusation and negativity or to remain in shallow and wounding relationships. You might choose to ignore the suffering of those down the road or the God above your head.

Or you might remember the way Jesus sees you. As exceedingly good. More valued than all the sparrows in the air. Loved. Crafted with excellence. Capable of goodness and forgiveness.

Today, lean into the second way. Live under the light of the story that you are the exceedingly good, exceedingly loved, God-loving, people-loving person whom God created—the one whom Jesus sees underneath everything else. Will you remember the sparrows and trust that good news?

trying

"The very hairs of your head are all numbered." —Matthew 10:30

Do you ever feel like life is just one storm after another? Just one headache after another? Why can't life give you a break? As soon as you fix the car, the computer breaks. Your mom finally gets a good job, and your dad loses his. It feels like the world is taking the elevator to the fortieth floor while you take the stairs.

Jesus told his students that God was so incredibly attentive to every moment and worry of their life that God knew how many hairs were on each person's head. God is intimately acquainted with all of our striving and sorrow. Psalm 56, a psalm Jesus would have known and perhaps sung, says this: "Put my tears into your bottle; are they not in your book?" (v. 8). Every tear that falls is collected and recorded. It all matters to God.

God numbers your hairs and counts your tears and hears each step on the worn pavement beneath you. God sees you trying. God sees you pull yourself up from bed in the morning and collapse into it at night. God sees you hearing the bad news and going back to work and doing your best. God sees all the good work you do and the selfless things you do, and God sees the strength and resilience inside of you. God suffers with you with unconditional love and says that the trying is enough for the day. God awaits the invitation to come alongside you and give you strength; to renew your tired steps; to give you incredible hope.

So now, take one deep breath. Close your eyes and pray these words: "God sees me trying. I am never alone. We can do this."

rat park

Casting aside his cloak, he jumped to his feet and ran to Jesus.
—Mark 10:50

Researchers discovered that drugs were addictive by placing a rat in a box with two water droppers—one laced with heroin and one with regular, boring water. They consistently found that the boxed rats would return to the drugs and concluded that drugs became a physiological addiction.

More recently, researchers challenged the study. If you were all alone in a box all day every day, wouldn't you prefer a little heroin over water? So they built Rat Park with hamster wheels and rat toys for exercise, good food, and rats . . . lots and lots and lots of rat friends to play with and squeak with and scratch with, all day every day. And yes, in Rat Park the rats had access to drugs. But there, in the midst of the rats' profound social connection with others, their preference for drugs was nominal.

Addictions range from heroin to cigarettes to alcohol to pornography to gambling. Usually, addicts need things like interventions, clinics, medications, and anonymous groups. But universally, what we all need, and what our world needs in order to produce less addicts, is more Rat Parks—more deeply connected relationships where we feel safe to cast aside our cloaks. The blind man on the side of the road cast the cloak hiding him aside as he ran to Jesus, a beautiful demonstration of trust in this healer. He revealed his flaws, shame, and weakness to another person. Jesus looked at him and said, "Your trust has made you well."

We all need Rat Parks—communities of safe, loving people we can trust with our darkest secrets of shame, anxiety, and hurt. We need Jesus-like people whom we can trust with those things, because trust is what makes us well again and helps liberate our world from addiction.

My personal story has found such a community among other messy, imperfect, authentic, Jesus-following people—people who learned from Jesus himself to be healers. I pray that you find your own Rat Park, cast aside your cloak, share your pain, and find trust and connection with one another.

dopamine

But he went out . . . —Mark 1:45

When I was a kid, we played a video game called "Super Mario Bros." In the game, I controlled Mario as he ran across the board; I would push the jump button and he would hit his head on blocks and a prize would pop out, along with a "ding!" I would jump on threatening creatures and again hear more fun sounds. Eventually, I would defeat the board's boss and jump for the flag at the end, receiving fireworks, music, and a big count-up of points.

This is all about dopamine.

Dopamine is the chemical in your brain that tells you "You're happy!" every time you anticipate some kind of reward. Video games are brilliant because, beyond the mesmerizing graphics and fantasy worlds, you get consistent, small hits of dopamine (like working toward the "ding!") as you progress toward bigger challenges and rewards—that is, bigger hits of dopamine.

Social media is the same. Merely scroll with your thumb for more hits of interaction, entertainment, and "likes"—one long scroll in anticipation of dopamine. Television, too. Lie there on the couch as the images flash. Let the dopamine pour from the screen, demanding nothing from you.

The real world is not so good with dopamine. The real world is where you talk with actual people with no phone in your hand. The real world is where you leave your room and hang out in other places on campus or in town. The real world is playing sports, working a job, going on an actual date with an actual person. There is a lot more delayed gratification in the real world. You must work hard for the rewards. You must take risks involving actual consequences for any mistakes you make. In the real world, falling into lava pits are way worse than when Mario does it.

The one time Jesus told someone to stay quiet, they didn't. Mark's Gospel says the healed man "went out and began to proclaim his healing freely." This is the effect of a truly liberated, courageous, confident life found in Jesus. "He went out." It is a wonderful cycle too. The more you "go out" (away from the screens and your room) into the real world with real relationships, the freer and braver you become. The theme of the Gospels is that everyone who is touched by Jesus's incredible life "goes out" into the real world and celebrates with others.

It is easier to stare at your phone, stay in your room, or play games and watch TV. You get all the dopamine with none of the effort or courage.

But Jesus's good news draws us out into the real world where we discover a life far deeper, more meaningful, more thoughtful, and, yes, more rewarding than anything our screens could ever offer us.

flowers

"Carefully examine the flowers." —Matthew 6:28

When we bought our house, the little front yard was a small stretch of grass, from the sidewalk up to the oversized holly bushes hedging the white exterior of the home. I thought that was boring. With enormous effort, I yanked out all the hollies and replaced them with blooming azaleas. At the sidewalk, I built a terrace up the hill, complete with red brick retaining walls and expansive carpets of creeping phlox spilling over. At the curb, I planted a little dogwood tree.

During our first spring living in our house with the flat green yard, I never stopped on my way from the car to the front door. Now I stop.

For you, this week is likely a time of heavy stress, a threshold of enormous change and transition, or perhaps both. Jesus says this: "Carefully examine the flowers." For a Christian, it is literally a divine mandate that we stop and look at flowers and maybe at any pretty thing along the way.

This mandate isn't a terrible burden, however. Jesus teaches us that our heads have a way of veering off into tangled messes. We let ourselves get bogged down with worries and fears. But flowers are simple and beautiful without ever being fearful or worried. Matthew's Greek word for "carefully examine" might more literally be broken down as "learn through." Through looking at the flower, learn not to be worried. We so often get trapped in the mindset that we can breathe deeply and freely only once the big break comes or some kind of materialistic gain is made. Jesus smiles and waves that off. Just carefully examine the little flowers along the way, he says. Let it do something good to your soul.

The great wisdom of Jesus insists that you enjoy the little things along the path. That you permit them to shine light into your heart. That you look at things that are lovely, take a deep, cleansing breath, and remember that in all this mess, somehow God is near to you and faithful and doing good things all around you. There is goodness and beauty in this world. the flowers between the car and the front door neither toil nor spin, but they can help carry us very far when our feet feel heavy.

he withdrew

Great multitudes came together to hear, and to be healed by Jesus of their sickness. So he often withdrew into the wilderness and prayed.
—Luke 5:15-16

My wife was a special education teacher in a public school. She also ran a tutoring ministry at our church on Sunday afternoons to help at-risk kids, served on the church's missions committee, taught Sunday school, served on a board to organize an annual race to raise money for the hungry, and regularly consulted with a ministry in Romania that provided special education to needy children there. She was part of a local women's organization that helped the community, and she periodically participated in women's Bible studies at church. Oh, and she also had a toddler at home.

Eventually, she felt led to peel some of this stuff back, to say "no" to some great things so she could say "yes" to the things that matter most in life. Even though some of this stuff only took one or two hours a month, she realized that it all stacked up and ultimately robbed her of the goodness of life itself.

Luke tells us about how many people needed Jesus to heal them and speak with them, and Jesus would withdraw away from them. Jesus would tell desperate people "no" so he could slip away, get out in the woods, and pray. I think Jesus knew that if he didn't tend to his soul through prayer and time in God's beautiful, peaceful creation, he would falter and be less productive, less life-giving, to those who needed his gifts and passionate love.

Perhaps you have said "yes" to too many things—clubs, organizations, and people. You are faltering or unhappy, or you are not doing any one thing well. Perhaps you need to peel some of it back a bit, trim off some of the small things or big things that are making life too stressful and exhausting. Perhaps you need to decide to withdraw a bit so you can become a more joyful, life-giving follower of Jesus to the people you encounter on your journey.

Out of all your priorities, are you making time for prayer? Are you making time for being in God's creation (parks, riverwalks, etc.) as Jesus did in his life? In your life, may you serve your world, and may you always remember to withdraw when your soul needs it most.

the goose

> *"The wind blows where it wishes, and you hear the sound of it, but cannot tell where it comes from and where it goes. So it is with everyone who is born of the Spirit."* —John 3:8

Celtic Christians in the Middle Ages had a word for the Holy Spirit: *Ah Geadh-Glas*, meaning "wild goose." How could those Christians refer to God's Spirit as a silly animal? And then we have Jesus rambling about the wind. His words, written in Greek, have a double meaning. *Nooma* translates into English as "wind" and as "spirit." The "spirit/wind blows where it wishes," Jesus says. "So it is with everyone who is born of the spirit/wind."

Now it makes sense. A goose ambles in its own direction. It is impossible to predict or restrain. Waddling across riverbanks, gliding across mighty rivers, soaring through uncharted skies, the goose and the wind blow where they wish. What about you? Are you free?

the world around you will lead you in the most predictable paths. Without even realizing it, your life will be a statistic, guided by demographics, market forces, and marketing schemes you don't even notice. Big players pushing culture and politics know how to manipulate the masses without us realizing it. They know where we come from and where we are going.

And then there is the goose and those "born of the Spirit." They blow where they wish. Their vision for life is broad and unrestrained. They cannot be controlled because they do not fear; they are not anxious. Like the goose, they keep looking above for guidance that is bigger rather than reacting to whatever is in front of them.

I know it's awkward to go against the grain. It's hard not to laugh at some bad joke or to binge drink on the weekend. It's hard to prioritize faith in your life's schedule. It is easier to glide along the banks of the river downstream and be like everyone else. But no one who goes with the flow lives an inspiring life.

May you march to a different beat. Have a different vision. Speak with higher language. Value higher things. Keep the goose in your heart and the wind at your back.

May Jesus —not culture or peers or security or stuff or ease or all those sinister puppeteers behind the scenes—guide you as you step, as you swim, as you fly. May you surprise the people around you with something different and better. May you be the silly goose.

May

ancestors

"If you were Abraham's children, then you would do what Abraham did." —John 8:39

Those who believe are the children of Abraham. —Galatians 3:7

My freshman year of college, we buried my father's father. When I was thirty-three, we buried my mother's father. Very good stories were shared about both men. Certain things were left out. In both cases, it was a day of inheritance. I can explain.

I choose to see a lot of myself in those two men. Like Papaw Ron, I like to think that I am hard working, entrepreneurial, and curious. Like Grandaddy Jean, I like to think that I am a good pastor to people, that I embody the Lord's peace in a room, and that I encourage people in their journey. I've inherited good things from them both.

Jesus and all the Jews around him shared a common ancestor: a man named Abraham who gave to the world the gift of believing that there is only one God in this universe. Some Jews rested their laurels on that ancestry, like someone who can trace their genes back to George Washington and wants everyone to know about it.

But Jesus and Paul were interested in changing that conversation. They thought there was a certain freedom about ancestry that was matched by a responsibility of intention. They told us two things: someone's story is something you can inherit, and you can go to anyone's funeral.

Ancestry, they were saying, isn't necessarily biological. It is spiritual. To quote Ralph Ellison, "…while one can do nothing about choosing one's relatives, one can, as an artist, choose one's 'ancestors.'"[1] To paraphrase

---

1. Ellison, "The World and the Jug," in *Shadow and Act* (New York: Random House, 1964), 140.

Jesus, "If you're a child of Abraham you will act like him, and if you don't act like him I suppose you're really someone else's kid." I knew people who claimed my Granddaddy as their own because of some bad spots in their personal stories. That's a Jesus kind of thing to do.

It is important for us to situate ourselves into a larger story, to see the spiritual stream of which we are a part. If we are not intentional to root ourselves in some kind of grandparent or parent figure and their positive values, if we blithely assume we are some kind of floating, individual thing in the universe making our own way, then we are deluding ourselves. We are choosing to be blind to darker spiritual forces from our ancestry that are pulling on us. We need good spiritual ancestors to latch on to, follow, and build upon.

Isn't it interesting that Jesus and Paul never said, "Forget about Abraham! There's no point in thinking about your past! Think about now! Think about the future!" Jesus and Paul wanted you and I to be rooted in a long story from ages past. That's why we have to choose to make Abraham our father. That's why we have to choose to go to funerals and remember good stories about grandfathers and other good people.

In the way of Jesus, may you be intentional about choosing your ancestors. May you remember who they were and what they were about so that you may become a better ancestor to others one day.

wedding invitations

"Go to the roads on the edge of town and invite everyone you find to the wedding party." —Matthew 22:9

Recently, my cousin, who lives five hours away, decided to get married. It was kind of a last-minute thing. I think they got engaged a month before the wedding. A relative sent me a text message: "She's getting married! The wedding will be on the 29th!" I was excited for my cousin. I wasn't sure the date would work with our schedule or that I could make the huge sacrifices of time, energy, and otherwise to drive my family so far away to enjoy the awesome party. On top of that, I wasn't certain we were invited, and in the end we didn't make it to the wedding.

I have always been someone who felt deeply attached to church and Christian community. Flustered preachers warned me to tell people about Jesus or suffer the guilt of them burning in hell forever. Ironically, that made me never want to tell anyone at all. But Jesus talked about inviting people to a party—a huge feast of good food and music and laughter and conversation.

Church is Christian community. It is a space for people to love and care for one another, to spur one another on to live better and more connected lives, and to experience moments of transcendence, awe, and worship. These are all things every soul desperately craves and struggles to find in life outside of church. The title of an awesome book by David Dark sums it up well: *Life's Too Short to Pretend You're Not Religious* (InterVarsity Press: 2016).

Jesus wanted his followers to find the uninvited people, the people who felt unsure of themselves and left out of the group, and he wanted them to make everything crystal clear for those people: "You are indeed invited to the party, to the thing you have wanted all along." He wanted them to say this to such people:

"I know a party where everyone loves each other in the ups and downs of life, a place where you can grow and become your best self, a place with vaulted ceilings and beautiful music where you can experience the awe and transcendence for which you are wired to thirst. A place where you can finally connect with your Higher Power, the Living God, the Thing-That-Is-Bigger-Than-You. I want to invite you to the party. You can sit with me at the table or in the pew. I'll introduce you to every awesome person there. Come to the party. You are invited!"

Today, may you go to the edge of town where someone feels unsure and left out. May you invite them to the party of which they've always wanted to be a part. Life is too short to pretend otherwise.

352 quintillion

Those who hope in the LORD will renew their strength. They will soar on wings like eagles; they will run and not grow weary; they will walk and not be faint. —Isaiah 40:31

When a ship glides across the waters of the sea, it is surrounded by 352 quintillion gallons of water. For all you non-math majors, that's 352,000,000,000,000,000,000 (yes, eighteen zeros!) gallons pressing in on the few inches of hull between air and sea. With such a tremendous amount of water coming against a ship, how does it not sink?

The only ships that sink are the ones that let water into the hull. And comparatively speaking, they only let in a little bit of the massive pressure and content of the surrounding oceans. Consider your circumstances right now: the pressure of work or exams, issues with technology, issues with family, issues with friends or relationships, financial stress, a crippling past and an uncertain future. How will you keep gliding and not sink? How will you keep 352 quintillion gallons of stress, anxiety, and obstacles from getting into you and bringing you down?

I think of Isaiah's words. What happens to people who have hope in the Lord? Isaiah claims that their strength is renewed, that somehow they soar like eagles, that they can keep on running without getting tired.

Our faith in God comes from outside us, but it operates like it comes from within us. In that sense, it is different from other forms of strength. It is both/and, internal/external, and it makes us incredibly resilient, gritty, resurrection people in every conceivable circumstance.

Today, are you hoping in the Lord? Are you trusting in that voice and that Spirit that is above you, below you, behind you, before you, and within you? Are you stretching out your wings, trusting that the Lord's wind will lift you up?

I know you are surrounded by 352 quintillion gallons of water. I know it is hard. My encouragement is this: if you hope in the Lord, you will not let the water in. It will not pull you down.

Today, may you put your trust in the Lord. May you keep gliding across the waters and soaring like an eagle and running on and on . . . never sinking or falling or fainting.

surprised by goodness

"But a certain Samaritan, as he journeyed, came where he was. And when he saw him, he had compassion." —Luke 10:33

A lawyer was conversing with Jesus about the Bible, and together they agreed that loving God and loving one's neighbor was the most important part of faith. But the lawyer pressed Jesus about defining exactly who a "neighbor" was.

That's when Jesus told him the story of the "Good Samaritan." A man is beaten, robbed, and left for dead on the road. A preacher walks by and ignores him. A priest walks by and ignores him. Then comes the Samaritan. Who was a Samaritan? They were considered "half-breeds," half Jewish, half . . . something else. They worshiped differently. They acted differently. They believed differently. The running story of the day was that they were bad, terrible, evil, no good, impossible-to-trust people. "Those" people. And yet the Samaritan, not the preacher or the priest, was the "good" man, who saved an innocent stranger's life.

How do you understand the world? Who do you distrust? What group of people have you been taught were bad, or "idiots," or conniving villains out to get us all? Goodness surprises us in every place. You can find goodness in the people you hate and fear the most.

Discovering that goodness can help you love and listen and find peace and strength.

The news usually focuses on bad guys and bad stories and terrible things happening . . . it makes us feel like the world is a bad place. For every 1,000 Muslims or cops or politicians or teachers or soldiers or doctors or millionaire CEOs or homosexuals or black people or white people or somewhere-in-between people who are incredibly self-less, brave, generous and good, our news and our attention focuses on the one bad guy . . . the one bad Samaritan.

But Jesus tells us the story of the Good Samaritan. This is the story Jesus is telling. The world is not such a bad place after all.

In Texas in 2017, Hurricane Harvey dealt 125 billion dollars in damage and took the lives of 68 people. But what I'll always remember will be the lines, hundreds and hundreds and hundreds of people lined up to volunteer to assist and rescue, guys with fishing boats driving towards the storm to rescue from the waters. Some people died while saving the lives of others. Across the country millions of dollars raised. Bottles of water. Prayers. This is our world.

This is your community too. Maybe you feel neglected, betrayed, or disappointed by others. You are tempted to become jaded and quit. But you must remember the volunteers in Texas. You must remember the Good Samaritan. If you feel beaten up and left for dead, God's people are near you, ready to love you, embrace you, support you, "be a neighbor" in the most surprising of places. Let's tell a different story about where we are, who we are, and what kind of world we live in. In that story, we will discover a lot more hope for our life and for our world.

pronouns

"I pray they will be one, Father, just as you are in me and I am in you. I pray that they also will be in us." —John 17:21

I read about a large-scale scientific study that discovered a direct correlation between pronoun usage and heart attacks. That is, the more people used the pronouns "I," "me," and "mine" in their daily lives, the greater their chance of a heart attack and the greater their chance of dying from the heart attack if they had one. Conversely, those who talked more about "us," "we," "ours," and "you" in their daily lives were significantly less likely to have a heart attack or to die from it if they did have one.

Let that sink in for a second.

If you read Matthew, Mark, and Luke, Jesus doesn't talk about himself very much. He does not march around declaring himself the Savior and Son of God. He even resists his disciple calling him "good" (Mark 10). He announces a lot of good news for people. He says, "You are the light of the world." The Gospel of John is famous for its "I am" sayings because Jesus says the words "I am . . ." about eight times in its twenty-one chapters. Aside from that, Jesus did not use the pronouns "I," "me," or "mine" very much. The Christian tradition has even refused to think of God as an isolated individual. Rather, Christians have called God a "Trinity," a mysterious being that is both three in one and one in three, a God who has never existed outside of this holy inner interdependence.

These days, researchers are affirming most everything Jesus exemplified and taught. If you want happiness and joy, do not seek it. Instead, be like Jesus and focus on others, celebrating our interdependence—the idea that we are all in this together, that we are all fundamentally connected and the same, despite our differences.

Today, monitor your pronouns and your thoughts. Recognize that your burdens and pain are shared by the world around you. Be sensitive and empathize with what others might be struggling with or celebrating around you. Try to use "we" and "you" as much as possible. This is the way of Jesus and his final prayer for us. It is also, apparently, a good way not to die from a heart attack any time soon.

sledgehammers

"Neither this man nor his parents sinned; but that the works of God should be revealed in him." —John 9:3

I'm sure she only weighed about 100 pounds, but I handed the sledgehammer to the grandmother in my church. Together, we walked over to the church wall, and she started swinging as best she could, throwing the weight of the heavy mallet into the concrete brick.

We had been standing around talking and crying because a friend from our church had lost a grandson that morning, a stillbirth. Just two weeks prior, they had celebrated a baby shower for him in that very room. And now, two weeks from the due date, the baby was gone.

It just so happened that later that day, we would be knocking down a wall to open up more space in the church fellowship hall. Through tears, we were asking, "Why would God do this? What is happening? Why do such awful things have to happen?"

Two old ladies swinging at concrete with sledgehammers, taking out their anger at the world and its seeming lack of order and fairness. Seventy years old and still unable to tie things down and make them do what you want. Sometimes the world can feel like an awful place.

Humans, both modern and ancient, have often gravitated to the platform of pain with this answer: "God is telling us something, disciplining us, punishing us." But I tend to lean more toward how Jesus interprets the great pain of the world.

Jesus's disciples once asked him, "Teacher, who sinned, this man or his parents, that he was born blind?" Jesus answered, "Neither . . . but that the works of God should be revealed in him." When Jesus encountered pain, he saw an opportunity for God to use him to heal and restore. Jesus found meaning in the opportunity to rise to a challenge and reveal a human life that is selfless, compassionate, and Divine.

What will you do with the anger and pain you feel from tragedy and loss and injustice? Will you drive that sledgehammer of sorrow into becoming a more broken-open and compassionate human being? Or will you drive it into your own foot? Will you imagine a world with an angry god above, blame yourself, blame others? Will you fall into despair as you disparage yourself and your world?

In times of tragedy, Jesus calls us to allow others to rise up and show us God-like compassion and care. Let us receive it. Then, Jesus calls us to show divine compassion and sensitivity to those in need around us. This is the work of God: healing through compassion, receiving and giving and discovering something enduring and beautiful through the chaos of this imperfect world.

Instead of interpreting painful circumstances as punishment from God, let us imitate Jesus and see it as an opportunity for connection, compassion, healing, and trust in God and others. This does not protect us from pain, but in the long run it will heal us and make us better.

slanderous lies

> *"I tell you, on the day of judgment people will give account for every careless word they speak, for by your words you will be justified, and by your words you will be condemned."* —Matthew 12:36-37

If it sounds too good to be true, it probably is.

When I was around sixteen years old, I bought a book that convinced me that after reading it, I would be able to "speed-read" books, finishing entire volumes in under an hour, read a thousand words a minute, etc. I absolutely could not wait to achieve this new power. I could finish my homework in no time. I could start reading all kinds of books. I could become the smartest guy around. I imagined all the things I would learn.

I got ripped off.

That whole concept is ridiculous. Everyone's brain needs computing time. If anyone is reading that fast, they are skimming—not processing all the information appropriately. It was baloney. I never even finished the book.

We are quick to believe and share silly things, and Jesus knew this. He warned his followers about their words, the things they were passing along and spreading. We humans are lazy thinkers and careless speakers. We do not test the things we hear or the things we are taught or the things we assume. The result of our lazy thinking and careless words is that people get hurt. Good people are demonized by gossip. People wound others by being insensitive. Wise leaders are maligned for their misinterpreted decisions. The list is endless of the destruction wrought by people's quick and careless words.

Take this as wisdom: If it sounds too good to be true, it probably is.

If the fact or story makes your enemies look even more evil, it is likely untrue. If the fact or story makes your "side" look even braver, more selfless, or more innocent, it might be embellished.

You are not innocent if you pass along untrue information. You are accountable. "By your words you will be justified, and by your words you will be condemned" (Matt 12:37). You don't get a free pass for sharing destructive, untrue things, so think long and hard about what you hear and share. Our brains are tempted to adjust reality to our own emotions and preexisting understandings of the way things are. The thought of speeding through homework was so tantalizing for me that I let myself believe something ridiculous. I adjusted reality to my own emotions. You might do the same thing when you hear about something bad your best friend's ex-boyfriend supposedly did, or if a person of another color, religion, orientation, or economic background supposedly fulfills your stereotyped expectations. We get lazy with our thinking and believe things that align with our emotions and our worldview. And then, in our excitement, we pass those things along to others.

If you are hearing things secondhand (or thirdhand), you are not hearing them, and you can't justifiably share them. You will be judged for every careless word. Be careful of the gossip you spread. Be careful of sharing simplistic, political, social media memes. Be careful of the dramatized, "juicy" stories you tell. Be careful of pretending that you know things of which you are unsure. Be careful of being insensitive to people of other races, religions, orientations, and life backgrounds. You will be judged for every careless word.

Words have the power to heal or kill. It is rare that thoughtless, careless, unwise words do the healing. This week, may your words be thoughtful, wise, and true, and may they heal God's hurting, aching, suffering, oh-so-beloved world.

a helper

> *"But the Helper, the Holy Spirit, whom the Father will send in my name, he will teach you all things, and bring to your remembrance all things that I said to you. Peace I leave with you."* —John 14:26-27

I remember the day my daughter was born. We were living in my wife's hometown of Bucharest, Romania, in Eastern Europe. After being there just over a year, it was still nearly impossible for me to carry on a conversation with folks in the local language. I was scared. Romania is a poorer country. So many things could go wrong.

When the time came, we were on the seventh floor of our apartment building. We took our tiny, unreliable elevator down, where an ambulance met us. We both got in, and I watched with wide eyes as we sped through one of the most congested and maniac-driving cities on the planet.

What happens to us during these times? What happens when the test is coming, the relationship is ending, a life is passing, the loneliness is consuming, or the work and stress is never ceasing? Are we alone in our fears and regrets and shame and pain and anxiety?

We arrived at the hospital. Our doctor wasn't on duty, and they could not reach him. Another doctor looked at my wife and decided the baby was facing the wrong direction, the umbilical cord was wrapped around her head, and contractions were depressing her heartbeat. A C-section would be necessary to save the baby's life, and they prepped the operating table.

What happens to us during these times?

In the end, our doctor arrived at the last possible second. My wife delivered the baby in a tub using no medicine. Our child was perfect and healthy and amazing and fragile and awe inspiring . . . and did I mention perfect?

Through the whole ordeal, I understood nearly every word of Romanian that was spoken by the doctors. It felt like magic. We could have conceded to the C-section (we were pressured to do so), but we took a brave chance and held out. I could feel a presence, a divine energy pulsing within me, helping me rise to a momentous occasion.

The moral of the story is not that "everything turned out OK in the end." The moral is something that many would say is impossible and ridiculous and naive: there was a Spirit in that room with us, and we were not alone.

There is a Spirit available to you as well. You have to open your heart to it and believe it. You are never alone. Jesus had to leave his disciples to be crucified by the violence of our world, but he said that he did not leave them alone in this world. He left a Helper, an Advocate, an Encourager—"the Holy Spirit." This Spirit brings us God's peace in each of our daily trials and tribulations. This peace enables us to be better people—better Jesus followers. It makes us capable of serving and transforming the world around us.

You are not alone today. Open your eyes and your heart and hold on to that Helper as you walk with peace. Be alive and transform your world.

rise

"Do you want to be made well?" —John 5:6

I was at a lunch with friends, celebrating birthdays. Outside it was 90 degrees, but the roaring air conditioner had brought the temperature down to about -20 at our table. As we settled in and looked at our menu, we began to complain and shiver. We discussed clothing options. "Does anyone have a jacket in their car?" "I think I have an extra dress shirt you can throw on." We were so cold. We scoured the menu for the warmest-looking food.

Finally the waiter came. Without warning, one my friends said to him, "We need you to turn down the AC. This is way too cold. Can you take care of that immediately please?" We were shocked. Surely someone was going to spit in our food. We chastised our friend for being so rude.

But according to Jesus, he was right.

Jesus found a paralyzed man and he asked him what seems like a silly question: "Do you want to be made well?"

If you think about it, it is not so silly. We find excuses. We don't want to bother people. We convince ourselves that we deserve what is happening to us. The paralyzed man had been waiting thirty-eight years for someone to dip him into the healing pool. Instead, they stepped over him. We pay a company good money to sit in their freezing restaurant and suffer. We stay in a toxic relationship or don't fight for our marriages. Forgotten and discriminated groups don't stand up for themselves and demand justice. All the time, we sit in freezing restaurants and shush the people who speak up.

Before Jesus could heal the man, he had to ask him, "Do you want to be made well?" Because we can find some comfort in feeling sorry for ourselves. Sometimes there is something gratifying about being a victim. Usually, we are simply afraid.

Do you want to be well? Do you want justice? Do you want life-giving, healthy relationships? Do you want to be comfortable while you eat your food? Jesus says to you what he said to the man lying on the ground: "Rise, take up your bed, and walk" (v. 8).

You must rise. According to Jesus, it is OK to assert yourself. It is OK to ask for things. It is OK to have needs. It is OK to have wants. It is OK to want to "be well." You should fight for the things you want to achieve.

God created you with love and with excellence. Do not diminish that great gift of life. We best love others and glorify God when we are equals, not inferiors, to those around us. Who is pushing you over or around or not looking your way at all? What circumstances are holding you down? Even if you've spent thirty-eight years on the ground, I pray that today you rise.

back to here

Jesus [returned] to Nazareth, where he had been raised. On the Sabbath he went to synagogue as he normally did. —Luke 16:4

Every day for four years in college, I studied theology, psychology, biblical Greek, literature, and much more. All day every day, I would contemplate and muse and discuss and write about the greatest mysteries of the universe. Why has God let such terrible things happen in history? How can I help fix all the great problems of the world?

Then I graduated in May , at the bottom of the Great Recession, and no one would hire me, even with my fancy college degree. "Oh, you can tell me all about how Ellison's *Invisible Man* elucidated the existential plight of African American men in early twentieth century America? Great, that won't help you flip burgers here, so get a job somewhere else."

I cobbled through terrible jobs until I landed at JC Penney, fancy college degree in my back pocket. I was standing uselessly at my cash register one day when my manager approached me. "Skyler, do you see that toaster box on that shelf? It's slightly crooked. Can you go fix that?" His words crystallized for me the stupidity of where I was. I wanted to be in ministry. I wanted to be saving the world and helping people who were hurting, not twisting toaster boxes two degrees left to look busy.

For a year between college and divinity school, I was tormented by the uselessness of where I was. I was barely surviving on minimum wage and had a boring social life. What was the point of it all?

But think about Jesus Christ. He needed to return to his backwater, sleepy hometown to begin his history-altering ministry. And did you notice? "He went to synagogue, as he normally did." For thirty years, he had attended that synagogue with its so-so sermons and meh music and very normal Jewish families in the pews beside him, week after week. Six days a week, he worked in the hot sun, and one day a week, he sat in synagogue. Jesus needed to return to these things.

One day, you will need to return to the place you are in right now. You will need to return to this common ground to find yourself again and steer your path forward. You will finally see the beauty and importance of this time. You will discover that twisting toaster boxes on dusty shelves and driving home to cheap groceries and weird roommates shaped your character into someone able and worthy to influence the lives of others.

In life, we often find ourselves stuck in ruts where we don't want to be, caught between two mountaintops, waiting for the next big thing, wondering if we'll ever catch the dream and land where we aspire to land. But Jesus knew that in order to do great things in this world, he had to go back to that mundane place because the mundane place is where everyone else is. He needed to tap into the energy of Nazareth, of all those years in his hometown doing normal, boring things. Not in Jerusalem or Rome, but in that small place and in those quiet years. That was where he would find something profoundly redemptive for the world.

God offers purpose for the precise location where we currently are. Here, there is molding and shaping to be done within us. Here, there are important things before us. And if we will do whatever we are doing with all of our love and courage, if we will love as many people as possible with all that we have right now, if we will seek God day by day with hands that are calloused with work but open to the grace in this place, then we, like Jesus, will bring good news to the poor, liberty to the captives, and sight to the blind. We will let the oppressed go free. We will do incredible things. We just have to come back to here . . . to the ground beneath our feet.

boxes and stars

"Teacher, where are you staying?" He said to them, "Come and see."
—John 1:38-39

"So, are you the kind of Christian that believes all Christians should carry guns in order to shoot Muslims? Or are you the kind that believes all religions are relative and equal?"

Someone literally asked me that question once, upon meeting me. Do you see what he was doing? He stated two extremes of faith and wanted to back me into a corner. He wanted to see if I belonged in his box or the caricatured box he distrusted.

I think we do this all the time. We want to know what sort of assumptions we can make about someone else—do they belong in my box or the other box? It's a way of deciding whether we can trust someone. Are you a Republican or Democrat? A lot hangs in the balance. Which box do you belong in? Are you religious? Do you support same-sex marriage? Are you against abortion? Which box do you belong in?

These sorts of questions prevailed in Jesus's day too. Should Jews pay taxes to Caesar? Should Jews draw the sword against the Romans? Do you believe in resurrection after death? Yes or no? Which box do you belong in? We want simple answers to what are usually complex and sensitive questions. We want to reduce almost infinitely mysterious and complicated human beings into simple, easy-to-understand boxes.

Jesus almost never gave a straight answer. Once, his disciples asked him where he was sleeping that night. Even then, he answered "come and see." Jesus always answered questions with his own question, with some odd parable or story, or by answering a different, more important and deeper question. No yeses or nos. It must have been incredibly aggravating to his disciples. The Gospels record 307 questions asked to Jesus but only 8 straight answers. How radically different from his followers today.

I want to be like Jesus. I want to see the issues of the day as complex and complicated, and I hope I can keep asking the deeper questions. "Come and see." Let that be my answer if you want to know my opinion. Come and observe my life, my actions, what I do when no one is looking. "Are you pro-life?" Observe how I treat the lives around me. "Are you conservative?" Observe the things I conserve with my speech and actions.

Let us be like Jesus. Let us view the people with whom we share this world as evolving, fluid, sojourning human beings—more mysterious than the stars of the sky. Let us see people in place of issues. Like chicks emerging from eggs, let us step outside of the boxes that talking heads on cable news and social media have squeezed us into. We can rediscover our own smallness—the wonder and mystery of people and life and God's creation. We can imitate Jesus's profound, indiscriminate love for all. Boxes and stars, boxes and stars . . . your world will exist like one or the other. Consider what David Dark writes in *Life's Too Short to Pretend You're Not Religious*:

> When I label people, I no longer have to deal with them thoughtfully. I no longer have to feel overwhelmed by their complexity, the lives they live, the dreams they have . . . . The mystery of their existence has been solved and filed away before I've had a chance to be moved by them or even begun to catch a glimpse of who they might be. They've been neutralized. There's hardly any action quite so undemanding, so utterly imaginative, as the affixing of a label. It's the costliest of mental shortcuts. (InterVarsity Press, 2016)

ready. set. fail.

Yet in all these things we are more than conquerors through him who loved us. —Romans 8:37

I'm probably the world's expert at failing. I host a program and no one comes to it. I give a sermon and realize later that it made no sense. I misread some social cues and embarrass myself. I forget that my wife is always right.

Growing up, I guess I was naturally decent at most school subjects and naturally decent at some sports. But I was never great at anything and quite poor at many things. As an adult, I question myself, my success, my abilities, and more. And I feel like I regret about 75 percent of the things I say, so I often try to keep my mouth shut and my ears open.

I fail.

Do you feel like you fail at things? Do you feel like you aren't good enough? Do you question your abilities or worth? Do you want to give up, or do you find yourself not even attempting certain things?

Paul tried to tell people about Jesus, and instead they stoned him until they thought he was dead. He tried going on a journey by ship, and his ship sank. Close friends betrayed him. People he invested in turned on him. He lost all the prestige and respect he once garnered as a Jewish teacher. He struggled with guilt. He would start a new church, and all those people would do awful things to one another. He kept getting knocked down.

But he knew that even if life knocked him down ten thousand times, he was going to get up ten thousand and one. He knew that God loved him without limit, without fail, and that nothing could ever, ever, ever separate him from that great, divine love. Everyone makes mistakes, but defeat and failure are ultimately a choice we make. Truly, we only fail when we give up.

So Paul just kept waking up each morning, working hard, loving harder, and trusting in God's faithfulness even more. Whatever you have "failed" at, whatever has been done to you in life, no matter how unfair life has been or how limited your resources or talents seem to be, you can be "more than a conqueror." You can overcome. You can get back up again. You can do great things for your world and for God. God loves you, and God is with you.

Jesus people are not conquered. We refuse to allow failures and tragedies and difficulties to beat us or diminish us. We are conquerors. *More* than conquerors. We overcome each of our challenges because God will never give up on us and we are never alone.

Today, get back up. Get back up tomorrow! Get back up every day. You are loved without limit, so become the conqueror you are supposed to be.

beloved

"This is my beloved son, in whom I am well pleased." —Mark 1:11

I remember the week my life was changed forever. My wife gave birth to a perfect baby boy. Our three-year-old daughter, our parents, our friends and our church welcomed him into this world with joy and adoration, celebration and food, smiles and hugs and kisses. He was beloved and a source of immense pleasure to all who encountered his seven-pound body with a head full of hair.

He was useless. He could not mow the grass or shoot a free throw or graduate from college with honors. He was just a baby, and in that time he mostly just slept and ate and wet himself. Admittedly, he was pretty good at those things.

A baby is vulnerable. He is utterly dependent on others, insufficient in and of himself. For this reason, we fall over ourselves, we cannot contain ourselves, we find ourselves totally captivated by babies. We are driven to hold, cuddle, and nurture them in their state of total dependence.

It is ironic, then, that we are so repelled by being vulnerable ourselves. We don't like to admit that we are wrong or ask for forgiveness. We don't like to ask for help. We want to be strong, right, and independent. Similarly, we insist on the perfection of others. We are unforgiving when they put their foot in their mouth, behave rudely, or even make selfish life choices.

I think Jesus understood, in a way no one else ever had before, how vulnerability was necessary for authentic loving relationships. And that is why he insisted so much on grace, forgiveness, and mercy: he knew that grace and vulnerability go hand in hand. If you are gracious, you promote trust and vulnerability in others. If you are vulnerable, you can catalyze grace in others.

May you learn from my infant son. May he teach you the great power of vulnerability, of bearing yourself up, of confessing your shortcomings to others. May he teach you to love others, not based on how useful they are but on the incredible and marvelous fact of their existence.

God spoke his pleasure and love over Jesus before Jesus performed a single miracle or taught a single lesson. Before Jesus was tempted by the devil, God's love was declared and guaranteed. May it be so among us. Let us patiently guarantee our love for one another, like a father to his son. Let us live vulnerable lives with one another, like a baby in his parent's arms.

silence

Very early in the morning, while it was still dark, Jesus got up, left the house and went off to a solitary place, where he prayed. —Mark 1:35

I lived in Bucharest, Romania, for two years. The Eastern European city of over 2 million is people stacked on top of people—one of the most congested and crowded cities on the continent. Its soundtrack is a chorus of car horns, trams rolling on rails and ringing their bells, and Romani blaring their manele music on big speakers. It is a very loud city.

I remember the first time it snowed. The filthy, grimy city was buried in five feet of perfectly white powder. The graffitied walls and trash-strewn streets turned into a magical and beautiful winter wonderland, and, perhaps most spectacular of all, all the sound was buried with it. No cars. No people. No music. No bells. Only silence. One felt obliged to speak in soft tones while tromping through the now-marvelous streets of the city. My heart soared. I discovered new energy and my mind was cleared. The silence and beauty of the snow had worked deeply into my soul.

Yet as time progresses, silence is an increasingly precious and rare jewel in the sands of our lives.

Take prayer, for example. Two generations ago, prayer was much more commonplace. Days were bookended by time spent on one's knees, giving thanks to God and requesting God's intervention in the workings of the world. But even for religious people, prayer is disappearing. We cannot bear the silence. We cannot look away from our phones. We cannot help wondering "What am I missing out on right now?" Prayer is not a noisy thing, but we modern humans are addicted to noise.

Jesus regularly sought out silence. Crowds followed him everywhere he went, and it was difficult to be alone, but he made it happen. He arose and left the house "while it was still dark." His quiet times were specifically for the sake of prayer, for expressing his wishes to God and sharing his heart.

Let us imitate Jesus. Let us regularly seek out that marvelous silence that a snowfall imposes on us so rarely. Let us prioritize our relationship with God, praying for the people we love and praying about the things that burden us. Let us reset our alarm clocks and become committed to a practice that will lift up our hearts and shape our world for the better.

Saturdays and Sundays

One of them, an expert in the law, tested him with this question: "Teacher, which is the greatest commandment in the Law?" Jesus replied: "'Love the Lord your God with all your heart and with all your soul and with all your mind.' This the first and greatest commandment. And the second is like it: 'Love your neighbor as yourself.' All the Law and the Prophets hang on these two commandments."
—Matthew 22:35-40

I heard a story of a man named Clayton working with a client who told him he needed to assist their team the upcoming Saturday in order to complete their project. Clayton responded, "Thank you, but I'm so sorry—I've dedicated all my Saturdays to my wife and my children." The client was furious and stormed off. However, the client returned after consulting his team and said, "We've worked it out, and the team has agreed that we can all come in on Sunday and complete the project." Clayton answered, "Thank you so much for doing that, but I'm so sorry. I cannot come to work on Sunday. I've dedicated all my Sundays to God."

According to the story, the client didn't fire Clayton.

Have you ever stopped to carefully and deliberately choose your priorities? What and who is most important? What is the correct order? How will this be represented in your investments of time, money, energy, and attention? If you do not do this, if you do not give great thought and care and prayer to the question of what is most important in your life, the loudest and pushiest voices around you will.

The Jewish expert of the law was wise to ask Jesus about what was most important, and it seems to me that Jesus had already thought it through. Loving God is most important, and loving your neighbor is second most important.

Our culture, I think, has ignored Jesus's wisdom. We have everything out of order, and indeed we have paid a terrible price for it. Parents put work before their family, or spouses prioritize their children over their own marriage. On a typical Sunday, the majority of self-professed Christians are not in church. Everything else takes priority over God.

All of this probably sounds a lot like a curmudgeonly man complaining about the world around him, and maybe that's partly true. But I've made many mistakes for many years and thought a lot about these words from Jesus. I've been married for over a decade, have two kids, and work in a career I love. Ultimately, my choice is this: to make my relationship with God my first priority, my relationship with my wife my second priority, my relationship with my kids my third priority, and the work God has given me to do my fourth priority. Everything else comes after all that.

If we are not spiritually formed and centered and grounded and guided by our Higher Power, we fail to love our spouse well. If we do not model an affectionate and peaceful marriage for our kids, they will struggle to have successful relationships in their own lives. If we don't show our kids that they are more important to us than our jobs or money or friends or hobbies, they will become lost within themselves. If we do not take great pride and care in our work, the world around us and within us will suffer in the wake of our irresponsibility.

Don't you see? Love God first. Love your neighbor second. Choose your priorities with purpose. Jesus says that everything hangs on what we decide is most important in life.

June

religion

Jesus said, "Go, show yourselves to the priests." And as they went, they were cleansed. —Luke 17:14

It can be hard to attend church—to wake up on a weekend morning or dedicate an hour in the middle of a hectic, stressful, overly busy week. And even harder is doing life with other people who can be too old, too different, too boring, or too obnoxious. What's the use of church of anyway? Organized religion is difficult and inconvenient, to say the least.

Jesus was the king of interior spirituality. Read his classic the Sermon on the Mount. He was all about private prayer and inward morality. But there is simply no question that Jesus remained firmly committed to organized religion, despite its hiccups. Notwithstanding his criticisms, Jesus deferred to other priests and participated in synagogue and temple worship. He was part of the synagogue system—he was a Jewish rabbi. His followers sustained that commitment. The book of Acts and all of the New Testament epistles begin with describing not if but *how* they organized themselves into a religious family.

Jesus sought to build religious community for his students: community where people were healed, taught, and liberated from the demons inside them, the things that stole their lives away. Jesus himself was a religious teacher and healer, organizing people around him. Within that institution, Jesus charged his followers to serve one another and the world.

There is no record of Jesus establishing an incredible show for his followers each week, a star preacher with rocking electric guitars or stunning organs. For Jesus, the crucial focus was the community formed around God and God's good news. When faith is personalized and individualized—like when someone says, "Every once in a while, I'll say a prayer in my head or go on a nice hike or read an inspirational book"—it is vulnerable to becoming shallow, passive, peripheral, and most of all self-generated and unchallenging.

If faith or spirituality is about something larger than ourselves, we need the sacred books (Scriptures) that existed for millennia before us. We need religious traditions that preceded us by centuries. Most of all, we need the regular community of "brothers and sisters" and teachers who are outside of ourselves—loving us, encouraging us, and caring for us in times of need.

This week, hear Jesus's message. Show yourself to your priest (or pastor), face to face and in the flesh. If you're in a new place and it's hard to find a church "just like" your old one, or if your past experiences with church were bad, maybe try something new. On the way there or back home, you just might find yourself cleansed and healed.

spilling salt

> *"Salt is good; but if salt has lost its saltiness, how can you season it? Have salt in yourselves, and be at peace with one another."*
> —Mark 9:50

In my mind, I was thinking about the cute girl from first period. Five minutes later, I was thinking about lunch. And five minutes later, I was making weekend plans in my head. High school chemistry was boring. I didn't even have friends in that class. I didn't care about it. I didn't want to be there, but all I had were more boring classes, laps at swim practice, and time on my feet at my fast-food job. I had all of this to endure in the hours and days ahead.

Life can often be bland and colorless or difficult and sad.

One solution is to cover all your food in salt. You can make life exciting with French fries and fast burgers and fried chicken. Another solution is to keep scrolling the vivid social media screen. Or you could buy more stuff or drink lots of alcohol. There are many ways to spice things up and make an otherwise boring or sad life exciting.

Jesus teaches an alternative path, and that's a good thing. Because using junk food to make life good will ultimately wear you down and destroy you. That's also true of screen addictions and the empty and destructive promises of partying. These things are mirages in the desert. "Have salt in yourselves," Jesus said, "and be at peace with one another."

When we live prayerful lives of deep and constant gratitude, when we daily make others feel good by sharing our gratitude for them, we create salt within ourselves. There is a direct and short line between exercising our gratitude muscles and feeling joyful, making others joyful, and having more peace in our relationships. Salt is inside of us, spilling all over the place.

Ask yourself why you feel the need to endlessly scroll on your phone, eat junk, or buy more stuff. Then practice lots of gratitude today. Go out of your way to pray prayers of gratitude to God for every conceivably good thing in front of you, and go out of your way to express a big thanks to every conceivable person you can. Be ridiculously and weirdly grateful, even towards people you thought you didn't care about or with whom you feel bitter. People love being around grateful people, and people who are grateful end up loving their lives. It's like salt on potatoes. Gratitude seasons the world and brings peace between us.

The world around you and within you needs you to have salt in yourself.

terrible and horrible and awful

Then their eyes were opened, and they recognized him; and he vanished from their sight. They said to each other, "Were not our hearts burning within us while he was talking to us on the road?" —Luke 24:31-32

On certain days or weeks, I feel like the whole world is careening toward inexorable doom. Usually, it follows a nice cocktail of global natural disasters, terrible decisions from politicians, tragedies happening to people I know personally, and bad or potentially bad circumstances in my own life. Have you ever felt like things going on in the world were terrible and horrible and awful?

Two millennia ago, two men were walking down the road feeling like everything was terrible and horrible and awful. As a people, they'd had their land occupied by foreign oppressors for centuries. But recently, an anointed man had appeared on the scene during their annual festival. This was a festival where they celebrated a time when God's anointed one delivered them from their enemies many centuries before. But this time, their supposedly anointed man had been executed. He didn't overthrow anybody. All their hopes and dreams were crushed. Life would go on as normal.

Terrible and horrible and awful.

A third man came up beside them on the road, and for hours they discussed the big events of the last week. The third man explained that all of these things were just part of God's story—a painful dip before a glorious reprise. When they arrived at their home in Emmaus, they invited him in for dinner and he ate with them. Suddenly, they realized that all day they had been talking with Jesus, the Anointed One who had been crucified and buried. Right then, he vanished from sight. They had spent the day talking with the tangible sign that resurrection was right in front of them, that the bread of life was right in front of them, that the light of the world was right in front of them. Their hearts had burned the whole time with that fire, but they had ignored its crackling warmth and light while they muttered about the terrible, the horrible, and the awful.

In the swirl of things being so bad, what is right in front of your eyes? You need to have faith, but you can see it. It is the risen Lord. It is resurrection and it is life. To share Brian McClaren's prayer: "I'm here, God. You're here. We are here together."[2] Pray that prayer under your breath. Most of the awful things are distant in your past, distant in some possible future, or distant across the broad skin of the earth. Right here and right now, the mundane things right in front of you are probably quite lovely and good. For a moment, don't shake your fist at the God of Friday's cross or plead with the God of Easter Sunday. See how God is present to you right here and now. Come back to this moment and see how good it is on this precise road you are walking.

I am here. God is here. We are here together.

patience

> *He took the blind man by the hand and led him out of the village; and when he had put saliva on his eyes and laid his hands on him, he asked him, "Can you see anything?" And the man looked up and said, "I can see people, but they look like trees, walking." Then Jesus laid his hands on his eyes again; and he looked intently and his sight was restored, and he saw everything clearly.* —Mark 8:23-25

What would Jesus do? Jesus would spit in your eye.

This is a weird story. Jesus wants to heal someone, but (1) he has to remove him from his village, (2) he has to put saliva in his eyes, and (3) the healing doesn't work the first time.

Other times in the Gospels, Jesus raises the dead, walks on water, heals blindness and illness, and even resurrects from the grave himself—always with a simple word or gesture. Why does Jesus have such difficulty with this

---

2. McClaren, *Naked Spirituality: A Life with God in 12 Simple Words* (New York: HarperOne, 2011), 36.

blind man? Or, put another way, "Why did this man have such difficulty getting better?"

Sometimes I get frustrated with people. (Um, all the time.) I wonder why this guy can't get his act together. I wonder why that girl is still so hypocritical about her faith. I wonder why people behave with incompetence, selfishness, and apathy. I see people squander incredible opportunities. In these moments, I am tempted to judge and accuse. I am tempted to assume that they are indefinitely "blind."

But I remember this story. Unlike with others, Jesus had to go way out of his way to heal this man. Usually, he didn't need to drag people out of the village to heal them. But that's what it took with this one. Usually, he didn't need to put spit in people's eyes. But that's what it took with this one. Usually, his miracles worked the first time. But it took two tries with this one.

Jesus was patient with the blind man's long journey toward healing. He recognized that this man had a unique life story that required a unique relationship.

Will you be patient with others? Instead of throwing up your hands or judging their incompetence or misbehavior, respond with positivity, care, and respect. Believe that they can grow and change and become something better.

If they need more love, patience, and effort than others, then so be it. If you must drag them from the village or spit in their eyes or try, try, try again, then so be it. If some journeys toward healing are longer than others, then so be it. In the end, the blind man saw everything clearly. Jesus's patience and care paid off.

Perhaps it will be so with you and the people around you as well.

sunshine and shadows

And when they had sung a hymn, they went out to the Mount of Olives. —Mark 14:26

Sitting where I sit (doing ministry with college students), I have received an unfair portion of bad news recently. Lots of sad things have been happening all around. It is unfair. Painful. Depressing. I feel that I have been sitting among many shadows.

You too may have experienced your own hard and dark and long shadows in life—recently or even right now. These difficult things can challenge our faith in the idea of a good God. The shadows can challenge our sense of continuing forward in life. Maybe it becomes difficult to see any goodness at all.

As a dark cloud laid upon me, I decided to try singing something cheerful and spiritual. I tried many new and old worship songs. Finally I found one:

> This is my Father's world,
> the birds their carols raise,
> the morning light, the lily white,
> declare their maker's praise.
> This is my Father's world:
> he shines in all that's fair;
> in the rustling grass I hear him pass;
> he speaks to me everywhere.[3]

Somehow, it gave me a big boost, and I sang it over and over again. And at to church on Sunday we sang this one:

> God of beauty, truth, and goodness, Lord of wisdom yet unknown,
> grant us strength to match the vision as we come before Your throne
> . . .
> Sing a joyful alleluia, Praising God in all you do,
> and remember as you witness, God is singing over you![4]

My eyes closed and my heart swelled and I held on to the words for dear life.

Jesus told his disciples that he was about to be betrayed, and right before they departed for the Mount of Olives, the place of his betrayal and arrest preceding his torture and execution, they sang a hymn together. Jesus prepared himself for his darkest moment by singing to God.

When life is weighing you down, imitate Jesus and his students. Find the sacred songs that celebrate the goodness of life and the good God who is mysteriously behind it all. Listen to them, hum them, sing them alone, sing them with others. Find the sunshine behind the shadows. Remember that indeed, the shadows prove the sunshine. We mourn broken things only because we are blessed enough to have experienced happy and lovely

---

3. Maltbie D. Babcock (1901).
4. Wesley Forbis, "God of Beauty, Truth, and Goodness," in *Celebrating Grace Hymnal* (Macon, GA: Celebrating Grace, Inc., 2010).

things. When the shadows come, sing about the source of life and love—the light that shines behind them and illuminates a world that is, after all, still incredibly beautiful.

faith and heart

> *"Why do you reason because you have no bread? Do you still not perceive or understand? Are your hearts hardened? Do you have eyes, and fail to see? Do you have ears, and fail to hear? And do you not remember?"* —Mark 8:17-18

When I was in college, I minored in Spanish. I thought the language was neat, but mostly I wanted to be a preacher when I grew up, and everyone told me I would need "marketable skills" in case I needed a regular job while "preaching on the side." I studied abroad a lot to improve my Spanish—a summer in Chile, a month in Mexico, a month in Costa Rica and Nicaragua. I invested a lot in learning the language.

But do you know what? Not once have my Spanish skills ever made me marketable for anything.

We humans look at our lack of bread. We make decisions based on the current lack and on the perceived lack of the future. In Mark 8, Jesus has just fed over 4,000 people with nearly nothing for the second time. Now, the disciples have traveled across the lake in their boat and forgotten to bring bread. They are anxious, thinking Jesus might be upset about not having enough.

Do you hear how incredulous Jesus is? He cannot believe their lack of faith. He cannot believe how easily they have forgotten the way faith fed 4,000 just now and fed 5,000 before. He cannot believe how we plan for the future, thinking there will be no bread. He cannot believe we form our decisions based on what we lack instead of on what is possible through faith and heart.

While I pursued Spanish, I studied other things I loved: English literature, religion, Greek, psychology. I pursued my dream and went to divinity school, where I spent three great years asking hard questions about God and preparing for ministry. I ate my nerdy heart out. Now I do what I love—I do ministry all day every day and go to work with joy.

In life, you will have many voices insisting that you reason based on what you and this world lack. Voices will talk about job markets and salaries. Voices will insist that "there is not enough." But remember what faith and heart can do.

Follow your heart, your interests, your passion. Do not seek fame. Do not seek money. Do not seek the approval of others, for these are not noble things. Our world (and yes, its markets) is looking for people who are unapologetically passionate about whatever weird thing they enjoy. If you truly love it, you will passionately study it, work hard at it, and crave mastery of it. You will become a master of it after a long time, and you will provide value to the world through it, and someone will pay you—maybe even a lot—to be into whatever weird thing makes you tick. Today, may you hear Jesus's voice begging you to believe in God's abundance.

Roger

Jesus began his ministry at about thirty years of age. —Luke 3:23

I once met a guy named Roger, who now reminds me of other people I occasionally meet.

Roger was a sixty-year-old pretending to be twenty. He tried to dress as if he were twenty, in spite of his leathered skin from too much suntanning and his flushed face from a lifetime of too much alcohol. At sixty, he still wasn't very invested in his kids or a particularly meaningful career, and he definitely wasn't investing time, money, or energy into serving his community. Roger wanted to have fun and live it up without all that serious "adult stuff."

The culture that you and I live in idolizes the twenties—that age when your body is young and people supposedly drink and date and have money to blow. Maturity (30+) is associated with boring "suit and tie" jobs, an obsession with money, or a boring lifestyle as servants to children. It's associated with unhappiness.

The Bible does not talk about Jesus's twenties at all. Everything significant about Jesus's life happened after his twenties. Apparently, his twenties were so incredibly boring and uneventful that there was nothing worth mentioning in any of the four Gospel accounts. Jesus did not have a "career job" until he was thirty. Jesus was not "famous" until he was thirty. As a Jewish rabbi, his youth would have consisted of tremendous studies and hard work, memorizing Scripture and studying to become a teacher.

I loved my twenties. I did crazy, unforgettable stuff. But in my thirties, it just got so much better and more significant. Often, I'm in bed at 9 p.m.

I change diapers, read bedtime stories, fix leaky faucets, and wear ties. I drive a very old Honda Civic. But I'm hitting my stride in my career, and I'm in love with my kids and my wife.

I am persuaded that, just like with Jesus, my life and the mark I am going to make is just getting started. Jesus's life gives us permission to think of our twenties as a happy and hard time of preparation rather than of frivolous spending and trivial relationships. The good news is that a life of following Jesus gets better with age instead of worse and more desperate.

Let us celebrate and work toward a mature, responsible adulthood where we can finally and joyfully make a mark on our world with something of meaningful substance.

Don't be like Roger. Be like Jesus. Learn, work, and love, and find deeper and deeper joy with every season of life.

the beginning of murder

> *"You have heard that it was said to those of ancient times, 'You shall not murder'; and 'whoever murders shall be liable to judgment.' But I say to you that if you are angry with a brother or sister, you will be liable to judgment; and if you insult a brother or sister, you will be liable to the council; and if you say, 'You fool,' you will be liable to the hell of fire . . . therefore . . . first be reconciled to your brother or sister."*
> —Matthew 5:21-22, 24

Pop! Pop! Pop!

I woke up at 3 a.m. to the sound of far-off gunfire. My heart rate quickened and my stomach turned in knots. I was in my home, my wife asleep next to me, and I knew that something terrible had just happened. Anxious, I vigorously followed the local news the following day, and soon enough my instinctive feelings were verified: a sixteen-year-old girl had been murdered in the street a few blocks away.

Jesus lived in a time of violence too. Research suggests that the time of Jesus was far more violent and bloody than ours is today. Jesus was a teacher of what we call the Old Testament, and he found a limitation in its teaching. Telling people "do not murder" didn't go far enough in terms of curbing violence. Jesus saw that the violence all around us begins a long time before anyone swings a sword or pulls a trigger. It is hard to tell a murderous person, "No way, dude, you're not supposed to do that—it's against the rules."

People become violent after insults are thrown around. They throw insults after they feel angry, and they feel angry after their sense of connection and trust is severed. Jesus understood that we humans hate feeling lonely, unsafe, not good enough, powerless, or inferior to others. We hate those feelings so much that we mask our pain and fear with anger. We dwell on the feeling of anger in order to push the other feelings aside. We channel that anger into insults. Eventually, we might even channel it into violence.

"Therefore, first be reconciled to your brother or sister." This is how Jesus people cure the malaise of violence. We seek reconciliation where there is disconnection, and we do that by building trust and connection with others. Like Jesus, we always respect feelings rather than dismiss them. We seek connection over isolation. Equality over power. Forgiveness over judgment. We do not demonize our adversaries—we find their goodness and start there, because we cannot be reconciled to someone whom we have labelled a "fool" or monster. We do not give anger a foothold in our relationships.

I hope I never hear of another sixteen-year-old girl breathing her last breath. I want less violence in my world because I believe it is loved by a good God. How do we bring murder to an end? We find it at its beginning and we stop it there. As Jesus says, reconciliation is the thing for which we are each held responsible in a world torn apart by murder.

the devil

> *Then the* LORD *said to Satan, "Have you considered my servant Job? There is no one on earth like him; he is blameless and upright, a man who fears God and shuns evil." "Does Job fear God for nothing?" Satan replied. ". . . But now stretch out your hand and strike everything he has, and he will surely curse you to your face."* —Job 1:8-11

Would you like some unsolicited relationship advice? If your partner is causing 99 percent of the problems, if your partner represents 99 percent of the crazy, if your partner has made 99 percent of the mistakes . . . stop trying to fix your partner. You don't have a 99 percent problem; you have a 1 percent problem. Focus your energy on the 1 percent you can do something about. Focus on yourself being and doing and getting better.

Satan is first introduced in the ancient Jewish story of Job, and I think most English translations of Scripture get things wrong here. The original Hebrew calls him *ha satan* ("sah–than"), literally meaning the adversary or the accuser. A satan is an accuser or enemy, not someone's personal name. In Job's story, there is an innocent man, and an accuser walks up to God to talk about the man. The accuser focuses on criticizing and complaining. "Yes, he looks nice, but surely he wouldn't be if his circumstances were different." The accuser has nothing to criticize about the real Job, so he creates a straw man to knock down. This is classic, desperate gossip. This is something we have all done. It's easier to make a good man look bad rather than deal with our own issues.

The accuser doesn't come to God for help in working out his own issues. He's got his nose in Job's business for some reason. Probably, it felt good to worry about someone else instead of himself. I know I can feel gratified when I convince myself someone "out there" is more of a mess than I am. What Job and the accuser expose about me is this: when I am anxious and afraid and hurt, when the world is changing and my life is in transition, I start looking for others to push down with little gripes: my spouse, my family, my church, my colleagues. I start throwing darts in my mind or start talking about someone behind their back. I don't want to go to people directly and share my heart with them. It's easier to become the accuser who draws triangles instead of direct lines and who makes straw men to knock down.

Think about how stressful things are for everyone around you. The epidemic of anxiety is spreading around us like wildfire. The fruit hangs low for each of us to make triangles and straw men and never bother asking what we can do or where we are responsible. So remember the old story of Job and the accuser and which one of them is eventually remembered as the devil. "Ask not what your country can do for you," one of our presidents said. "Ask what you can do for your country." I could replace "country" with "marriage" or "church" or a lot of different things. Where have I been wrong, and what can I do to help?

May you focus on your own 1 percent. May you draw direct lines instead of triangles. May you ask what you can do instead of asking what others can and should do and aren't doing for you. May you strive to be less like the accuser and more like Job.

holes in the sky

"Happy are those who don't see and yet believe." —John 20:29

Have you ever asked yourself the question (as I have), "If God is real, why doesn't God prove it to the world? Why doesn't God just rip a hole in the sky, wave to everybody, throw out some candy to the kids, and then zip it up and check back in occasionally?"

It's a great question, but it requires a bit of a loop if we sit with it honestly.

In his letter to the Ephesians, the apostle Paul talked about "salvation by grace through faith." It was a way of saying that as long as we strive to prove ourselves worthy of God's love, we make a mockery of what love is. If love is conditioned on proving oneself, it isn't love in the first place. We can't have love if we don't have grace. Grace is free, unmerited favor and love. Some of us struggle to trust this grace—that God's love for us and also other people's love for us is secure, even when we perform poorly.

There is a flip side to grace through faith. If we are not offering grace for others to receive with faith, do we believe in grace in the first place? When we stop offering love to people because they are cranky or immature or we feel unsure of their motives, we are not offering grace. If people have to prove that they are cool enough, nice enough, or enlightened enough to have our love, we are not offering grace. There is no faith or trust in our relationships.

And this brings us back to God tearing a hole in the sky and throwing out peanut butter cups. At a certain point, we have to second-guess what's going on in our hearts when we talk about proof. There isn't a lot of trust or love or grace in proof. If I'm demanding that God earn my love by proving God's existence, you might say I'm not offering free, unmerited favor and love to God. And I'm stuck in a mindset of my love being something that has to be earned by God—and by everyone else too.

I respect and honor all who are in a place in life where belief in God feels impossible. Doubt has been a major theme of my own spiritual journey. Our questions about God often come from serious places of pain and rigorous and thoughtful questions. But in my journey, I have decided to set everyone, even God, free from the demanding chains I was creating. I choose to trust in God and God's grace for me, even when the sky is the same, uninterrupted blue. I have to live a life premised on faith, not works; on grace, not proof. That faith, that trust, will open me up to a world of abundant grace and save me from some turbulent and unforgiving waters in life. I think that's what Paul meant. I think it's what Jesus meant too. Happy are those who don't always have to see and yet still choose to have faith.

salt

"You are the salt of the earth; but if salt has lost its taste, how can its saltiness be restored?" —Matthew 5:13

Yesterday, on a road trip, I swung through the McDonald's drive-thru and they handed me the only two good things on their menu: a big, icy Coca-Cola and a box of fries. Nearly 700 calories of deliciousness. Those fries were just what I needed to get me home. Each hot bite lit me up with its salty, greasy goodness.

One time, Jesus went on top of a little mountain (a big hill), and all these people followed him to hear what he had to say. They were peasants . . . fishermen and farmers and craftsmen and women and children. Almost everyone in the crowd did not know how to read, had never left their village, and had little surplus income. Their lives could be swept away at the whim of the Roman oppressors, a farming accident, a disease, or a child's birth. Their lives were frail and unnoticed by the world. Most were uncultured, ignorant, poor hillbillies. They mourned, they were meek, they were hungry, and they were persecuted. Jesus looked at these people and told them they were blessed. He told them that they (not the rich, powerful elites in the big cities) were the salt of the earth.

In my mind, salt is about the only good thing fast food has going for it. Salt is what makes fake food taste real, crummy food taste good, and boring meals taste exciting. Woe to the world if there were no salt!

Jesus looked at this crowd of hillbillies scratching their armpits, picking their noses, swatting flies, and he told them that they were what made life good for the whole world. They were blessed and a blessing. They were salt. They were the "light of the world." Jesus said that if they lost their saltiness—the thing that made them who they were—life would lose its zest to the detriment of all people. Jesus restored their dignity. Jesus saw their God-given value when no one else did and reminded them of it.

Think of your world and the people in your life. Who is living in the shadows and margins? Who are the hillbillies? The thugs? The rednecks?

The poor? The ignored? The obnoxious? The losers? Whose life matters "less"?

Find them. Make a choice to see the salt in them and the light to which even they are perhaps blind. If all their lives they have received messages that they are insignificant and unworthy and less than and a burden on society, you can spark change when you imitate Jesus and say to them, "You are the salt of my life and our world."

spilled milk

> *To some who were confident of their own righteousness and looked down on everyone else, Jesus told this parable: "Two men went up to the temple to pray, one a Pharisee and the other a tax collector. The Pharisee stood by himself and prayed: 'God, I thank you that I am not like other people—robbers, evildoers, adulterers—or even like this tax collector. I fast twice a week and give a tenth of all I get.' But the tax collector stood at a distance. He would not even look up to heaven, but beat his breast and said, 'God, have mercy on me, a sinner.' I tell you that this man, rather than the other, went home justified before God. For all those who exalt themselves will be humbled, and those who humble themselves will be exalted."* —Luke 18:9-14

When our son was four months old, he was the cutest, fattest, jolliest little man ever. Stubbornly, he refused to nurse directly from his mother, insisting instead on drinking strictly from bottles. This wouldn't have been so bad except that the bottles began to leak milk all the time. Having a baby is joyful but also very stressful. It is much more stressful when every time you try to feed your baby, half the milk spills all over you and him. In our duress, we shouted and cursed and accused the bottle company of being employed by incompetent morons. Who would engineer such low-quality bottles that made a huge mess every time the baby ate? Stress, stress, stress. Anger, anger, anger. Stupid bottles.

One week, my mom watched our kids for a few days in another state while my wife and I went on a short trip. When the kids returned home, I was unpacking their bags and pulled out our baby's milk bottle. I noticed that its rubber nipple had a tighter, better seal against the bottle than it normally did. I looked closer. Mom had simply pulled the rubber nipple a little further through its plastic ring and brought it to the place where it was designed to fit snugly. No more leaks.

All this time, all we had to do was tug just a little bit harder on that rubber nipple, and we could completely eradicate a problem that was truly plaguing our lives. This could be an object lesson on how hard it is to live life as a stupid person. How dumb could we be?

When you are confronted with problems in your relationships at home, school, or work, do you seek to solve them through blaming others and assuming your innocence? Or do you look long and hard at your attitudes, your actions, your thoughts, and your emotional control? It feels better to overcome our obstacles by looking down on others. It is a lot harder to look within ourselves and ask, "What did I do wrong to contribute to this problem?"

As my wife and I sought solutions for the leaking bottles, we spent more energy blaming "the stupid bottle company" than asking ourselves, "What am I doing wrong? How can I do better?" We paid a heavy price for focusing on the perceived faults of others rather than improving our own. Blaming others almost never solves anything.

Part of the heart of Jesus's message is that we are all sinners. We are all good, but we are imperfect and make big mistakes all the time. We are no better than anyone else. Tax collectors were the epitome of hated and sinful people. Pharisees were the esteemed saints of the day. Jesus flipped the script because the tax collector owned up to his wrongdoing while the Pharisee blamed others. The tax collector would have done a better job preparing his baby's bottles because he looked within instead of cursing others.

What problems are you facing today? To what extent are you responsible? Jesus challenges us to overcome life's struggles by admitting our own mistakes and improving ourselves instead of judging, blaming, and condemning others.

keep fishing

"I'm going out to fish," Simon Peter told them, and they said, "We'll go with you." So they went out and got into the boat, but that night they caught nothing. Early in the morning, Jesus stood on the shore, but the disciples did not realize that it was Jesus. He called out to them, "Friends, haven't you any fish?" "No," they answered. He said, "Throw your net on the right side of the boat and you will find some." When they did, they were unable to haul the net in because of the large number of fish. —John 21:3-6

Jesus had just been executed by the occupying foreign army—the Roman Empire. That was a tough pill to swallow for Jesus's followers. They had hoped he would be a "Messiah," someone who would overthrow the Roman occupiers. Things had turned out to be a huge and tragic disappointment.

What do we do when we experience disappointment, loss, and tragedy?

Jesus's students returned to their old jobs of fishing. This was a night-shift job that concluded at daybreak. Their first night back brought them even more disappointment. They caught nothing all night long. Their Messiah was dead and business was dry—disappointment, loss, tragedy.

Then Jesus, resurrected from the dead, showed up on the shore the morning after. Consider for a moment what Jesus did not say: "Look, guys! It's me! I'm OK!"

No, Jesus was interested in something else. "Throw your net on the right side of the boat." Get back to work. Get creative. Catch some fish. When life is hit by disappointment, loss, and tragedy, our emotional response can be a physical sluggishness and a lack of motivation. Despair seeps into our bones. We ask, "What's the point?"

Jesus challenges us to rise up in such times. The best thing we can do is keep fishing. Keep trying. Keep working. Show up. Dress well. Stand tall. Shoulders back and chin up. Jesus stands not too far off, speaking to us, telling us that our feelings matter, life is hard, and that it is important to talk out our feelings with people we trust. But the world keeps spinning and the people around us need us—so "throw your net on the other side and give it another shot." You are not pretending everything is normal. You are keeping things running until everyone can arrive at the new normal. You can embrace your difficult feelings while putting one foot in front of the other.

How can you help those around you who face disappointment, loss, and tragedy? Keep fishing. Do it well so that they don't have to bear the burden of everything else falling apart too. This is how you are strong for them. Do your best at whatever you do.

Jesus shows us that we are not alone. There is a Voice at the shoreline cheering each of us on after the long, hard night.

air is grace

"Look at the birds of the air, for they neither sow nor reap nor gather into barns; yet your heavenly Father feeds them. Are you not of more value than they?" —Matthew 6:26

You do it 25,920 times a day. You don't even think about it. And you're probably doing it wrong.

I'm talking about breathing.

Ideally, a human would take ten or fewer breathes a minute. Usually we take sixteen to twenty. All of this "over-breathing" wastes lots of our precious energy, makes us stressed, tense, sick, cancer-prone, emotionally out of balance, and less cognitively functional. Sigh.

We have this great gift of air all around us. We can relax, breathe from the belly, and absorb it—let it fuel and heal us. What do we do instead? Grab for it like it's some kind of scarce resource. We lose faith in its presence with shallow breaths that refuse to trust that if we exhale for a whole four seconds, the air will still be there when we breathe in again.

I think of Jesus's words, "Look at the birds of the air." They are the same words I used to hear from my excited three-year-old every day. She was amazed by the robins in the yard and the hummingbirds floating outside our window.

This incredible force of Creation, "air," is all around you, and it is free. It is grace from God. It upholds the soaring and carefree birds and brings life into our lungs, and it carries clouds and blows through the leaves and caresses our faces, and it is good and it is free.

This air is for you and me—even more than it is for the birds—and it is from God. Sometimes in quiet times of prayer or moments of high anxiety, I will "box breathe": inhale four seconds, hold four seconds, exhale four seconds. My spirit and mind become clear and calm. It's amazing what this grace of air can do.

Life can be hard. Stressful. Heavy. Fast-paced. Stop and remember to breathe. Remember that air is grace. Drink it in and be at peace.

treasures

"Where your treasure is, there your heart will be also."—Matthew 6:21

I broke a pencil one time. This was interesting to me, because seven days before a kid in my youth group had broken my guitar. The total destruction of my most beloved thing (the guitar, not the pencil) had stirred up intense and enduring suffering. I had been depressed and furious and even a little upset with God's capricious unfairness: "Why would you let this awful thing happen to me?" And now my pencil had snapped uselessly in half. Even here, a ten-cent pencil was somehow controlling my well-being.

This is a universal truth of life. If we spend any money on something or invest any time into something, it begins to own and control us, no matter how small that investment is. So into what are you investing your time, money, thought life, and energy? Where is your treasure? Anything can be taken away from you, but some things go more easily than others.

You can invest a lot of effort into chasing a crush only to be rejected and heartbroken. You can work, stress, and sacrifice to buy a car or laptop or phone only to suffer their loss through theft or damage. You can work hard to enjoy popularity only to have that betrayed, tarnished, faded. The result is heartbreak and misery.

But Jesus talked a lot about a different "age" or "kingdom" that could come into our lives—an eternal one. He said all of us could store treasure there: "treasures in heaven."

Where your treasure is, your heart also will be. Through Scripture reading, prayer and meditation, and worship, you can invest in building your character every day to develop its strength. No one can take that away. Like Jesus, you can serve, love, and help others. No one can take that away. Cultivate a deep and mature faith in God. No one can take that away. These are the kinds of treasures that mysteriously and paradoxically bring deep and simmering joy to you while saving the world all around you.

Our culture celebrates a young adult life that stores up all kinds of "treasures." Most of these are easily stolen from us at worst—and endure for only a moment at best. If you follow this path, your heart will rise and fall, break and bend, with the swelling tides of life's fortunes.

Do something different in this season of life. Choose simplicity in the way of the world's typical pleasures and treasures. Focus on forming your inner self, laying down your life for others, cultivating your faith. These are treasures you will carry for the rest of life and eternity.

July

Skyler's fence

"You are my Son, the Beloved; with you I am well pleased."
—Mark 1:11

If you can crunch through the traffic on Kingston Pike, you might arrive at a particular office building, in the back of which you will find a parking lot, within which you fill find a fine-looking, wooden, privacy-fence enclosure. On the pavement next to said fence you will discover a huge blob of paint. That is how you know you have discovered "Skyler's Fence."

I graduated college in the rock bottom of the Great Recession. No one was hiring. My uncle Lonnie was running an HVAC business up in Knoxville. He took me in, showed me the ropes. We climbed on top of dozens of roofs and into air ducts and cleaned AC coils and even did some routine maintenance work for a few properties. Lonnie was full of jokes and political commentary, and he always kept a fairly hot and mundane job lively and fun. But he was full of something else too: he was full of grace.

When he offered me a job in the most sluggish economy possible, I brought zero experience to the trade. I broke things and bent things and required endless explaining. I helped build a fence and dropped an entire bucket of paint, splashing everywhere for all to see. Lonnie gave it the honorary title "Skyler's Fence."

After my summer with Lonnie ended and I moved on, Lonnie was always telling me, "You're a good guy, Skyler." He said it with deep sincerity, and I always searched for his motivation to say such a thing. I mostly just showed up and tried to do whatever he asked. We had sweated out the summer rooftops of Knoxville together, and he was affirming me even when I didn't deserve it, old man to young man.

Before he began his ministry work, Jesus was baptized in the Jordan River. God announced that God was "well pleased with him" and that Jesus was "beloved." Immediately afterward, Jesus was tempted in the wilderness and proved himself to be faithful. Why didn't God say God was well pleased with Jesus after Jesus proved himself in the wilderness temptation? Why didn't God say God was well pleased with Jesus after his ministry had been successful? Because this was the grace of affirmation. Before Jesus did anything to "deserve it," God affirmed him with grace.

I have tried to imitate this with my children. I have tried to imitate my uncle. My kids have been klutzy and confused, but I have affirmed them in grace anyway. Their drawings were terrible. Their bicycle skills minimal. Their grammar hilarious. "Great job, kid!" I've shouted with a heart full of love. And when their wilderness comes, they will be confident, knowing they are loved. When their work begins, they will succeed with a strong sense of this firm foundation—that they are beloved whether they succeed or fail.

Let it be so with all of us. May we encourage and see the goodness in people around us . . . especially those who are younger. Even when they don't totally earn it, let us demonstrate God's grace. You can be an older sibling, be someone who works with kids, or just be around younger people. Let us affirm the unproven. Let us love them into beauty. Today, let us all be like my uncle that summer and exhibit the grace of affirmation.

enough

> *Jesus's mother said to him, "They have no more wine." . . . Jesus said to the servants, "Fill the jars with water. . . . Now draw some out and take it the master of the wedding." . . . The master of banquet . . . said, "You have saved the best till now!" Jesus thus revealed his glory and the disciples put their faith in him.* —John 2:3, 7-8, 9-10

I'll never be good enough. I'll never have enough. If I only had enough _____, I could be happy. But there's never enough.

We live in a world of scarcity and competition, where wedding organizers serve water, wishing they had more wine. The feeling of not having enough is like a cornerstone to how our world understands itself and operates. In everything from economics to politics to marketing, to the way we feel when we look in the mirror, at our bank account, at the car we drive, at the grades we receive, or at the attention we get from our peers in school, we feel that "It's not enough."

This tough feeling lurks within all of us. It produces shame and fear and anxiety within us, and then it causes us to act desperately and destructively and opens us up to the manipulations of those in power. We hurt ourselves and each other as we try to compensate to feel valued, respected, and loved.

Jesus's message spoke directly to the heart of this problem. When he turned water into wine at the wedding in Cana, he was announcing in a concrete way that God's kingdom was arriving on Earth. It was a new way for the world to operate—not based on scarcity and competition but on abundance and generosity, connected to a generous Creator. A community of people where there is always enough. Where we are always good enough and have enough and are loved and valued enough. The kingdom of heaven is the kingdom of enough. It is a place where competition and anxiety and insecurity-based advertising fall apart. We look at our skin and our shape and our possessions, and our envy and bitterness drift away. Our contentment fills us up. We look at our lives and we say, "It is enough and I am at peace." The good news announced by Jesus is this: the kingdom is here, it is now, and it is available to you at this moment (not after you die up in the sky).

So today, hear Jesus's declaration: in Jesus, there is enough. Your water is wine. Your party gets better, even with those same stone jars you've always had. You are good enough. You are beautiful enough. Worthy enough. Skinny enough. Strong enough. Smart enough. Loved enough. Respected enough.

You.

Are.

Enough.

Worthiness is your birthright in this new world that Jesus inaugurates—a kingdom that is here and now and available to anyone who will let go of their anxious struggling and fall into its embrace with vulnerable faith.

foreigners

> *"Take your inheritance, the kingdom prepared for you . . . . For I was a foreigner . . . and you welcomed me."* —Matthew 25:34-35

I will never forget the day I brought my two-week-old daughter to the US Embassy in Bucharest after her birth in a hospital just down the road. At the time, my wife and I were missionaries in Romania. I held up her tiny body before an officer who swore her into US citizenship. In that moment, so many incredible privileges were bestowed upon my daughter. The most powerful army in the world now stood at the ready to defend her life and liberty. Untold wealth awaited her adulthood. Freedom was hers, an "easy" life. On our way out, we walked past 200 Romanians sacrificing, risking, clamoring just for a chance to visit our distant home country.

My daughter had not risked her life to escape any country, had not traveled through lifeless deserts or jungles full of malaria, had dodged no bullets, risked no attack dogs or torturers or mafias. She had endured no hunger. She had not been pulled from the arms of her father by men with guns or put in a jail cell. She was never accused of infesting a country or bringing drugs or stealing jobs. She paid no fee, passed no test, declared no allegiance—claims even her own immigrant grandparents could not make.

With gratitude, I watch her now in her oversized, beautiful home, giggling at her toys, her eyes sparkling. Tonight she will go to ballet class. Yet she, like myself, did nothing to earn any of this. Our planet is unfair and painful. I weep for it. Trusting in God, I resolve to make it less like hell and more like heaven, and to do so with Christ's peace in my heart.

I'll start with gratitude. I am grateful that over thirty years ago, a family arrived on the United States' shores from a distant refugee camp. They risked everything to escape a country destroyed by communism and revolution. I'm grateful for each one of them but most especially for their youngest daughter, my wife. My in-laws are so hardworking, honest, and wonderful. I'm grateful for the immigrants who teach and work around me and the immense intellectual and cultural capital they bring to my community. I'm grateful for the immigrants in my church congregation. I'm grateful for the immigrants who pick my tomatoes in sweltering fields and the immigrants who patch up the scorching roofs in my city and the immigrants who save the lives of people I love at the hospital down the street. By the way, I'm also grateful for tacos and shawarmas and egg rolls and gyros and salata de boeuf. Immigrants are loved and appreciated and welcomed by me.

Jesus welcomes immigrants too. After all, Jesus fled genocide in his birth town Bethlehem to become a refugee in Egypt. As a child, Jesus and his parents immigrated to a town called Nazareth in northern Israel. And when asked, "How can we go to heaven when we die?" Jesus responded, "I was a *zenos* [a foreigner/immigrant], and you gathered me in . . . whatever you have done unto the least of these, that you have also done unto me."

We imitate Jesus when we welcome the foreigners among us. Our coworkers, fellow students, teachers, neighbors, the guy grilling our burgers and the woman discussing our lab results. We imitate Jesus when we celebrate their cultures (on their terms), when we are curious about their food and history and way of life. We imitate Jesus when we appreciate diverse languages. We imitate Jesus when we are grateful for immigrants' presence amongst us. We imitate Jesus when we refuse to judge immigrants based on sound bites and the media.

We remember that Jesus judges us on this principle: did you greet the foreigner with privileged prejudice and disregard and guns and suspicion, or did you greet them—did you greet Jesus—with open arms?

what is normal

> *"You have heard that it was said, Don't commit adultery. But I say to you that every man who looks at a woman lustfully has already committed adultery in his heart. And if your right eye causes you to fall into sin, tear it out and throw it away."* —Matthew 5:27-29

Here is my first question: What is normal?

When I first moved to Romania to serve as a missionary, I had to make a decision about the apple core in my hand. Bucharest was a city covered in trash—newspapers, paper cups, garbage bags all over and from everyone. I have always hated littering, but the leftover apple was wet in my hand and would leave a sticky mark if set down somewhere in the car. If I threw it on the street, an animal would surely make it disappear soon enough. I rolled down the window, ready to toss the core. All the litter outside made it feel normal. Expected. Maybe even kind of respectable.

I recently heard a story about a young woman who was drunk at a college party. A man had sex with her. That is, he raped her. She couldn't give consent in that situation. Something very serious and wrong and broken happened there. Apparently, this is a common story. Something like one-fifth of American women are raped or experience attempted rape. And here is my second question: Is there something pervasive in our culture that makes people think it's OK to violate others or to look the other way when it is happening? Is there some kind of litter in the streets that turns makes throwing trash on the ground acceptable?

This is a complex, multifaceted issue, but I know that when Jesus wanted to say something about the subject of adultery, he talked about lust. He said that dwelling on the inner state of desire is equal to adultery. They are the same. I think he was going for shock effect, because he went on to say that you should rip your eyeball out before you lust. Jesus dreamed of a world where men and women took their natural feelings of lust and surrendered them to God instead of dwelling on them or feeding them. This is a hard thing to ask mere mortals to do. But if it sounds too hard or legalistic, I suggest climbing in a hot air balloon to look at our world from 2,000 feet above, just for a moment.

We have created a world where one-fourth of internet searches are related to pornography, and about 40 million Americans regularly visit those sites. Researchers are demonstrating the frightening truth in Jesus's wisdom about lust, finding that the pervasive habit of watching porn is addictive for the brain, that it steals intimacy from couples, that it contributes to more affairs and more divorce, that it causes men's brains to see women as objects to be used, that women are trafficked for its production, and that this 98 billion dollar "industry of lust" contributes to more sexual aggression and rape in our culture. Indeed, it would be better to tear out our eyes.[5]

We have to hold predators accountable when they hurt other people. But in a culture where everything and everyone has become so sexualized, we must ask ourselves hard questions about how our own behaviors are also littering the streets.

What is normal?

I remember rolling up my car window and waiting for a trash can to come along, wiping the apple juice from my sticky hand, not realizing until years later just how important that decision was. Normal people have a choice to choose the good in the small things. We can surrender our lustful feelings to the graceful compassion of God. We can refuse to play along to

---

5. Yumeng Ren and Jieru Xu, "Online Porn: Here's Some Facts You Probably Didn't Know," Ruggles Media, October 25, 2017, web.northeastern.edu/ruggles-media/2017/10/25/online-porn-heres-some-facts-you-probably-didnt-know/; Donald L. Hilton Jr. and Clark Watts, "Pornography Addiction: A Neuroscience Perspective," *Surgical Neurology International* 2/1 (February 21, 2011): 19, doi.org/10.4103/2152-7806.76977; Gary Gilles, "How Pornography Distorts Intimate Relationships," MentalHelp.net, mentalhelp.net/blogs/how-pornography-distorts-intimate-relationships/; Megan K. Maas, et al., "A Dyadic Approach to Pornography Use." *Journal of Sex Research* 55/6 (2018): 772–82, doi:10.1080/00224499.2018.1440281; "How Porn Can Normalize Sexual Objectification," and "'I Didn't Know If They'd Kill Me,'" Fight the New Drug, accessed March 23, 2023, fightthenewdrug.org/how-porn-can-normalize-sexual-objectification/ and fightthenewdrug.org/what-happened-when-this-jane-doe-was-trafficked-by-girlsdoporn/; Whitney Rostad, et al., "The Association between Exposure to Violent Pornography and Teen Dating Violence in Grade 10 High School Students," *Archives of Sexual Behavior* 48/7 (2019): 2137–47, doi:10.1007/s10508-019-1435-4.

the locker room talk. We can shut off the things on the internet that lead to people getting hurt. We can speak up when we see something that doesn't look right and refuse to blame victims. We can be a positive influence in the right direction.

This week, may you use the time and choices and influence God has given you to create a different kind of normal. The little things we call normal can make a big difference.

dress well

Let us not love in word or speech but in truth and action.
—1 John 3:18

Do you love yourself? I certainly hope so.

I don't do this well. I don't love myself the way I should. It makes me feel poorly. It makes me serve God, others, and my world less fully.

In one season of my life, I knew that God loved me, that others loved me, and that I was worthy of love. But there is a difference between knowing something is worthy of love and loving the thing. I was feeling lousy, like the demands of work and family were controlling my life. I was out of shape. I had serious back issues that diminished my ability to take care of others, especially my small children.

So on the first day of the new year, I started working out in the mornings, four days a week. I had a newborn baby at the time, and I had to plan out every minute of my day in order to make sure I had enough time to squeeze in a thirty-minute workout. It was tough. In under a month, though, I felt better. I felt that I was taking charge of my life—like I was in the driver's seat again. I felt that I could take on the constant challenges of life and ministry. As I strengthened my core and lower body muscles, my back issues went away, so I was better able to care for my wife and kids. I was better able to serve others in ministry.

If you don't take care of something, you don't love it.

There's a difference between knowing something is worthy of love and loving the thing. You say that you love your family. Do you tell them? You say that you love the poor. Do you help them? You say that you love yourself. Do you take care of your body, mind, and soul? Do you eat well, exercise, read, and pray?

I had to confess a hard truth about myself: I was using the difficulty of my schedule as an excuse to avoid responsibility. I had been accepting my life (that is, my life choices) as "OK." That lack of taking responsibility was corroding me and thus hurting my family and my world. Our culture equates "accepting something as it is" with "love." But that is not love. That is acceptance. If you don't take care of something, you don't love it.

This is a call to love yourself well. To do what it takes to get to the gym. To discipline yourself to read. To go to worship this weekend. To dress well. To brush your teeth. To stand tall. To work hard. Every day. If you don't take care of something, you don't love it.

Do you love yourself? I certainly hope so.

crazy uncles

> *"My kingdom is not from this world. If my kingdom were from this world, my followers would be fighting."* —John 18:36

We all have a crazy uncle. (Well, some of us *are* the crazy uncle, I suppose.) I'm talking about the guy who speaks his mind too much, always has something stuck in his teeth, has the most offensive opinions, drinks too much, or who knows what else. But some of us have difficult stepparents. Or immature siblings. Some of us have changed so much while away at college that it can be difficult to step back into our families of origin. Even though family is good, sometimes family is hard instead of easy.

Jesus's life and death would make a terrible blockbuster film. When the big, bad Roman troops and Judean leaders came in the dark of night, Jesus's disciples didn't fight back. They didn't swoop in. They didn't dodge bullets. Peter pulled out his sword, took one swing, and successfully cut off an ear. Jesus reached out and healed the guy. Big whoop. They were all wusses, it seems.

Or maybe not.

Maybe the bigger person is the one who bites their tongue. Maybe the bigger person is the one who is patient with offenses. Maybe the bigger person is the one who vulnerably reaches out and heals the one who is coming at them. Maybe the bigger person is the one who chooses to be Christ-like, regardless of how devil-like someone else is treating them, even when it feels like someone else is crucifying them.

This is a call to choose peace, to put away your sword with your family. May you be a presence of God's Spirit in the chaos, just like Jesus was on the night of his own arrest. Your family is hurting. They are anxious about jobs and relationships and medical diagnoses and the meaning of life, just like the rest of us. Perhaps in that pain and angst, they lash out or spin out a little, especially during the holidays. Don't fight back. Offer a kingdom from a different world. Be like Jesus; be a force for peace, hope, and healing, even if everyone around you is fighting.

more freedom

> *Jesus said to him, "Away from me, Satan! For it is written: 'Worship the Lord your God, and serve him only.'" Then the devil left him, and angels came and attended him.* —Matthew 4:10-11

I once was in a bike crash that ruined my back. I could hardly move. It would take me five full minutes to get up from the couch, and I couldn't lean over or pick things up. This wouldn't have been so bad, but my wife and I were raising our two kids and two foster boys . . . three of whom were still in diapers. It was the lockdown of the Covid pandemic—we could not get any help or send the kids to school.

I was in pain and paralyzed, but my wife was solely responsible for keeping everybody alive and well. My paralysis was leaving my family with an enormous challenge. What I wanted to do was to crawl in a hole and feel sorry for myself, stare at screens all day, take pills, have someone bring me snacks. I wanted to avoid causing any pain to my body. But if I just lay there and didn't aggressively address my injury, I faced a lifetime of back issues and would be unable to help my family.

I was free to make the choice, but love called me to choose less freedom, to do things I didn't want to do. I forced myself to help even when it was uncomfortable. I learned various stretches and calisthenics to do daily to strengthen and repair my body. I hated all of it, but I cared for my family and today I am healthy.

Jesus chose forty days of fasting in the desert, refusing the food he very much wanted to eat. Then, he was made three offers from the devil—nice offers. Jesus would have enjoyed the gratification, attention, and control the devil was offering, but he refused it. Jesus knew that he was not free to do whatever he wanted if he wanted to love you and me. Jesus gave away total freedom for the sake of love.

Our culture celebrates the freedom of young adulthood. The media is saturated with images of young people living a fun and free life. College and your twenties are supposed to be for big trips and nights out, right? But this unrealistic view hides a darker truth—that freedom comes at a high cost and often produces less freedom and joy later on.

Jesus invites his followers deep into the desert, to live a life of sacrificing little freedoms and pleasures to better love the world into God's kingdom. To practice self-restraint and self-denial in the little things for "big-picture" freedom. To live a life spiritually liberated to focus less on self and more on God and others. To create more freedom through choosing less freedom along the way.

Where is God calling you to practice greater self-restraint for the sake of love?

empty crosses

> He said, "Father, if it's your will, take this cup of suffering away from me. However, not my will but your will must be done." Then a heavenly angel appeared to him and strengthened him. He was in anguish and prayed even more earnestly. His sweat became like drops of blood falling on the ground. —Luke 22:42-44

How do you prove your love?

Let's say you're in love with a guy named JaGorky. (What were JaGorky's parents thinking?) JaGorky is confident and cool and cute. You've been dating a while; you're thinking long term. JaGorky is also kind of helpless. He needs you to bring him food. He won't do his laundry, so you do it for him. And JaGorky belittles you sometimes. He can be disrespectful and even calls you names, followed by, "I was only kidding!" It hurts, but JaGorky insists that you need to "lighten up."

True love is willing to tolerate some pain, right? Think of Jesus and how he took his cross for us! Jesus endured pain and abuse for us. Many of us "take up our cross" to serve a spouse, a parent, a sibling, a coworker, or the poor. We prove our love to God by suffering and sacrificing for God. We remember Jesus, and he inspires us to press on in our sacrificial love.

This is the part where I (carefully) call "bull."

Remember Jesus's prayer. Jesus agonized in his prayer, hopeful that his suffering could be averted. Jesus did not want to go to the cross. He was so stressed about the suffering he would endure that he prayed to avoid it, got a little snappy with his disciples, and even sweated blood. Jesus did not want to go to the cross, but he was willing to do so if necessary. Jesus did not model a life of suffering love. Jesus modeled a life of joyous partying, feasting, healing, teaching, and restoring people's lives. Jesus never lived joyfully at the expense or risk of others' well-being; He discovered life-giving joy in loving others, and that was his hope for each of us. Jesus died to save us from sacrifice, to pave a way for an abundant life and a peace that demands no blood.

As a husband, I must constantly sacrifice my selfish and usually trivial desires to experience something deeper and better. In the times when my wife and I confront illness and tragedy and, yes, one another's crankier moments, more sacrifice is required. But we do not seek sacrifice or glorify sacrifice, and we do not prove our love through sacrifice. Our love is proven through day-in and day-out affection, service, sensitivity, and support for one another. Our love shines brightly through our willingness to sacrifice, but we do not glorify it and we certainly do not demand it.

Jesus died on a cross to rid the world of crosses. Jesus sacrificed himself to be the final and last sacrifice—no more sacrificing lambs, no more sacrificing people, no more sacrificing ourselves. Jesus died to save the world from glorifying suffering and martyrdom and the myth of redemptive violence. So his earliest followers stopped sacrificing animals at temples and began a revolutionary new religious practice—"the sacrifice of praise." They would let their worship of God be sufficient proof of their love. They would "take up their cross" by following Jesus.

Today, my church has a large, empty cross at the front of its sanctuary. It is a compelling reminder of the good news that God, through Jesus, is shaping a world where one day every cross fashioned by evil men will stand empty. That empty cross calls into question any human or god or JaGorky that insists on or celebrates suffering. True love requires no such proof. It rests in trust and lives in joy, and it is a truly wonderful thing.

belonging

"He said, 'I will get up and go to my father, and I will say to him, Father I have sinned against heaven and before you; I am no longer worthy to be called your son; treat me like one of your hired hands.' So he set off and went to his father. But while he was still far off, his father saw him and was filled with compassion; he ran and put his arms around him and kissed him." —Luke 15:18-20

I am unworthy of acceptance and belonging.

Have you ever felt that way? Maybe you felt embarrassed or afraid or disconnected. Maybe, even without realizing it, you resorted to blaming someone else or going into denial when things got bad. You were trying to avoid feeling small and terrible. This happens to me all the time.

I speak in public a lot, and sometimes I put my foot in my mouth. Then I feel unworthy of acceptance and belonging. I compare myself, my abilities, and even my interests with those of others, and I feel like the odd one out. Unworthy of acceptance and belonging. I compare myself and my life to the pictures I see on social media. Unworthy of acceptance and belonging.

Jesus told a story about a young man who had a good life but ruined it all. He abandoned his family and squandered his wealth. He was reduced to isolated, abject poverty. Knowing that he had ruined his relationship with his father, he decided to hang his head in shame and ask to be a servant, not a son, on his father's farm. To his surprise, his father was filled with compassion. His father ran to him. He embraced and kissed him. In a dramatic twist, the son discovered love, acceptance, and belonging—the things he wanted and needed all along. These things were always available to him, but he had looked for them in all the wrong places.

Your soul longs to belong. Your soul longs for people who know your imperfections, goof-ups, insecurities, and struggles and still love and embrace you. If success, money, sex, fame, or fun are on your mind, behind them lies the soul desire of deep, intimate relationships and community, where each person stands as a dignified equal. Unconditional belonging is the thing your soul needs, and it is the thing everyone around you needs you to offer them. Today, there are people in your community who are like the father, offering you unconditional acceptance and belonging, but I wonder if you run to them. Like the son, are you wandering off, looking for belonging in "more exciting" places?

I want to be the son. I want to move towards the people who offer me unconditional belonging, who set me free to truly be my truest, most authentic, most wholehearted self. I want to choose the kinds of friends, the kind of church family, that treats me like the father treated the son.

I want to be the father. I want to be the one who accepts people just as they are. I want to run to them and embrace them, even when they are still stumbling in the darkness of shame. I want to create a community of friends (especially in my church) that offers belonging to everyone, where no one has to try to fit in.

What kinds of relationships will you choose? What kind of relationship will you offer? Hear the wisdom of Jesus. Discover and create a world of true and deep and liberating belonging.

threshold

But Mary stood outside the tomb weeping. —John 20:11

When I was sixteen, my dad made me join the swim team. Swimmers wear what appear to be underwear and then swim for hours in endless circles among chemicals and Lord knows what else. So I thought it was dorky and didn't want to do it. I treated it like a joke, goofing around at practice while middle school boys and girls swam laps around me.

I call this "the threshold of the tomb."

Mary, a disciple of Jesus, was devastated by his arrest and execution. Jesus had died a cursed death, with a whole mob shouting "Crucify him!" The people coalesced to pronounce him guilty—a shame, a sham, a criminal. Yet Jesus was a savior to Mary, and she thought he was surely the hope of Israel and the whole Earth. Mary lived in dark times, and the one light of hope had been snuffed out. Mary visited Jesus's tomb after her Sabbath day to mourn and honor his death. When she arrived, she found the stone covering the tomb's entrance rolled away and his body gone. "Someone has desecrated and stolen his body," Mary thought. In that spot, Mary broke down and wept. This empty tomb meant that just when she thought things couldn't get any worse, somehow they had.

After a few weeks of flapping about in the swimming pool, getting beat by seventh graders, I started having second thoughts about the swim team. "If I'm stuck here, I might as well make the best of it." I started applying myself, working hard, curiously studying how to improve my stroke. I slowly but dramatically improved my speed. I started dominating practice and winning races. I went from drowning klutz to Michael Phelps (OK, not really Michael Phelps). I became so good at swimming that I went to regionals and state, joined the summer swim team, and swam my senior year as well. I became team captain and broke school records.

I have no doubt that Mary bore tremendous emotional pain when she took the next step into the tomb. Yet once weeping Mary stepped past the heartbreaking threshold of the tomb, she discovered something glorious on the other side. Jesus's body was gone—that was true. But two dazzling angels from God challenged her: "Why are you weeping?" She turned around to find Jesus. Jesus was risen! Jesus was alive! Everything changed in an instant at the very center of her suffering.

The threshold of the tomb is the most painful place, and it is where most people get stuck in life. They despair because things have been terrible, and now it appears that things are even worse. They accept the obstacle as it is.

Because it is harder to step toward the pain (the tomb), they remain on the outside, weeping and despairing. Mary had the courage to move toward the thing that was so painful. Only through that did she discover resurrection. In my (admittedly, far more trivial) story, it was only by throwing myself fully into the place I didn't want to be that something truly positive emerged.

When things are bad, do not despair, do not run away, do not become bitter, and do not be afraid. Confront the pain and step toward it. Face the challenge. Walk past the painful threshold into the darkness of the tomb that you face. Angels and resurrection await you on the inside.

"The very cave you are afraid to enter turns out to be the source of what you are looking for." —Joseph Campbell[6]

resurrected life

"Put your finger here; see my hands. Reach out your hand and put it into my side. Stop doubting and trust." —John 20:27

There is nothing harder for me than to admit serious mistakes, wounds, and limitations. I can admit the trivial stuff, like "I said the wrong thing" or "I'm not exactly sure how to perform heart surgery." But I deeply struggle to admit my darker moral failings, share my embarrassing moments, or confess that I don't know something "men usually know about," like all the rules of football or who won the last NBA championship. I often internalize emotions instead of showing them because I tell myself it's weak to reveal the heart. In short, I try to present to the world a "resurrected me." Someone who has walked through the fire and come out put together: smart, funny, nice, happy. We all do this in some way.

The story of Jesus's resurrection speaks powerfully to the fables of invulnerability that we tell ourselves and our world. Jesus was shamefully killed by his whole world uniting and agreeing that he was a petulant fraud, a scourge, an inferior nuisance that should be tortured to death and thrown

---

6. *A Joseph Campbell Companion* (New York: HarperCollins, 1991), 24.

away. Crucifixion was the most embarrassing way one could die. So when Jesus resurrected from the dead, how did he recover from that?

He didn't hide it. Wounds from the nails and the spear were still visible on his body. Thomas insisted that he could not trust Jesus unless he saw those wounds. He understood that the basis of true trust and intimacy is being honest about our vulnerabilities. That is what our souls need most to truly come alive. Jesus invited his friend into the heart of his deepest, darkest pain. It wasn't enough for Thomas to see it from a distance. Jesus invited him to physically touch his wounds, to deposit his hand into the spear wound on his side: "Stop doubting and trust me."

This is what resurrection life looks like: connecting to God and trusted people by inviting one another into our most vulnerable spaces. It's letting someone see when we're scared or wrong or don't have all the right answers or feel insecure. It's choosing to confess that "this is painful and confusing" instead of choosing blame in times of stress. A resurrected life is one that can say, "Put your hand into my side and feel my pain." A resurrected life is one that reaches out and touches the scar and says, "You're not alone in your pain, and I understand."

Jesus couldn't and wouldn't post pictures of his scars on Instagram, and he certainly didn't share them on his first date. Jesus did not cheapen his wounds by oversharing them with anyone. But he had a long relationship with a close student and friend named Thomas, and they connected in this way. So who is your Thomas? Are you building this level of family and friendship in your life? Is this the kind of relationship your church is cultivating with people? Do you invite God into your wounds and your pain? Jesus demonstrated that this is resurrected life: vulnerable, connected, alive.

biscuits

> *As soon as Jesus was baptized, he went up out of the water. At that moment heaven was opened, and he saw the Spirit of God descending like a dove and alighting on him. And a voice from heaven said, "This is my Son, whom I love; with him I am well pleased."*
> —Matthew 3:16-17

I was standing at the threshold of my front door. For a moment, I was frozen. I was a senior in high school. I was taking two AP classes, narrowing my college search, selling KFC on the weekends, serving as captain of the swim team and captain of the school choir, working on the lead role in the senior play, serving as an FCA leader, and playing in my youth group's praise band on Wednesday nights. I kept good grades and never missed church. I was a busy boy. Each night I would get home, shovel down some dinner, and shuffle off to my room to study until I passed out.

That morning at the threshold of my door, I held a sausage biscuit my mother had cooked for breakfast. She was a good mom. She believed that cereal was junk, and she needed all four of her kids to eat a hearty breakfast to start the day. She woke up early and made us biscuits.

Standing at the threshold, I flinched at the tidal wave of a day before me. Considered all at once, it was too much to take on. But then I remembered the love represented in the biscuits. All of the affection, support, encouragement, sacrifice, and discipline I had received for eighteen years from my mother who had, even that morning, sacrificed to support me. With that kind of grace behind me, I could take on all of it and remain victorious.

The biscuits remind me of a baptism. When Jesus came up from the water, he hadn't yet started his ministry. He hadn't yet beaten the devil. He hadn't yet proven himself faithful on the cross. He had proven nothing. Even so, his Heavenly Father affirmed him, encouraged him, and loved him. I think that conscious awareness of God's unconditional and limitless love and grace gave Jesus the confidence and strength to heal and bring light to all the darkness around him each day.

My parents were also very flawed and imperfect at the parenting gig. They did things and didn't do things that did not serve me well in life. This is true of every parent on the planet! So from the beginning, Jesus's followers have always believed in "re-parenting." We love our imperfect parents, but we also receive a new, heavenly parent, who is God. As followers of Jesus, we awaken to our daughtership and sonship to God through prayer, the reading of Scripture, the weekly listening to this good news being preached. Each day, we sit, close our eyes, and whisper these words: "Thank you, God, for loving me. Thank you for being well pleased with me. You grieve my bad choices, yet you love me no matter what. You respect me. You like me. You find joy in who I am. You are with me. You support me. And so you hold me to the highest standard of love and integrity because you believe in what I can do when I am connected to you." Over time, this is a life-transforming prayer.

We hold the biscuit in our hand and remember that with this kind of love spoken over us each day, our inner striving can cease. We don't have to be victims anymore, and we can take on challenges with integrity. We can suffer hardship and injustice and still demonstrate compassion to others.

tables

The Pharisees and the scribes were grumbling and saying, "This fellow welcomes sinners and eats with them." —Luke 15:2

"Social suicide." That's what my friend called associating with a particular fraternity on our college campus. She intuitively understood that if people saw her hanging out with them, the "in" crowd would put her on their level—as a loser, weird, desperate.

Have you ever felt that way? You don't want to be rude, but you don't want to be seen with a certain person. Or maybe you felt like you had to be sure that you scheduled your lunch to be with a group you knew because you couldn't be seen eating alone. And I'm sure that you, like myself, have seen someone eating alone in the dining hall as you hustled along to your own table of friends.

Religious people like myself think of "faith" as looking like this: "I'm pretty responsible, I try to do the right thing, I try to go to church, I try to say some prayers, and I try to be nice to everyone. You know, I try not to sin."

What made Jesus so unique and special among all the religious giants of world history was his commitment to hanging out with all the wrong people—to what my friend called "social suicide." Jesus hung out with the most awkward people. He treated them like normal human beings. He was interested in who they were and what their story was. Jesus encouraged them and shared good news with them as he passed along the bread at the table.

What if religious folks like myself thought less about following a long list of rules parsed out from the Bible and more about this one rule: hang out with all the wrong people? Welcome the annoying, the awkward, the lonely, the weird, the sad, the different, and the people on whom everyone else turns their backs. Leave the ninety-nine at the party and sit with the one who has been excluded. Don't follow the crowd. Don't be popular. Stop obsessing over "what and who can benefit me," and hone in on "how I can bless others."

What if we made a decision to live an extraordinary life? To do the thing that no one else is doing? To life with purpose and meaning and impact? Everyone needs someone else to see the goodness and worth in them. Everyone needs someone else to enjoy their company, even when it requires some intentional effort. And if you imitate Jesus and welcome far-off people to your table, you can live that kind of life.

Do want to follow Jesus? Well, who sits at your table?

a deserted place

When daybreak arrived, Jesus went to a deserted place. The crowds were looking for him. —Luke 4:42

NOISE. That is our life, isn't it? A constant input stream of sounds and visual information.

Watch people walking around at the store or some other place. Everyone is either talking to someone else, listening to headphones, or staring at their phone screens while they walk. Even when I am in my house, I struggle to leave my phone somewhere. I keep it in my pocket. There are screens everywhere, speakers everywhere, people everywhere.

At the same time, life is hard, isn't it? Our "to do list" is unending, people are mad at us, we feel like a disappointment, and life can steal precious things from us. So many of us struggle with feeling anxious, a thousand "what ifs" and doomsday scenarios endlessly playing out in our minds. There is so much pressure. How can we cope? How we be strong and victorious?

I think of Jesus, with thousands of people coming after him every day during his ministry. They brought to him demons and mean, criticizing leaders. At the drop of a hat, the Romans might have decided to execute him, or an angry mob could have attacked him. In some ways, he was alone, vulnerable, and pushed to the edge.

In these intense weeks of Jesus's life, the Gospels record him withdrawing from the noise and finding quiet spaces in nature. The Scripture is silent on what he did there. But we can imagine that he prayed, meditated, or possibly just enjoyed sitting and taking it all in—the stunning beauty of everything around him.

What about you? I know your life is challenging too. So do you imitate Jesus? Are you finding those moments, be it five minutes or five hours, to withdraw? Are you taking time to talk with God about the burdens on your heart? Are you going for walks outdoors with no phone, to unplug and reset?

Scientific studies consistently report that these kinds of practices—prayer, meditation, and nature walks—function like free medicine to lower stress, anxiety, and depression and boost energy, productivity, and compassion.

Make a decision today. When will your "daybreak" be? Where will your "deserted place" be? Will you pray, meditate, or just walk in nature?

blind guides

If you were blind, you would not be guilty of sin; but now that you claim you can see, your guilt remains.—John 9:41

I remember being in college, feeling called by God to move into the poorest, most dangerous neighborhood in town. Everything was arranged, but I hadn't told Mom and Dad yet. I was certain they would think I had lost my mind. I stewed and agonized about telling them my plans.

Jesus heals a blind man on the Sabbath and the pharisees, a group of men that everyone around respected and admired, couldn't believe it. They argued with the man's parents and even the man himself! They said he was lying that it was Jesus who had healed him, or that he had been born blind at all. They had opinions about the man's own story of what God was doing in his life. They were sure he was still seeing things unclearly.

You will likely find no shortage of people who want to fix you and tell you how to live your life. They will happily tell you what you should do or where you should go. They will want to speak for you and see for you.

But Jesus comes to the man and offers him a direct relationship with himself, and that is what Jesus offers you as well. You can (and should) invite wise people to offer a listening ear and good advice, but there is only one person who will be stuck with the life you choose to live. The pharisees claim to see so clearly that they can see for the healed man. In turn, Jesus tells them that they are the ones blind. The moment you try to see for someone else, he is saying, you become blind.

I was so worried about charting my own course and doing this strange thing of moving into a struggling neighborhood. I spilled my guts and told my whole story to my parents. They said, "OK." They didn't freak out at all. I followed the call and lived a great adventure that made a great impact.

May you hold the opinions of the people around you who want to fix you with a loose hand. Jesus comes to you directly to be your guide. May you discern and follow the faithful voice of God within to do brave and good things with your life.

August

birds

"Look at the birds of the air." —Matthew 6:26

This morning, as I often do, I took a sunrise bicycle ride with my one-year-old son riding in a trailer behind my bike. It was a gorgeous morning. I loved cruising down Main Street, past historic homes with their gardened front yards. But the part that took my breath away, as usual, was the trail along the river. With a low, warm sun in the cool air, we raced alongside the water, the hawks and geese and ducks, the squirrels and robins, the waterfalls and trees. All of these things felt like they offered God's embrace. I live a fairly high-pace life; I juggle many responsibilities and do some stressful things. But there is no question that these bike rides renew and restore me; they keep me connected to the Source of Life. They grant me equilibrium and balance to make me a more "high-functioning" person.

But have you seen the news? In the last fifty years, the population of birds in North America has declined by over 30 percent; about 3 billion less birds are alive today than when our grandparents were growing up. There have been massive fallouts of sparrows, warblers, blackbirds, finches, larks, and juncos. Bird experts write that we have converted so much forest and grassland into farm and city, and we spray so many pesticides on our crops and backyards, that our birds have nowhere to live or eat, and they are poisoned even when they do.[7]

"Look at the birds," Jesus says as he teaches his followers how to calm their anxious hearts. In this modern era of social isolation, screen-staring work, and disconnection from the outdoors, our anxiety has skyrocketed. So we must hear Jesus's words again. We must pause and look at the birds and the trees and the rivers and the flowers. We must enjoy God's beautiful creation for the sake of our own hearts.

---

7. Cornell Lab or Ornithology, birds.cornell.edu/home/bring-birds-back/.

I fear that if we do not look at the birds, we will not care to raise our voices to protect them. And if we value the future well-being of our children—their opportunity to "look at the birds of the air" in their moments of anxiety—we will protect these birds for them. We can spray our lawns less. We can eat more local and organic food. We can plant more trees and cut less down. We can reduce and reuse and recycle the things we buy. We can write our legislators and ask them to conserve wildlife and its habitat. And we can ride our bikes to remember how beautifully God designed each piece of creation.

Will we obey Jesus? Will we look at the birds? If we do not protect them, I fear we may not have them around much longer.

college culture

Do not be conformed to this world, but be transformed by the renewing of your mind. —Romans 12:2

The loneliest time in my life was my sophomore year of college. My freshman year, I studied too much. Then the next year I became an RA in a freshman dorm while my friends moved on to other places. To those with whom I lived, I was perceived as an authority figure. To those with whom I was friends, I was far off and less relevant. In my loneliness, I felt exceeding pressure to connect with others. I lowered my moral standards and rationalized my bad choices. I wouldn't say it out loud, but I so badly wanted to be connected to people. I felt a painful, gaping void within.

This is true for many of us—even those perceived as popular and put together. God has so strongly wired us to be intimate, connected people, people who relate authentically and vulnerably to each other. In the inevitable gaps of connection and our surges of loneliness, we cave to the easy pressures and pleasures of this world.

The (false) expectation of college culture is pervasive drinking, sexual promiscuity, and skirting "adult responsibilities." These are wasteful, shallow, uncreative, and damaging ways of attempting to connect with others. They come at a big cost to ourselves, our community, and our future. Yet conforming to a cultural pattern makes us feel a little more "OK," less vulnerable and insecure.

Jesus and the Apostle Paul dared to live their lives differently. They did not conform to their cultural patterns and expectations. And each of us has the choice to be our own, unique self. We can choose to make our life our own, to enjoy the things and people that truly make us happy, to live in such a way that lifts others up and glorifies God and is at peace. We don't have to conform to someone else's idea of what college or young adulthood should be about.

But heed this warning: when your mind isn't being renewed from above, you have little choice but to conform to those around you. Our hearts are incredibly hungry for deep, authentic connection and purpose, so we must remember to connect to God through prayer and church community. We must sing religious songs. We must create friendships with those who share similar life values and principles. In college, these faith practices sustained me and protected me from making even worse decisions. This is how God renews our minds from the inside out, and it is how we are able to be like Jesus and Paul: we can dare to be different and shine a light of love, integrity, and faith into this world.

Today, may God transform you by renewing your mind so that you might have the strength to be your own amazing and unique self rather than straining to conform to the patterns and expectations of this world.

Zebedee

Jesus saw two other brothers, James the son of Zebedee, and John his brother, in the boat with Zebedee their father, mending their nets. He called them and immediately they left the boat and their father, and followed him. —Matthew 4:21-22

One time, our one-year-old son got sick with croup. At night, his airway was inflamed and constricted. Each breath was an intense struggle for air—for life! He was suffering so much. He (and we) barely slept. Our parental impulse was to rush him to the emergency room. But our first child had once endured the same thing, so we forced ourselves to calm down and just lie awake all night long until the morning, when we could see a doctor for medicine. Ronella and I were scared for our son. And in my fear (and our 4 a.m. exhaustion), I got a little snappy. I wanted Ronella and my son to do exactly like I wanted and what I felt was best. I wanted to be in charge, in control.

Have you ever been scared for someone? Or have you ever felt scared or unsafe about a relationship—a friend, a colleague, a boyfriend or girlfriend, family, or especially a child? Often, in our moments of fear we are sure we know best and we become controlling. It is helpful and consoling to envision ourselves in the driver's seat.

And that is why Zebedee is messing with my head today.

In two verses, Jesus strolls up, calls Zebedee's two sons, and walks away with them. I have this mental picture: an early morning on the lake, a fisherman standing in his boat, silently watching his two sons—his whole life and future—walk away with this traveling rabbi named Jesus. In my head, Zebedee is left profoundly empty-handed. I imagine Zebedee had everything planned out and set up for his boys. They would take over the fishing business, have a good life, and care for him and his wife in their old age. They would always be together.

Sometimes God has greater plans for those we love than we can imagine. And we can't control their destiny or the fiery calling within their hearts to "go." We have to respect the gifts God has placed in other people, enabling them to manage the scary moments and choices as competently as we can.

The world is a scary place and life can be hard, and if we can just get the people we love to do exactly what we think is best, it takes the edge off of our fear. But I think of Zebedee at the shore and how Jesus calls those around us to do their own great things and take big risks in the adventure of life. I have to be like Zebedee. I have to give my loved ones freedom, even in the scariest moments. I have to center myself in prayer and accept the rocky and even painful paths of life.

Legend has it that John died in his old age, leading the church. But James was executed less than fifteen years after Jesus called him. There are no guarantees. Can we courageously accept that risk? Can we respect the freedom of those we love? The freedom Zebedee granted to let his boys pursue their adventure helped change the entire world for the better. May it be so with each of us.

in you

> *"Those who drink of the water that I will give them will never be thirsty. The water that I will give will become in them a spring of water gushing up to [abundant] life."* —John 4:14

In today's dollars, John D. Rockefeller was worth well over 300 billion dollars. (In comparison, Bill Gates is worth one-third that much.) The guy owned whatever he set his eyes on, and no one could tell him "no." The world was his playground. Nothing could ever go wrong. A reporter once famously asked him, "Mr. Rockefeller, how much money is enough?" How did the man who could buy anything he wanted, ten times over, reply? "Just a little bit more," he said.

That is the answer for all of us, isn't it? "I just need a little bit more." That's how much money we need to have enough. And it is not just true of money. If you are single, you likely also think, "I will be happy when I find and marry 'the one.'" Surely, if you can marry the one with the face of a Hollywood star and the heart of a saint, you'll both live happily ever after! If you are married, you might think, "If my spouse would straighten up, we could both finally be happy." To be happy, we need a little more stuff, better partners, a few more friends, an easier job, or a little more free time. "Just a little bit more."

Jesus makes an astonishing promise. He offers us an astonishing gift. He offers us water that will forever fulfill our thirst. But that's just the beginning. It will become its own fountain within us. That life-giving water will burst forth and give us and our world the abundant life for which our hearts have so endlessly ached.

To read Jesus's words and hear him saying he will magically confer joy into your heart is to tragically mishear him. He is saying the opposite. This is a teaching that happiness, "eternal life," is only something that gushes up from inside you. It is not something that comes from outside circumstances and people. No one else and nothing else can make you happy. We generate our own abundant life by living in gratitude, loving and helping others, and most of all by loving and serving God. Jesus taught us to live with compassion, peace, and faith. To pursue that kind of life is to find a fountain in our own hearts, to be content with exactly what we have in front of us.

How much money is enough? I answer the question with another question: "How I can I offer you compassion, peace, and faith? That will be 'enough' for me." When we offer water to the world, we discover a fountain overflowing within our own hearts.

never lose heart

Then Jesus told them a parable about their need to pray always and not to lose heart. He said, "In a certain city there was a judge who neither feared God nor had respect for people. In that city there was a widow who kept coming to him and saying, 'Grant me justice against my opponent.' For a while he refused; but later he said to himself, 'Though I have no fear of God and no respect for anyone, yet because this widow *keeps bothering me, I will grant her justice, so that she may not wear me out by continually coming.'" —*Luke 18:1-5

I recently attended a program that included a free dinner from a local restaurant. We could order whatever we wanted, just as long as it was under $9. Awesome! Free food is the best food. But it wasn't for another couple in attendance. The husband wanted something extra expensive, and the wife wanted something below the $9 threshold. So they raised a fuss to try to bend the rules. My skin was crawling. How tacky can someone get?

But this is who I am. I don't complain. I don't fuss. I don't ask for things. I don't express anger at people. Usually I don't disagree with people, even if I disagree with them in my own mind. The result is that most people like having me around because I'm flexible and accommodating. And many of you are just like me! You hate conflict. You're "a really nice person."

But Jesus tells us a story about a widow. With a dead husband in an ancient world, she was powerless. She depended on a fair justice system to ensure her survival. But an unfair judge didn't care and wanted to pass her by. Jesus says she would not play Mrs. Nice Gal. She stood up for herself. She argued. She fought. She refused to be flexible. She wasn't nice. And she wouldn't shut up about it. She never lost heart. She never gave up.

We live in a good world with good institutions and good people. But sometimes people abuse us and neglect us. And sometimes the system lets us down. Stand up for yourself, Jesus says. Never lose heart. Don't let people push you over, knock you down, and pass you by. Don't ever let someone disrespect you. Never lose heart.

Pay attention to your relationships. Are you letting someone take advantage of you? Are you letting someone talk down to you, say mean things to you, manipulate you, or even hit you? Are you letting someone get away with racism or sexual harassment? I know it is hard to confront someone. I know it is hard to start a fight. I know it is hard to be angry. Your heart wants to cave in on itself. But never lose heart. Listen to the unjust judge. You, like that old, poor, powerless widow, can make a change. You can love yourself the way God loves you. You are worth fighting for. But if you won't fight for yourself, who will? No one. Never lose heart.

Today, you have a hero. Your hero is an old, destitute woman. Will you choose to believe that you deserve justice? Will you believe that God loves you, that you are worthy of love, and that your worthiness is something worth fighting for?

broken grace

"Since [the servant] was not able to pay, the master ordered that he and his wife and his children and all that he had be sold to repay the debt. At this the servant fell on his knees before him. 'Be patient with me,' he begged, 'and I will pay back everything.' The servant's master was moved with compassion for him, canceled the debt, and let him go. But when that servant went out, he found one of his fellow servants who owed him a hundred silver coins. He grabbed him and began to choke him. 'Pay back what you owe me!' he demanded." —Matthew 18:25-28

Hit the pause button and read Jesus's story again. This time, notice the pattern in the story: First, the servant is in massive debt. Second, the forgiving master says payment of the debt is no longer required. Third, the servant goes out to demand payment from others so that he can repay the master.

Do you notice the pattern now? The servant tries to pay someone who doesn't want to be paid. He refuses to believe he has been forgiven, so he refuses to believe he is free to forgive others. After all, if he owes his master nothing, he has no reason to choke his friend and demand payment from him.

If I'm being honest, I resonate with this tortured servant. I live in a pretty gentle world, but I've always been hard on myself. Even if my master is moved with compassion for me, cancels my debt, and lets me go, I still feel like I need to pay the bill. I have to fix it, like my life depends on it.

I wonder, are you hard on yourself? I always thought I could be hard on myself and go gentle on everyone else. I thought I could be demanding and vicious with the man in the mirror so he would improve, while being gracious with others. Jesus says this is a delusion. It doesn't work that way.

If we put ourselves under pressure to earn our way, without realizing it we will become a sort of monster. We'll become demanding and judgmental of others. We either operate in a world of grace for ourselves and for all, or there is no grace at all for anyone. Our souls cannot manage it both ways. We may not even realize we're doing it, but our kindness will be shallow, and in reality we will choke our neighbors with our demands and our lack of grace.

Jesus's parable shows us that we have to go back to the source—receiving God's grace and compassion for ourselves. Every day in prayer, we have to be intentional to remember that we are loved and that we belong, without condition. Even when we screw up or fail or embarrass ourselves or do something awful to someone else, our belonging to God and to the good people God gives us is secure. This is why I begin each day repeating the prayer, "Thank you, God, for loving me." The good news is that when we are secure in our sense of belonging to God and to others, we become more effective and responsible than ever before. We are motivated by a sense of purpose instead of insecure desperation. If we want to be compassionate with others, we must start with receiving God's compassion for ourselves.

seasons

For everything there is a season, and a time for every matter under heaven:
a time to be born, and a time to die;
a time to plant, and a time to pluck up what is planted;
a time to kill, and a time to heal;
a time to break down, and a time to build up;
a time to weep, and a time to laugh;
a time to mourn, and a time to dance;
a time to throw away stones, and a time to gather stones together;
a time to embrace, and a time to refrain from embracing;
a time to seek, and a time to lose;
a time to keep, and a time to throw away;
a time to tear, and a time to sew;
a time to keep silence, and a time to speak;
a time to love, and a time to hate;
a time for war, and a time for peace. —Ecclesiastes 3:1-8

Life transitions are inevitable. Life transitions are hard. And life transitions are life-defining.

Many of you are still trying to wrap your head around the fact that you are in college now or are living away from home. Maybe you're attending college but still living with parents, negotiating what it means to live at home as a young adult.

There is a time for every matter under heaven. This is inevitable, but it can be tough. There is a time for our loved ones to die, a time to move away from family, a time to change our worldview, a time to accept our first professional job, and a time to depart from that job. There is a time to fall in love and a time to learn the painful lesson of how to mend a broken heart. For everything there is a season.

Author Rob Bell said that we can see each life transition as either a divorce or a graduation.[8] How will you see your transition into a new season of life? As a painful and tragic divorce? Or as a hopeful, life-changing, stepping-up new discovery, a life-defining burst of opportunity, a graduation?

Change is death. There's no getting around that. You lose something, probably something profoundly intimate and beloved. So what will you gain? That part is in your hands.

Life transitions are life-defining. In these moments, we can see ourselves at our finest. We can choose gratitude, optimism, hope, and hard work. Like the season we leave behind us, we can forego pessimism, blame, despair, and an endless pining for the time and place and person we had to move on from. We can graduate from life transitions as better, stronger, more mature people.

For everything there is a season. We lament the passing of summer and embrace with hope the cool autumn. A new and beautiful season awaits us.

character

Character produces hope. —Romans 5:4

When my kids were little, I loved giving them gifts. The magic of gifting toys inspired me as a father to want to give them lots of other things, too. I wanted them to be proud of their clothing, our home, our cars, and our jobs. I wanted them to have great vacations, and most of all I wanted them to have the best education. I wanted them to be happy now and forever.

As we become adults in college and beyond, we seek for ourselves a good life. It's what we hope for. But Paul reminds us that when it comes to toys and cars and trips and parties and schools and careers, none of these things give us hope for a good life. All of these things are great, but they ultimately leave us empty-handed.

Character produces hope.

A lot of studies have revealed that happiness cannot come from the aforementioned good things. Joyful people live with gratitude, faith, and loving relationships; they have character. And a lot of experts in a lot of things agree that character (self-discipline, humility, hard work, respect for

---

8. Rob Bell Interview, January 20, 2020, Kickasspirational Podcast, season 3, episode 2, kickasspirational.podbean.com/e/season-3-episode-2-rob-bell-interview/

others, etc.) produces the real stars in sports, musical performance, business, leadership, medicine, and more. The stronger your character, the better parent, leader, professional, and citizen you will be in life. Those with lots of talent and little character often produce some hype, but they fade out quicker and with more destruction. We are both happier and more successful when we have strong character.

If you want hope, get character. Character produces hope.

Character is a muscle that must be exercised and formed every day. No one gets a free pass. Either we work on it regularly, or we don't have it. We grow our character through loving and positive relationships like family and religious community; through daily spiritual practices like prayer, meditation, and religious singing; through serving and sacrificing for others; and through study of things like Scripture or other good readings. Like physical exercise, building our character is hard work. We must devote ourselves to it all our lives and work hard to instill it into our kids.

I'll get a few cool toys to give my kids this year for Christmas, but at the top of my list and between now and December, I'm trying to instill in them strong character. I'm trying to be a man of character myself. That is the greatest, most hopeful gift we can give ourselves and all those we love.

gentle

"I am gentle." —Matthew 11:29

I have never been one to be gentle with myself. I have vivid memories of yelling at myself after failed high school races. Of deep insecurities amid constant social comparisons. Of endlessly striving to out-perform, out-cool, and out-nice everyone around me. Of berating my own lack of personal holiness. Of always seeing my deficits and minimizing my assets. How many times have I muttered the terrible words "I hate myself"?

I don't think I'm alone in my harsh self-whipping. You're probably often oppressed by your own inner critic, too. You probably try to be nicer to others than you are to yourself, too. You probably reserve your most bitter poison for your own cup, too.

"I am gentle," says Jesus. I want to tell you something I have learned: you can only love others as much as you love yourself. And if you don't heal your wounds, you'll bleed on people who didn't cut you. Jesus says, "I am gentle."

I thought that beating myself up, crucifying myself, and diminishing my inner goodness and worth was a good way to compel myself to become a better Christian and person.

Jesus has a very different idea. Jesus says things like, "You are the light of the world," and "Come to me all who are weary, and I will give you rest." He kept walking up to people and saying, "Your sins are forgiven," before they could repent or ask for it or jump through some crazy religious hoop to prove they wanted it.

Jesus understood that under the kind light of his gentleness, we are free to become what we want to be and who God wired us to be: loving, faithful, wise. Shame and guilt and threats manage outer behavior, but gentle compassion sets the heart free and transforms our entire lives from the inside out. We can calmly assess our setbacks and mistakes and resolve to make things right and do better next time.

You can only love others as much as you love yourself. To me, this is a gospel truth. Jesus is gentle with you. Are you gentle with yourself? In the face of your failures, inadequacies, sins, and generally embarrassing and awkward moments, Jesus is gentle with you. Are you gentle with yourself? I have decided to be at peace and walk this kind of path with Jesus. I invite you to walk it with me. It is a wonderful way to live.

God, You are gentle with me. You are compassionate toward me. Thank you for loving me. Set me free to receive your love every day. Amen.

pages

Now so it was that after three days they found him in the temple, sitting in the midst of the teachers, both listening to them and asking them questions. —Luke 2:46

As his custom was, he went into the synagogue on the Sabbath day, and stood up to read, and he was handed the book of the prophet Isaiah. —Luke 4:16-17

College is hard. In my senior year of college, I was reading almost 900 pages of material a week. And I had tons of other work commitments in addition to all that reading. But how in the world could anyone read 900 pages a week, week after week? How in the world can we commit ourselves to extraordinary levels of studying so that we can excel in school and never stop growing, even after we graduate? I think this is less a question of how and more a question of why. I think our biggest hindrance to more reading and studying can often be one of motivation and purpose.

Consider Jesus. He was a rabbi. He traveled around Israel, and people wanted to hear him teach about living life and being faithful. Some of them even followed him around, becoming his students (disciples). Education was incredibly important to Jesus, his life, and his ministry. Education is an important part of how Jesus became the one who offers life-changing wisdom to us even today, in this totally different world.

An interesting passage from the Jewish Mishnah speaks to the education Jesus undertook:

> At five years of age, one is ready for the study of the Scripture, at ten years of age one is fit for the study of the Mishnah . . . at the age of fifteen for the study of Talmud . . . at the age of twenty for pursuing a vocation, at the age of thirty for entering into one's full vigor . . . . (Avot 5:21)

The text suggests that education and apprenticeship continued until age thirty. Scholars say that Jewish boys at that time ultimately would memorize the entire Hebrew Bible, and the Gospels record Jesus constantly reading, teaching, and debating the texts of Scripture. He was a man of books and letters and words and reading. Indeed, his only boyhood story in the Gospels features him learning in the temple.

Every class you take in school (and everything you read) is a golden opportunity to expand yourself, to learn and grow and become someone more useful for God to help the world. Not all college classes, not everything you read, is intended to be directly applicable to the job skills you will need one day. More important is how your classes build you up as a person, how they broaden your mind and strengthen your character.

If you're in school this year, receive the gift and do well. Be like Jesus and dive into studying and reading, listening and asking questions, learning and growing. Your education is something no one can ever take away from you. A curious life steeped in learning is a life that can transform us into more Christ-like people of peace, faith, and grace. It is a life more useful to God to redeem the brokenness in our world.

responsibility

Bear one another's burdens, and in this way you will fulfill the law of Christ. —Galatians 6:2

I remember one day of my freshman year of college. I rolled out of my dormitory bed and strutted across campus to my first class. It suddenly occurred to me what I had put on. I was wearing hiking boots with dark blue sweatpants, a Spider-Man t-shirt, and a jacket. But it was warmer than I expected, and I cinched up the pant legs to my knees. I looked like a complete moron.

At the time, I thought I was pretty cool for looking so crazy. But later, I would look back on that day with a flash of embarrassment. I think of where I am now. I try to be presentable. Now I have professional job. I'm a husband and a dad. I pay a mortgage and I have neighbors. I vote and I go to church. I want a meaningful life that makes the world a better place. I want to give my whole life to loving God and loving others.

Paul says that when we carry one another's burdens, we fulfill the law of Christ. In other words, when we take care of others, when we carry others, when other people can depend on and rely on us, when other people can trust that we are responsible, we are fulfilling Christ's vision for our lives.

Are you carrying the burdens of others? Can other people trust that you are responsible? Love and responsibility are inextricably bound, Paul is saying. Seemingly nonspiritual things like waking up on time, keeping a calendar of appointments, doing your best in school, working hard, being sensitive to the needs of others, and serving others every day are extremely spiritual. Responsibility is at the heart of love, at the heart of Christian living. From page one of the Bible, God is seen as responsibly creating and sustaining God's world—the God in whose image we were created.

I also want us to think about alcohol and how it relates to love. If we are drunk, where is love in this? Folks will often suggest, "I'm not hurting anyone getting drunk with friends." That is proven untrue through many needless and tragic deaths every year. But where is responsibility in it? We assign "designated drivers," that is, people who will be responsible for us because we know that in a state of inebriation, we will be unable to care for others and probably even unable to take responsibility for ourselves. We intentionally do something irresponsible. The more we drink, the more we lose our innate inhibitions and sense of boundaries, which are vital to healthy relationships and love. Drink by drink, we become more physically and cognitively disabled, unable to regulate ourselves. We cannot carry others' burdens. We cannot carry our own. We become a burden for others to take care of.

In college, I got into rock climbing, camping, and hiking. I played a lot of guitar with musician friends. I did a lot of front porch sitting. I was active in church, and I did volunteer work every single weekend. I also worked a lot. Yes, I did (and do) drink a beer or two from time to time. But I had to exercise creativity and courage to carve out fun stuff that didn't include getting drunk. Still, I had an awesome time in my twenties.

And I stayed safe. I helped a lot of people. I built a stronger resume. I had money for things that mattered more than expensive hangovers. All of that did and does help me carry the burdens of those in need. I made that choice because I was taught to live like that by the adults in my life. It spared me a lot of grief. Now I'm passing that wisdom along.

Hear Paul, pass on the second drink, and build something awesome with your life and for God's world.

It is not for kings, O Lemuel. It is not for kings to drink wine or for rulers to desire strong drink. For they will drink and forget what is decreed, and pervert the rights of all the afflicted. —Proverbs 31:4-5

tomorrow

> *"So do not worry about tomorrow, for tomorrow will bring worries of its own. Today's trouble is enough for today."* —Matthew 6:34

As I was finishing divinity school, preparing for a life of ministry, I felt very anxious. I did not feel that I was setting myself up well, establishing myself for success. I was worried that down the road, my "career" would not materialize. I compared myself to others who seemed so put together. They had accomplished things and achieved great things. Me? Not so much.

Are you ever worried about tomorrow? Post-graduation. Your next job. Finding "the one" you are to marry. Or the doomsday news. You look around you, and it feels like others are so much farther ahead of you. You feel certain your "tomorrow" is going to be a lonely and disappointing disaster.

I sat in the office of a school counselor named Chris. His job was to help folks like me in their ministerial vocation. I shared my burdens with him, looking for answers. What should I do? What strategic steps can I take to ensure my path? What do I need to do to avoid hardship and suffering and disaster tomorrow?

After I spilled my guts, Chris paused. He put his hand to his chin in that "thinker" pose. With a concerned head tilt, he asked, "Have tried praying about it?" I, the guy studying the Bible every day to prepare for a life of ministry, of leading others and caring for others, was instantly hot with embarrassment and a punch in my gut. Pray about it?

No. I had not done that.

Today, you can focus on worrying about tomorrow, or you can focus on your work. So first, pray about it. Trust God with tomorrow. "God, I trust that you are with me always, and you are always faithful and good. God, I trust that I am never alone and you are always on my side." After you pray, work hard . . . work really hard. Be the best you that you can possibly be. Pour yourself into your work and the troubles of today, and be successful in what you do. Make great grades. Be a great friend, family member, citizen, and follower of Jesus. Do your work, and work on yourself. Jesus doesn't talk about a worry-free life. He says focus on today's worries, today's "troubles," today's work.

When I start to get worried about the future, I breathe deeply and trust God to be near and go with me into that future. Then, I put my hand to the plow and get to work to build something great today. We must work hard on today's challenges. And we must trust God that tomorrow, God will be faithful, God will be with us, and so all will be well.

unmeasured

"Do not judge, or you too will be judged. For in the same way you judge others, you will be judged, and with the measure you use, it will be measured to you." —Matthew 7:1-2

With a carload of my college friends to impress, I was doing donuts in my 1994 Rodeo in the church parking lot, late on a Friday night. The ridiculous Christians who belonged to this church, with its ostentatious steeple and fountains and gardens and massive glass panels, with its overdone Prayer Room high up in the air—I didn't like them. I could throw a rock from their glitzy church to the train tracks, where just on the other side sat the poorest neighborhood in the city, one that desperately needed love and resources, and this church did nothing to help. Unlike this church, I was deeply involved in the lives of the poor families who lived there through a weekly ministry of friendship, food, and prayer. I knew that I had figured out what this Christianity thing was all about and that this church had missed the mark. And I relished the opportunity to show off a little and hand it to those hypocrites.

I hope this disturbs you the way it does me when I look back on it.

Have you ever talked bad about someone or made fun of someone, and to your horror you realized that they were right behind you, hearing it all the whole time? That terrible, sinking feeling is hard to live down. Or have you ever been around someone who seems to constantly gossip, criticize, make fun, or complain about others? You begin to wonder if they are doing the same about you when you're not around.

"With the measure you use, it will be measured to you." When I spend my energy evaluating others, assessing others, judging others, and measuring others, Jesus teaches that it's going to come back around. Others will feel defensive. They will feel a need to evaluate me, assess me, judge me, measure me. I will create a culture around me of conditional love, of vigilant defensiveness, where no one feels comfortable or at ease or like they belong.

Imagine you are at your funeral, sitting in the pew, listening to someone share their remembrances of your life. The speaker says this: "Not once in our entire life together did I ever hear him/her say one negative thing about someone." Wouldn't that be an awesome thing for someone to say at your funeral? Wouldn't that be an inspiring life you had lived? What if we were people who took seriously Jesus's teaching to "not judge"? What if we focused on the goodness in all people instead of the bad? What if the people around us constantly heard us offering praise, compliments, encouragements, and appreciations? What if we surprised people with good words about our enemies—the people who offend us, let us down, hurt us, and irritate us?

I'm so embarrassed by my actions that night. I was arrogant and cynical and judgmental. I don't want to live a life of others measuring me, criticizing me, judging me. And I realize that I am happier, more joyful, and more at peace when, instead of measuring, criticizing, and judging others, I fill my heart with gratitude, love, and a recognition of the mystery that none of us have everything figured out, but we're all doing the best we can. I want to look within and work on me. I want to leave others' faults unmeasured and instead fill my heart with appreciation, peace, and joy.

friends and missions

"Come, follow me," he said, "and I'll show you how to fish for people."
—Mark 1:17

My senior year of college, the duplex we lived in was pretty awesome, and it quickly became a popular hangout spot for our circles of friends. It had a great front porch and a back deck and easy access to other students' apartments. A perfect "bro" pad! People were at my house every night, and usually it wasn't quiet enough for me to go to bed until about 1 a.m. They weren't wild people—our hangouts were pretty mellow. People would just come over and hang out, mostly with my roommates. I spent a lot of time studying or, more likely, spending time with my soon-to-be fiancée.

During that same time, I participated in a ministry every Saturday morning that brought groceries to families in the poorest neighborhood in town. We spent a few hours each Saturday sharing friendship and a prayer—the love of God—with these families. Over the years, we had experiences and memories that were at times hilarious at other times hard.

I graduated college a long time ago. The friendships I built from a shared purpose, a common mission, and mutual values of faith and service endure to this day. I stay in relative touch with those folks (admittedly its mostly through my wife). But the friendships from hanging out at the house (and the dorm before that)—the ones where I had some good laughs and fun times—quickly dissipated with time and distance. I can hardly recall the faces of some of the people who spent hours and hours in my home.

At the beginning of Mark's Gospel, Jesus begins his ministry journey. He starts bringing good news to people's lives. His first step is to gather friends. Essentially, Jesus says, "I have this mission, and I want you to join me in it." Simon and Andrew, and then others, see the vision and join the mission. Ultimately, Jesus will say to them, "I have not called you servants but friends." Jesus's closest friends were often foolish and confused. They even abandoned him at his crucifixion. Yet in the end, they rallied together to spread Jesus's message, often at the cost of their own lives. After Jesus was gone, they stuck together to create something beautiful and life giving for the world that still endures two thousand years later. All told, Jesus built his friendships through purpose, and he found purpose through his friendships. Jesus spent a lot of time with friends eating and drinking and enjoying life. But at life's most basic level, Jesus was on a particular mission to help others, and he built his incredible friendships through this mission.

Often we might feel like we lack friends or that our friendships lack a certain quality. Jesus started with the mission God had placed on his life. He got busy doing good work in the world and rallying friends to his side to join him in it. Good people dropped their nets and followed him. That is where true bonds are forged. That is where real memories are made. When you suffer together to create something beautiful and life giving for the brokenness in our world, you create deeper, more authentic friendships; you find friends you would be willing to die for. What mission are you calling people to your side to accomplish in our hurting world?

possibility

"Ask, and you will receive. Search, and you will find. Knock, and the door will be opened to you." —Matthew 7:7

My childhood was one of privilege and blessing and lots of love and laughter. It was also a childhood with lots of "nos" from Mom and Dad. No, I will not give you money if you didn't work for it. No, I will not buy junk food for the house. No, we will not buy a go-kart. No, you cannot go to that kid's house, and heck no, you are not going to that party.

I was very blessed, it turns out to have strict parents. They understood that developing my character was more important than me getting my way. They were raising me to become a responsible adult, not a perpetually pleased child.

Many of us have been told "no" all our lives in other ways. Maybe we had strict parents, but maybe our "no" came in other forms: "No, you can never be popular because you are too _____," or "No, you can never have what you want because you come from a broken family," or "No, you could never do that when you grow up because you are not _____ enough." People in our lives may have been repressive or uncaring. We might look back on a lot of doors slammed shut in our faces, but regardless, the outcome is the same. We become "nice folks" who just duck our heads and accept whatever life and people throw at us. We assume the good life and the good things are for other people.

Jesus was speaking with a crowd of oppressed Jewish families. Their lives were often controlled by corrupt Jewish leaders and the military presence of the Roman Empire. People who have always been told "no" eventually stop asking for anything. They stop dreaming. They stop hoping. They stop seeking good things. Jesus understood that such an outlook, a perspective that stopped even trying, was doomed to allow injustice and despair to conquer the world.

Jesus taught his followers to be people of hope. Be people who never stop asking for good things in life. Never stop knocking on the doors of opportunity, blessing, and community. Jesus did not say, "Every time you ask for something, you will get it," as is often interpreted. Jesus said that the people who receive things are only the people who ask in the first place. Never cease to open yourself to the good, the better, the possibility that life could tell you "yes," that a door might finally swing open. Be a person who always dreams big dreams of wild and crazy things and works hard to pursue them.

September

worry

"Who among you by worrying can add a single moment to your life?"
—Matthew 6:27

One time in college, I worried about something so much that it magically got fixed. I needed a $2,000 transmission in my car, and I mulled and agonized over it so long that voila—suddenly I had a free, new transmission and the problem went away.

I wish this were true. I wish that by worrying about things, I am accomplishing something. But the truth is that I am not. I cannot fix anything by worrying about it. I cannot improve my life, I cannot give myself more time in the day or add years to my life, and I cannot "fix" the person I love by worrying.

Jesus's question makes us look within at how foolish our behavior is. When we catch ourselves worrying about the exam, the relationship, or the bills, we must repeat Jesus's question to ourselves: "Who among you by worrying can add a single moment to your life?"

What am I accomplishing by worrying?

Pay attention to your heart. If you are worrying, let it go and do the thing that solves problems—work. Face your problems head on. Get to work on the solution, or get to work on doing the hard thing of embracing that which you cannot change.

above

"Very truly, I tell you, no one can see the kingdom of God without being born from above." —John 3:3

My friend was upset about our new manager and his system of doing things. She was anxious and talking fast. She was plotting ways to overcome our terrible situation. I too, became upset and stressed. Over a period of several weeks, I sank into a pit of worry and self-righteous anger. It wasn't until maybe a year later after I left this job that I realized something: deep down inside, I had liked the manager. I realized I had allowed the anxieties of others to infect me and alter my own perspective.

I think we do this all the time. If folks around us are negative, we unconsciously become negative. If folks around us are angry or anxious or scared, we easily pick up those signals without realizing it, and then we feel the same way. We look at the same selection of information to rationalize our negativity and rationalize our feelings, but deep down it's more a product of those around us than a result of our actual circumstances.

I don't want to be a puppet of those around me. I don't want to be a victim of circumstances my whole life. I want to rise above them. I want to live a different kind of life, to do the opposite, to be a force for good! I want to infect the people around me with positivity, joy, peace, and moral conviction.

Jesus talked about the "kingdom of God." The kingdom of God was the idea that there could be a community centered on worshiping God and loving one another. A place of peace and justice and faith. That is something we all would like to see. Less road rage. More smiles for the checkout clerk.

Jesus says that the only way to see our relationships become like this, like heaven on earth, is to be "born from above" (also translated "born again"). To be born from above means to be guided by higher principles instead of endlessly reacting to circumstances and people around us. Our moral and spiritual DNA is born from spiritual convictions—they can only come from the teachings of Jesus. These higher religious principles offer us deeper convictions for how to rise above the fray around us. It can take us years to grow and mature into a strong sense of higher religious convictions, of coming to deeper terms with our heavenly DNA, but we must actively choose to pursue this path.

If all I ever do is react to the people and circumstances around me, I am incapable of being a leader, incapable of making an impact. In the midst of my manager's transition and turmoil, I could have been a calm, non-anxious presence that considered the long view, that offered peace, hope, and moral conviction. But I did not claim my heavenly birth. I rejected my spiritual DNA and clung to my earthly birth. Jesus teaches me to step back and ask, "Where is God in this? What does Jesus say here? How do I feel about this?" We can only answer these questions through regular and intentional prayer, meditation, and worship. Those are the spaces where we withdraw from the infections around us and look above, where we rediscover our heavenly DNA. It is there that God illuminates the proper path within ourselves and the proper path forward toward the kingdom of God.

prayer and compassion

Looking into heaven, Jesus sighed deeply and said, "Ephphatha," which means, "Open up." At once, his ears opened, his twisted tongue was released, and he began to speak clearly. —Mark 7:34-35

"Just letting you know I'm thinking of you and praying for you. You know I'm praying for you." I hung up the phone and saw the time marker—two minutes, thirty-eight seconds. That was the entire conversation. Just checking in with family members, church family, and friends. So simple and easy.

The Hebrew word for compassion is *rachamim*, the root word of which is *rechem*, or "womb." That is to say, compassion is imitating the phenomenon of a mother's incredible love and inextricable connection, for and to her unborn child.

In *The Book of Joy*, Douglas Carlton Abrams says that feeling compassion for others is necessary to live a life of joy and meaning:

> When we help others, we often experience what has been called the "helper's high," as endorphins are released in our brain, leading to a euphoric state. The same reward centers of the brain seem to light up when we are doing something compassionate as when we think of chocolate. The warm feeling we get from helping others comes from the release of oxytocin, the same hormone that is released by lactating mothers.[9]

Compassion produces joy, so practice lots of compassion when your joy is at stake. How do you practice compassion? There are so many ways. You can sacrifice to give to others—money, time, resources. You can serve your family or your community, or you can advocate for legislative change. You can offer kind words to people. All of these are important and meaningful ways of showing compassion.

---

9. The Dalai Lama, Desmond Tutu, and Douglas Abrams, *The Book of Joy: Lasting Happiness in a Changing World* (Leicester: Thorpe, Isis, 2018). 270.

Jesus touched the man's ear, sighed with him, and prayed for him. In that moment, Jesus and a suffering, deaf, mute man were deeply and spiritually connected. Prayer was essential to how the Great Physician healed "all who came to him." Prayer always catalyzed Jesus to action, to serve and heal others more.

When we pray for others, we weigh their suffering upon our own hearts and offer it to a compassionate God. We say, "How can I pray for you?" and someone opens up about their suffering. We become connected to one another in vulnerable and meaningful ways. We move past the surface level and become connected at a deeper, spiritual level. We pray and remember their suffering. We do not go about our day and forget it. Prayer builds up stores of compassion within us and saves our hearts from the misery of "me, me, me."

Praying for others and with others will procure joy in our hearts. Do you have a community of friends that regularly comes together to pray for one another? Are you reaching out to those in need to offer prayers? What a life-giving, joy-giving practice for our troubled hearts in these challenging days.

family

You, my brothers and sisters, were called to be free. But do not use your freedom to indulge the flesh; rather, serve one another humbly in love.
—Galatians 5:13

"No."

And the waterworks and wailing began. To tell my two-year-old son "no" was to break open his little heart. It was deeply painful to his feelings.

My son's agony over being prevented from doing something (from playing with Daddy's power saw, for example) was amusing and cute to me. I like to think that I am so evolved, so much more mature. But the truth is, we adults are not so different. The slightest hint of someone else controlling our lives is anathema. It's why so many of us struggle to respect our police officers, pay our taxes, or stay married. I myself am the absolute worst offender. I always think I know best, that "I'm so smart," and I distrust the competencies of others. My inclination is to be above the rules and determine my own destiny. I would like to think I am much more evolved than my two-year-old, but I'm not so sure. I get pretty pouty when anyone tells me "no," too.

The Apostle Paul was confronted with this dilemma early in the Christian movement. "Christ gave us freedom from the law! Free, free, free!" the early Christians said. Indeed, Christ had made them free. But for Paul, freedom could only be a servant to love. Freedom was not a Christian's highest value. Instead, humbly serving one another in love was.

He is right. When my five-year-old daughter was in time-out and would weep and stomp about not getting her way, I would sit on the floor with her. I would say, "I don't always get my way, either. I don't always get to do whatever I want to do. Because that's what we have to do in a family. We have to give up our wants sometimes and listen to one another."

America is all about some freedom. And that is fine for America, I suppose. But followers of Jesus are called to something higher—to live free but to subjugate some freedoms to love. We are called to humbly serve one another, even when it costs us some freedom. We American Christians struggle to understand that our freedom can never be pure and total. We cannot be free to murder people or to behave so recklessly that others could get killed, for instance. Family, community, citizenship—love never robs it all, but it does infringe on our freedoms. Love constantly asks us, "Please, can you refrain from this or that?" "Love is not rude. It always protects," Paul said.

You cannot have a healthy relationship, marriage, church, family, or country until you realize that freedom is great, but it is not supreme. Love is supreme. Humbly serving one another, sacrificing freedoms here and there—that is not the way of my young children, but it is the way of Jesus. So I am trying to live less like my little ones who are still learning and more like the Teacher who has taught me for so many years.

the dark

"Just as Moses lifted up the snake in the wilderness, so the Son of Man must be lifted up, that everyone who believes may have eternal life in him." —John 3:14-15

I had a friend who was so brutally beaten by his father that his back was broken once in his father's rage. My friend had to admit that their relationship was complicated, but while he endured a childhood of abuse, he was still working on honoring his father as a biblical commandment. I sensed some avoidance in his story, like he couldn't come to terms with admitting his father's failure as a parent. How would his contorted view of his father affect his ability to be a father himself?

There is a great scene in the movie *The Empire Strikes Back*, the second Star Wars film. On the swampy planet Dagobah, Luke Skywalker notices a cave that makes him feel the presence of cold and death. Yoda tells Luke, "In you must go," and says he won't need to bring in any weapons. When Luke asks him what is in the cave, Yoda replies that the only thing in the cave is whatever Luke brings in. Inside the cave, Darth Vader pops out and attacks. Luke strikes him down only to realize that it isn't Darth Vader—it is himself under the dark mask. Luke, it turns out, brought not only his weapon but also fear and anger into that dark, cold place.

There is also a great scene in the Jewish book of Numbers, when God's people are wandering in the foreboding desert wilderness. Cursed with venomous, biting snakes because of their endless complaining, they cry out to God for help. Moses raises up a bronze snake, and anyone who looks at that metallic icon of their plight will live.

And this brings us to our final scene. Who raised up Jesus on the cross? Did God put him there? Or the devil? It was people who crucified Jesus. It was me. This is not something I want to face. I don't want to own the ugly parts of my story or the potential evil of which I am capable. I don't want to admit, even to myself, that I have been humiliated or afraid or brokenhearted or guilty. I don't want to see my face underneath the supervillain's mask or think about the time I was bitten by a snake.

But Jesus says that we must look to this cold, dark, deadly moment. We must face it in order to find eternal life. We have to enter the cave and leave our armor behind us. We have to look at the snake that bit us all those years ago. We have to look at a Messiah who is naked, bloody, vulnerable, and in agony.

We cannot choose what is true about our own story or the world around us based on what is comfortable or what we want to be true. We cannot minimize the harm done to us in our own story or minimize the harm being done to others around us. We are wired to avert our eyes from the crosses and serpents and caves in the dark corners of our hearts. But a Messiah being strung up on a cross is undeniable spiritual gravity. It forces us all to finally look at the ugly things we have pushed out of our minds without processing them. It is only when we finally face, head on and with eyes wide open, the hard things of our story and of our world that we can finally break through to resurrection and salvation.

Today, what is the uncomfortable truth you have pushed into the cave? What is the hard thing you must do but want to avoid? In you must go. Look upon it and live.

ugly demon

"The voice of your brother's blood is crying to me from the ground."
—Genesis 4:10

Confess your sins to one another and pray for one another, that you may be healed. —James 5:16

It was a dark evening when I hopped in my car to run a quick errand. I turned onto the next street in my neighborhood and saw a young man in a hoodie coming out of a car. I had never seen him before, and I became suspicious. Did he belong here? Was he rifling through someone's car stealing cash? As I drove, I briefly considered calling the authorities just to check it out. But I caught myself. "He's Black," I told myself, "and you're being ridiculous." Sure enough, a week later I saw the same guy getting out of the same car in broad daylight, walking to his house.

Until I was nineteen years old, there were few people of color in my life. My experience was mostly relegated to television, the news, and other cultural things, like pop music. Most of the Black faces American culture pushed in front of me were poor, criminal, or of low moral standards. Culture didn't show me the hard-working, educated Black men doting on their wives and loving their kids and mowing their lawns.

I was (mostly) taught and I did believe that all are equal, regardless of skin color. I always told myself, "I'm not a racist; I don't see color." But an undeniable part of my story is that most Black bodies that culture pushed my way were ones less trustworthy, less capable, and less noble.

White supremacy is the view that people of color are less trustworthy, less capable, less noble. They must prove and earn what white people are freely given. It is the view that Black people are something to distrust, and it is the history of the colonizing West with its race-based slavery, Jim Crow oppression, and current mass incarceration of African Americans. Centuries of blood cry out from the ground beneath our feet.

So I am not a white supremacist, but white supremacy is an ugly demon I've got to look at. Around me, yes, but also, within me. You too—we're born into the same world with the same history. It is possible that somehow, unlike myself, you have magically risen above all of this unscathed. That you have always held the exact same level of trust and respect and openness for people of color as for white folks. You've never been extra suspicious, extra afraid, or a little more apathetic toward someone's suffering. If so, I commend you.

But the more we white people keep insisting, "I'm not racist, we're not racist," the more blind to our racism we risk becoming. All of us need to see that the tragic sin of white supremacy is prowling at our own gate. That the blood of so many innocent Black Americans cries out to God and to us from the ground. That all of us have sinned and fallen short of the glory of God. That it simply will not do to scapegoat the "white rednecks in the woods with rebel flags" or, conversely, to pretend there is almost no problem in the first place.

Jesus's wisdom and God's good news is that God forms all people in their mothers' wombs, equally and in God's own image. That if Black people are disproportionately failing in school, filling up jails, and dying in the streets, if our young adults of color don't feel safe jogging in their neighborhoods, wearing hoodies, or driving at night, it is ultimately the fault of white supremacy and not some inborn issue in African American blood or heritage. If we choose to stop poisoning the water, the fish will swim just fine. White supremacy is a sin that can be confessed, repented from, and redeemed. That is hopeful, good news.

You can scour the entire universe and never find God's unconditional, limitless grace and restoration. That is because it's only found in this one, small, narrow place—the place where your hands are open and you take responsibility for your choices, your actions, your life. God's healing lies in the thin place where we stop playing defense and playing dumb and finally tell the truth about our story.

I'm not seeking any reconciliation without first doing my own truth telling. I'm not facing anyone's demons but my own. I pray that you can join me on this hard journey toward redemption for ourselves and for the whole, hurting world. That is the narrow beginning of a wide and authentic hope.

had to

Jesus had to rise from the dead. —John 20:9

The floor was just a thin layer of carpet over concrete, hard against my back as I lay on it all alone. I never wanted to get up. I may starve and petrify, but I would not be forced to face the things around me and within me. Everything was too hard that night of my freshman year of college.

Have you ever said, "I refuse to get over this"? Or "I can never recover from this" or "There is absolutely no way to fix this"? Heartbreak, family betrayal, disappointment, money woes, school failure, harsh words, or the relentless ambiguity and anxiety of pandemic life . . . have you, too, ever lost hope in situations like these?

When Jesus, the Jews' purported Messiah, was killed by the Romans, Jesus's followers caved and fled. Only a few stood by him until his last breath. They were devastated, knocked down into the gravel of the arena. They couldn't get up and face the moment. The next Sunday morning, a few visited his grave to mourn him. They were shocked to find his tomb empty and couldn't believe that Jesus had risen from the dead. They couldn't believe that he had gotten back up from the humiliating and torturous abyss of execution by crucifixion. "They still did not understand from Scripture that Jesus had to rise from the dead," John wrote. But think about what the Scripture said: Jesus had to rise from the dead.

Jesus *had* to rise.

If Jesus did not rise, there was no vindication of Jesus's honor as an innocent man. There was no repudiation of sacrificing people. There was no conquering of death and despair. Mary would have kept weeping. Don't you see? If there is no resurrection for Jesus, there is no resurrection for the world. Jesus had to rise.

This is true for you and me too. When we fail to rise, when we close our eyes, breathe in the dry dust, and rest our cheek in the dirt, when the insults have landed so heavy and the news is so bad that we just decide to stay down, our surrender will inevitably present a black hole for others to fall into as well. Those around us will struggle, they will suffer, they will be knocked down by our quitting.

But our resurrection will inspire them. When others see us get back up, they will clap their hands. Their spirits will be strengthened. They will whisper to themselves, "I want to be like that; I can be like that." They will believe that the world is a good place and that they want to make it even better. Don't you see that we must rise?

Jesus has paved the way. If we have been "born again," received a heavenly birth, that means resurrection is in our DNA. It's like the chameleon's skin or the cheetah's legs or the bird's wings. Resurrection is what makes us who we are, and that's why you and I are going to choose to get up again.

Today, Jesus calls you to reclaim your resurrection identity and get back up. To be strong for your family, your community, and the world. Yes, times are hard and our graves are dark. But our world grabs its seat and stretches its neck and squints its eye to look toward you, and it watches. It is anxious as it waits to see what you will do. Like Jesus, so much hangs on whether you will rise up today. Will you reclaim this gift God has put within you? Surely your resurrection means a resurrection for many more.

loneliness

"*. . . that they may be one just as we are one.*"—John 17:11

I carefully preplanned sitting at a table and pulling out a book to occupy myself. I intentionally timed my entrance into the cafeteria to avoid standing in a long line. And once I shoveled my food down, I knew exactly where I was headed. I had the system down—no one would notice how alone I was. And this made me so sad. My sophomore year of college was the loneliest year of my life. At that time, I had not developed the social skills sufficient to navigate the unstructured, go-get-'em world of college life, and I studied and worked all the time instead of taking time to bum around with my peers.

I remember in 2020, the whole country was suddenly keyed in to the possibility that there are lonely and isolated people in this world. But loneliness is always pervasive—pandemics or not. Our world is full of lonely and isolated people. Older folks whose family and friends have died or parted ways. Younger folks who are unsure of themselves and unable to connect with others. Have you ever felt like you had no one to connect with, relax with, or share your deepest secrets with? If so, you tasted what many around you experience every day. All alone. All the time.

The doctor says this isn't good. Loneliness and isolation have dramatic ill effects on one's emotional and physical health. A "good life" is not lots of toys and money and cool vacations. It is a connected life. I even read that we die much sooner if we are lonely people. It's almost as if we were created in the image of some kind of triune God, like if we are not deeply, authentically connecting to other people, then we are out of whack with how we were wired.

I can't think of any other program in the modern world that heals this loneliness epidemic better than a small local church. One study showed that we live four years longer if we are actively involved in church than if we aren't. Some churches excel at connecting folks, creating a "spiritual family." And I understand that some churches are terrible at this. But in general, if you join a church, if you show up and participate, you experience deep connection with other people. Churches, these assemblies of disciples, weep with those who weep and rejoice with those who rejoice. They (try to) love unconditionally. They become "one" through the many prayer requests and visitations and funerals and graduations and childcare and the endless other life things in between. Good church is not shallow. Good-news preaching and hymn singing and Bible studies are about the precious things of life. Good church crawls into the deepest parts of ourselves, and we connect with others there.

The church is Jesus's remedy for loneliness and isolation and disconnection. It's OK to reach out to your church and dive in deeper this week. It's OK to connect with a pastor or a churchgoer for the first time in a long time. Anyone can join this. That's what makes it so special. Do you want to be less alone? Do you want there to be less lonely people? You can make a difference for yourself and for others. Jesus prayed that you would receive this gift he freely offers to you.

arrived

We know that we have passed from death to life because we love one another. —1 John 3:14

Today, I'm paying a mortgage on my house that is filled with a wife and two little kids and a dog. I have a career. I just need to make more income so that we can all live a little more comfortably. Then things will be good. I will have finally arrived at where I want to be.

Then things will be good. That was my mentality in high school, waiting for college. And when I was waiting to get a better car. And when I was waiting to move from general-education courses to major-specific courses. And when I was waiting to not be single anymore. And when I was waiting to get my college or graduate degree. The list goes on forever.

There's always a new horizon that we point to and say, "When I get there, I will have finally arrived."

But to quote James Bond, tomorrow never dies. The horizon is always there.

John charts a different course under the bright light of God's love. He says that we will have arrived—things will be good—not when we attain this or that equilibrium but when we make the choice to love one another right where we are.

This is a way of saying that we need to stop looking at the horizon and literally look at the people in the same room, the same home, the same community we are currently in and make the choice to enjoy and love those people. Try this: today, focus on complimenting people, focus on offering over-the-top gratitude to people, focus on noticing what other people are going through, focus on bringing in whomever is currently getting left out. When you stop focusing on what you're missing out on and instead focus on others, focus on what is right in front of you, you will be happier and at peace, and so will the people around you.

This is how we know we have passed from death to life. This is how we know that things are good. This is how we know we have arrived—when we love one another. That is all we need to live the abundant life God is offering each of us.

Loving God, thank you for making your peace and joy something I can live in today. As I work towards new horizons in life, point my eyes to the people I can lift up with love right here, right now. Give me strength to love them. Fill me up with your spirit of peace, joy, and love. Amen.

return to you

"If the home is deserving, let your peace rest on it; if it is not, let your peace return to you." —Matthew 10:13

I hear that anxiety is even more contagious than the coronavirus. By anxiety, I mean both ruminating on the past and worrying about the future, but I also mean the frantic, unsure, untrusting armor we put on in moments of conflict and pain. Lashing out. Running away. Becoming bitter and resentful. And this anxiety is contagious. It leaps from one person to the next unsuspecting person. Soon everyone in a household is sick with it, at each other's throats or blowing off steam in other bad ways.

Jesus's antidote is this: "my peace I give to you" (John 14.27). His gift of peace is the kind of gift that we can reject, but no one else can take it from us. I heard a scientist say that external circumstances can make our brains angry and upset for a total of three seconds. If we stay angry and anxious after three seconds, it is because we are rehearsing and ruminating negative lines and narratives in our head. No one can make us feel anything (longer than three seconds, that is). We can truly own and control this great gift of peace.

When we begin to receive and possess Jesus's peace, it will inevitably, every day, be met with anxiety and anger and misbehavior from others. Our choice is to either let this gift return to us—to remain peaceful, calm, regulated—or to choose to surrender it and let someone else's anxiety infect us. "Do not be overcome by bad but overcome bad with good," Paul says in Romans 12. We own the choice to act Christ-like no matter how others are acting.

The wonderful surprise here, the very good news, is that Jesus's peace is just as contagious as anxiety. We have the power, the opportunity, to become a contagion of peace to those with whom we live in these anxious days. And not through preaching, lecturing, or pathologizing the "crazy" people in our family. There are no judgements needed—just owning this gift of peace. Letting it return to us. Never surrendering it. We can't find peace by arguing with others or getting them to do what we want. We look within and we look to Jesus. We take responsibility for ourselves and stop trying to control other people and things. The infection of peace may take a long, painful time. It may take months! But it is Jesus's charge to all those who follow him: "If the home is deserving, let your peace rest on it; if it is not, let your peace return to you."

the logic of Jesus

"... *because they don't understand what they are doing.*" —Luke 23:34

I entered college as a wide-eyed Southern Baptist from a small town, and I wanted to be a preacher when I grew up. I had been trained to defend ideas rather than explore them. These were religious ideas including "one can never lose their salvation," "speaking in tongues is fake," and other ideas that, frankly, I couldn't care less to remember these days. I attended a college with a highly religious atmosphere, built by a Pentecostal denomination.

We all had to attend two chapel services a week, never have the opposite sex in our room, and promise not to cuss. Religion was the focal point.

I set out to prove all my surrounding Pentecostal friends wrong and build up my own religious ego. "Clearly, they were simply ignorant of what the Bible taught, or they were selfishly lying about the truth they knew," I thought. Yet I was surrounded by these "crazy" Pentecostals and they kind of wore on me. They were often very smart. They were often kind, generous, and sincere in their faith. I couldn't resist loving them, enjoying them, and respecting them and much of their tradition.

Jesus lived in divided times, much more divided and hostile than we experience today. His fellow Jews distrusted Samaritans and Romans and non-Jews and sinners and the poor. So over and over again, Jesus took every chance he could to point his finger at their enemies and show his followers the good in them. "Look at their faith!" he would say. "Look at their love!" Through his every step and word, Jesus proved that so much of our hostility and division is a product of misunderstanding and a lack of mutual goodwill.

It culminated on the cross. There was no miscommunication in that moment. "Those people" were killing him! Yet he prayed, "Father, forgive them."

Why should God forgive Jesus's killers? "Because they don't understand what they are doing," reasoned Jesus. That is not a very theological reason, and yet it's the one Jesus gave. Even in our enemies' worst moments, we must forgive them because the truth is, they don't fully understand what they are perpetrating.

Everyone is created in God's image, shaped and sewn by God in the womb of a mother, with great love and excellence. Everyone has been wounded and scarred and is trying to play defense or is simply shrouded in so much privilege that they have no idea what others are going through. They, just like we, are doing the best they can with what they've got, even if they commit great evil and cause pain in the world.

You'll never find the Lord's peace in blaming and hating and bitterness. Let it go. Who have you decided is evil or idiotic or the enemy? See the good in them. Sit at the table with them. And even if or when they pierce your side with a sharp spear, may you remember Jesus's logic of forgiveness.

the truth: part 1 of seeing clearly in unclear times

"The truth will set you free." —John 8:32

In 2020, the truth of COVID-19 (or anything else, for that matter) felt like a hard thing to come by. Some people thought we were all going to die the second we stepped out of the front door, and some people thought COVID-19 wasn't real. The death toll would ultimately reach 377,000 just that year in the United States. Other, more careful countries lost close to zero lives. Every day it seemed that we received different messages about washing hands, breathing air, wearing masks, the level of contagion, the probability of fatality, etc. These voices seemed so sure of themselves. Somehow, they were so certain that they could run things better and that they possessed the real truth of the matter.

How can we discern between what is true and false in this big world? Jesus offers a helpful parable on this:

> To some who were confident of their own righteousness and looked down on everyone else, Jesus told this parable: "Two men went up to the temple to pray, one a Pharisee and the other a tax collector. The Pharisee stood by himself and prayed: 'God, I thank you that I am not like other people—robbers, evildoers, adulterers—or even like this tax collector. I fast twice a week and give a tenth of all I get.' But the tax collector stood at a distance. He would not even look up to heaven, but beat his breast and said, 'God, have mercy on me, a sinner.'" (Luke 8:9-13)

In my life, I have learned that honestly seeking the truth of the matter is hard because I'm so prone to feed myself voices that reinforce my previously established views. Unconsciously, hearing "I'm right" or even "The people in power are wrong" becomes more important than the actual truth. It becomes nearly impossible to repent, to grow, to live in the real world because I so badly want to feel as confident and comfortable as the Pharisee. I don't want to be humbled, broken, and vulnerable like the tax collector.

But the gospel has constantly challenged me in life to remember that I am a sinner, and a very small one in a big universe, at that. I'm also beloved, not for my rightness or righteousness but simply because I am. For that reason, I have courage to say "They are wrong" less and work on saying "Maybe I'm wrong" more.

These days, I don't intentionally consume biased, unreliable, or non-credentialed media or news. I don't even listen to news coming from for-profit media companies. Because it only strokes my ego to say, "You are right! They are wrong!" This attitude is anti-gospel. Biased news organizations speak into our lives and shape our hearts. We become more gullible to living in hysteria or denial and to losing the narrow center where truth and redemption shine. We all easily take the bait because the power trip is so satisfying.

Yet faithfulness looks like seeing the world as it is so we can take responsibility for God's hurting world. Faithfulness looks like constantly praying the prayer, "God, have mercy on me, a sinner, a passing vapor in the wind." I see no faithfulness in choosing to let others subjectively arrange "facts" for me. I see no faithfulness in choosing to live inside an echo chamber, surrounded by supposed demons on the outside.

The great mystery of salvation is that those who confess they are sinful are the only ones who can become righteous. Those who confess they are foolish are the only ones who can become wise. May we be wary of any voice in our life preying on our soul's desire to hear, "You are righteous! You are wise! Those people are evil fools."

May God's unconditional love for us give us the courage to be vulnerable to the truth of the hour so we can calmly do what is necessary to serve our community and our world.

sell everything: part 2 of seeing clearly in unclear times

> *Jesus, looking at him, loved him and said, "You lack one thing; go, sell what you own, and give to the poor, and you will have treasure in heaven; then come, follow me." When he heard this, he was shocked and went away grieving, for he had many possessions.* —Mark 10:21-22

I recently learned that there is a group of people called "flat-earthers" who believe that planet Earth is literally a flat disc surrounded by a wall of Antarctica. For them, the Earth is not a sphere floating in space around a sun.

Good people believe this. They pay their taxes and feed their pets and use their blinkers before turning right. But you can show them pictures of planet Earth from space and point to the boat disappearing over the rounded horizon and it won't matter. They will not give up the idea of a flat Earth. They will not admit they are wrong.

I'm tempted to feel smug when I think about these folks. But I'm not sure I'm so much better off. Unlike the rich man Jesus spoke with, most of us must work hard our whole lives, painfully pinch every penny, and all the while watch the person down the street and on the screen make way more money than us and do all kinds of cool stuff we can't do. Even if we make enough to live comfortably, we will probably never be rich. The pain of that economic inequality is piled on by many other thorns in our shoes—we are not equally beautiful or equally popular, and our lives are marked by tragedy, heartbreak, and injustice. Many of us find a way to compensate for all that inequality and loss: we can be rich ideologues.

An ideologue is a dogmatic adherent to an ideology, a belief system. For example, "I'm a liberal" or "I'm a conservative." We can become rich in knowledge and arguments and full of great zingers to sling at ideological opponents. We can catastrophize with statements like "Our country is about to completely fall apart (if you don't listen to me.)" The playground term, if I recall correctly, is a "know-it-all." It feels good to know everything, doesn't it? To feel like you're right and other people are wrong? It's almost like being rich.

"Go, sell what you own, and give to the poor, and you will have treasure in heaven; then come, follow me," Jesus says. See that your intellectual mansion is a house of cards, and give it away. That's how you find the real treasure; it's the heavenly stuff. If you find yourself in a "conservative" disposition, vigilantly seek out the wisdom of "liberal" dispositions. And vice versa. Be diligent, always, in trying to prove yourself wrong. We can wrap a warm blanket around ourselves, surrounded by media and people that think like us. It's a cold and uncomfortable world when we keep pulling that blanket off. But the blanket makes us lazy thinkers. It covers over our eyes and diminishes our sight.

What if we each became addicted to repentance and learning and growth? What if we each became addicted to realizing we were wrong about something and shifting course? Surely that is a path we could all walk together in peace. The rich man was shocked and walked away in grief. But to those who can empty themselves of their wealth and follow Jesus, the discovery of peace and love and hope and trust in God awaits them . . . eternal life humming within ourselves and our communities, all across this little ball spinning through the big galaxy.

hopeful: part 3 of seeing clearly in unclear times

> *Then Levi gave a great banquet for Jesus in his house; and there was a large crowd of tax collectors and others sitting at the table with them. The Pharisees and their scribes were complaining to Jesus's disciples, saying, "Why do you eat and drink with tax collectors and sinners?"*
> —Luke 5:29-30

In the early 1700s, there was a smallpox outbreak in Boston. An African slave named Onesimus tried to explain to his master how, in Africa, they had successfully prevented such smallpox outbreaks for centuries. Africans deposited a trace amount of the disease into their blood prematurely, enough for the body to build up an immune response. His master, a pastor, agreed and tried to convince his colony to get "vaccinated" in order to save their lives. But most everyone refused. They simply could not believe that Black people could ever be, in any form or fashion, more advanced than white people. There was no way this African idea of vaccination could work. In the end, 280 Americans agreed to the practice and nearly 6,000 said "No thanks." Fourteen percent of those who refused the African remedy died that year from smallpox, seven times the rate of those who bravely tried it. Ultimately, what killed these Americans was not smallpox. What killed them was an inability to see hope come from people of color. Their own distrust and prejudice killed them.

The Pharisees were determined to save Israel through their intense spirituality of separating themselves from all who were perceived as impure and sinful. If a tax collector or "sinner" had offered a Pharisee a smallpox vaccination, they likely would have said "No thanks" as well. And what if they offered them a banquet? What if they offered them love, fellowship, and food? Still, the Pharisees and scribes would have said no. They had no trust and saw no hope in and for sinners and tax collectors.

The easy route in life is to extrapolate the bad in people, anticipate doom, and judge it all from a distance. But Jesus, who no doubt had been and would be wounded in his own life, bravely did the opposite. Like the first Bostonian purposefully placing smallpox into a cut in her arm, Jesus saw past the anxiety and fear around tax collectors and sinners. He said, "Follow me," and he sat at the table with them. Jesus was hopeful about their future and about what might happen when rabbis like himself became friends with sinners. The story ends with Jesus enjoying a great banquet and the grumpy Pharisees and scribes off to the side, muttering and complaining with empty bellies. They were highly educated people, but they don't look so smart in this particular story, do they?

These days, social media, the news, and even many pulpits are filled with warnings about "the scary direction we are headed" and a focus on the bad in people and in the world. Conspiracies abound about people plotting to rule our world. But, just like the belief that people of color cannot offer innovation to white people or that we need to stay away from sinners, this is unclear thinking. We are using the fearful, anxious, animal-like part of the brain, and so the more objective, executive part of the brain is shutting down. We are not rooted in possibility and hope and trust. We are living in fear and anxiety, and anxious people do not think clearly.

There are many terrible things happening in our world right now and perhaps more directly in your own life. And I"m not saying we should take any of those things lightly. But think of those racist Bostonians and those frowning Pharisees and what they missed by only seeing the terrible and the scary. Don't you see how muddled our thinking becomes when we focus on the bad and live in distrust? Maybe the only truly sane people in this world are those who hold on to a little hope in and for all people and all situations, no matter how scary and hard things have become.

on the ground

> "Aren't two sparrows sold for a small coin? But not one of them will fall to the ground without your Father knowing about it already . . . . Don't be afraid. You are worth more than many sparrows."
> —Matthew 10:29, 31

Some folks are fighters, but I am what you call a "withdrawer." In times of conflict, my natural inclination is to withdraw, to keep my mouth shut, to fume, to judge, to prefer bitterness over talking it out. Instead, I stuff it down and patch it over with distractions. In my fear, I have allowed things to simmer for years, made unhealthy choices, and failed to actively love others who needed it. When things are complicated, scary, or painful, it is safer and easier to withdraw.

But withdrawing is terribly destructive. We poison and callous our hearts, our relationships become abusive, and injustice is perpetuated as those with a voice offer nothing but averted eyes to the voiceless.

For Jesus's first followers (who were Jews), their relationships were becoming ripe with conflict. Their fellow Jews with whom they had always lived, worked, and worshiped did not agree that Jesus was their long-awaited Messiah. Arguments, slander, name calling, and even violence swelled and swelled. Whether a Messiah had come or not was a deeply precious question. It was about something tremendously sacred and existential, and how one answered the question made one vulnerable. "Is it true? Are we finally being redeemed?" Faced with hostility, judgment, and conflict, it was easier and safer to withdraw and remain silent and leave the Jesus question unacknowledged.

Nearly all of Matthew's tenth chapter represents Jesus's compassionate response to his disciples' anxiety around this terrible conflict. In Jesus's world, hunting sparrows for a morsel of meat was simple and common. When you found a sparrow, you hurled a stick at it. When struck, the bird would fall to the ground in pain and confusion. You would rush upon the sparrow, catch it with your cloak, and kill it with a knife.

But you couldn't kill that sparrow until it hit the ground. And isn't that how we feel in our moments of confrontation and conflict in relationships? We feel like we are putting ourselves at the kill point—a sparrow on the ground. Maybe we say something mean because we cannot control our anger. Maybe we embarrass ourselves. Maybe we are dishonest about the pain we feel inside. Scariest of all, maybe the other person hurts us even more than they already have. We want life to feel like a free bird, soaring carefree through the air. Yet authentic relationships call for exposed and uncomfortable conflict. They must be brought down to the messy dust, the undefended earth. The ground is where Jesus draws our attention.

Jesus tells us we are free to put ourselves in this position of raw vulnerability—that generally speaking, our loved ones won't go in for the kill when we "tell in the light" what we have heard or felt in the darkness. But if they do, God's nearness, faithfulness, and love will restore us. Our worthiness is our birthright and will never be compromised, no matter how the fight goes down. We can have the courage to be vulnerable with our loved ones. We can disagree with people. We can confront actions that seem unfair or hurtful. We can be open and honest about our moral, religious, and social convictions. We can share what we feel and experience. This is the sparrow on the ground, exposed to discomfort and hostility—the messiness of possibly not saying every word exactly right or having things go sideways. God loves us and cares for us and will absolutely never leave our side.

That gives us courage to put ourselves out there and gently say the things overdue to be said.

When relationships are ripe for potential conflict and discomfort, we want to fly away, free and safe like a sparrow in the wind and the tall trees. But we can't. We can't run away forever—it all catches up with us eventually. The good news is that God is with us even on the ground, so we should not be afraid. Now is our moment to stand in the dirt and finally say how we feel.

October

drowned rats

> Then Jesus went up on a mountainside and sat down with his disciples. The Jewish Passover Festival was near.... Jesus said, "Have the people sit down." There was plenty of grass in that place, and they sat down (about five thousand men were there). Jesus then took the loaves, gave thanks, and distributed to those who were seated as much as they wanted. —John 6:3-4, 10-11

I heard a story about a mad scientist from the 1950s. He threw rats into water to see how long it would take for them to drown. Through experimentation, he found that if he saved them right before they drowned and then threw them in the water again the next day, they swam much longer before starting to sink. That is to say, rats who had been rescued once before had more strength to swim than rats who had never experienced rescue before. If you're sitting there thinking, "What is wrong with this guy? Someone call PETA!" then, according to the internet, you are not alone in such feelings. Still, the scientist felt he had learned an important lesson about the rat as well as the human condition: when we remember there is hope that someone will pull us out, we have renewed strength to keep swimming.

If you read the story of Jesus feeding 5,000 people in John 6, you might notice a little sentence John scrunched into the narrative: "The Jewish Passover Festival was near" (v. 4). Why did he write that? Why did he bring up something about a Jewish festival before returning to the narrative? It has nothing to do with the story.

Except that it does.

Passover is an annual Jewish festival to remember the days in Egypt, when death passed over the homes of the Jews and granted them liberation from their oppression. After that night, the great exodus took place. God saved the people from death and from their enemies. John reminds us of the nearness of Passover. He reminds us of God's faithfulness in the past and the miracles that can happen when we keep holding on to hope. In view of the 5,000 "hangry" people, John reminds us that God has pulled God's people out of the water before, so God can do it again.

What is your "passover"? When have you been scared in the dark and surrounded by enemies? What are some of the great trials in your life, and how did God get you through them? We must remember these times. In the face of hungry crowds and the mountains in front of us, we have to look behind us at our story. We have to remember the ways God pulled us out before, right before we sank.

The truth is, people who remember how they navigated their struggles before become stronger and more resilient in the face of every trial in front of them. We need to celebrate and remember our own passovers, looking back to the fights we had with loved ones, times of financial desperation, and setbacks in our school and career and remember how God got us through it. This will fill us up with the same kind of peace and strength Jesus demonstrated on the mountainside. This will make us into the kinds of people who can offer life-giving bread to a hungry world. And yes, this will turn us into rats that can swim for a very long time.

breath

> *And with that [Jesus] breathed on them and said, "Receive the Holy Spirit."* —John 20:22

During a phone call, my friend pressured me to do something in my ministry that I wasn't comfortable doing. He felt sure that he knew exactly what I needed to do, and he kept coming at me with the reasons I needed to do it. I tried to be patient and nice and reasonable, but instead I got a little defensive. I even raised my voice with him a bit. I later apologized for that. I was embarrassed that I had stepped into the stew of anxiety and reacted defensively instead of maintaining a cool composure, filled with God's peace.

Beginning in the first chapter of the Bible and ending with the last, the Scripture writers talk a lot about breath. The words *ruach* (Old Testament Hebrew) and *nooma* (New Testament Greek) are used nearly 800 times in the Bible. *Ruach* and *nooma* can mean "breath" and "wind" and "spirit." The original readers would have heard all those meanings at once when they saw *ruach* or *nooma*. In John's Gospel, God's *nooma*, that is, the holy breath or holy wind or holy spirit, comes to us through—you guessed it—breathing.

What is more intimate and interior than breathing? Pause for a moment, take a deep breath, and pay attention to it. Your breath is inside you, close to your heart and to your gut. Paying attention to it draws you inward.

When we focus outward on external circumstances, we spend our whole lives reacting. But a life turned inward is one that can operate above the fray. We can detach for a moment from the madness and connect with something (or Someone) else. So Jesus talks a lot about the *nooma*—the breath, the wind, the spirit. It is quiet and mysterious, and it does not depend on whatever peace or craziness is happening around us.

When we are stressed, distraught, heartbroken, angry, or tempted, Jesus invites us to pause and look inward for a moment, paying attention to our breathing. This practice can slow us down and help us remember God. We can and truly connect with God in a brief moment of prayer. The holy wind/breath/spirit, God's *nooma*, comes to us not in interpreting signs and omens in the sky but in that slow, intimate space within ourselves. Taking a moment to pay attention to our breath and then pray, even during a tense conversation, can reshape us into people of God's peace in the world.

broken pieces

"Let nothing be wasted." —John 6:12

Think of one of the most disappointing moments in your life. Maybe you got dumped or rejected or things didn't pan out the way you had hoped. I remember the rejection letter I received from my first choice for college. I remember failing at getting any good jobs when I first graduated. I remember some unrequited love in my youth.

The truth is that in life, our open hands are often left holding broken pieces. We experience tragic losses, injustices, and hurt feelings. We hold on to feelings of being inadequate and ashamed and alone and disappointed.

"Let nothing be wasted," Jesus says. He says this to his disciples, who are holding broken and leftover fragments of good things in their hands. "Let nothing be wasted."

These words are not preachy and tough. They are tender and gentle. Jesus speaks in a soft voice, looking at the brokenness and saying that there is still hope for good things.

When life runs me over, Jesus has shown me a better way. I no longer believe in "bad days." There are only "challenging days." And when my heart is met with disappointment and hard stabs, I hear these words from Jesus. How can I turn this challenge into something good for me and my world? How can this setback ultimately support me in my life goals? How can God redeem some of this? Always, there is so much to learn and gain from our pain. Jesus is not saying that God causes bad things to happen to us in order to teach us a lesson. Jesus is saying that when bad things happen in our lives, when our trembling hands are holding broken pieces, he comes to us with a spirit of peace and a hand on our shoulder and says, "We're not going to throw this away."

Let us take our pain, let us acknowledge our story, and let us give it back to Jesus to do something redemptive and beautiful with it inside of us. As the apostle Paul said in his letter to the church in Rome, "Suffering produces patience, patience produces character, and character produces hope" (5:3-4).

cathedrals and castles

> *"Unless I see the mark of the nails in his hands, and put my finger in the mark of the nails and my hand in his side, I will not believe."*
> —John 20:25

A friend of mine was touring New York City and decided to worship in an Episcopal church for the first time. He was curious about it. He walked to the church at the designated worship time and opened the door—or tried to. It was locked, so he tried the next door. It was locked too. He peered into the stained glass window and could see the congregation beginning the worship service inside. He tried another door and another door. They were all locked, with everyone worshiping safely inside. There seemed to be no way to get in. He went home. Increasingly, churches are locking their doors, arming their ushers, and posting guards because there have been instances of horrific gun violence in places of worship. There are no easy answers to the question of how to cope with such tragedies. We have to be guided by some important considerations.

Thomas couldn't believe that Jesus had risen. The only way he could believe was by seeing a crucified man—a wounded but resurrected man. He knew his Messiah was not impenetrable. He knew that a man without wounds claiming to be Jesus was a phony.

Resurrection people may consider the risk of becoming so overprotective that we compromise our witness. We can become so armored that we are no longer open. We have to take some calculated risks. Our churches have to welcome in some strangers and go on mission in the world among some people and places we can't perfectly control. If every door is locked and every members armed, we might look very different from the exposed Jesus on the cross, trusting God's resurrection for him. Thomas and all of those who are genuinely seeking resurrection, genuinely seeking the Living God, may find people who bear no scars or willingness to risk a cross less persuasive or inspiring. Our world needs resurrection, not fortification. Cathedrals, not castles. Wounded healers, not soldiers. Like Jesus, may you love the world with humility and vulnerability.

broken treadmill

> *"I will pray to the Father, and he will give you another Helper, that he may abide with you forever . . . I will not leave you as orphans."*
> —John 14:16, 18

We need friends who pray for us and encourage us to pray about things. When we are most anxious and stressed, many of us tend not to stop and pray. We become spiritually injured for a time. That's why having friends and pastors around us who can pray for and with us is tremendously helpful. That's why it's great to have friends and pastors who, upon knowing our situation, can encourage us to pray our way through it.

"Pray about it" is another way of saying "trust God." When our bodies are riddled with anxiety, when we are stressed about tomorrow or in the middle of a fight with a loved one, prayer is sometimes the last place our brain wants to go. We often don't think to stop, step back, and pray about it. Still, that is the solution. If we start exercising our "prayer muscle," it will work more easily for us over time. Prayer is a physical way of doing the spiritual thing of trusting God with our hearts.

Jesus promises you and me a Helper. John uses the word *paraclete*, which his audience would have interpreted as "advocate." The original is a compound word of "coming forth" and "alongside." The *paraclete* is one who comes forth to walk alongside you when you are in trouble. This *paraclete* that Jesus promises is not one who fixes everything around us; instead, the advocate comes alongside us and renews us from the inside, reminding us that we are not alone.

The Helper brings us inner peace and clarity and an awareness of the love that surrounds us. So pray about what you are facing. In the worst possible moments and days, pause to share everything that is going on, with brutal honesty, to your praying friends and to this Helper of whom Jesus speaks. Otherwise, you're won't get anywhere. You'll be stuck on a broken treadmill. Stopping to trust God with our struggles will break the cruel conveyor belt under our feet and set us free to run straight through whatever lies before us.

the perfectionist

"Come to me, all you who are weary, and I will give you rest."
—Matthew 11:28

I just want people to like me.

How many times has that been the motivation undergirding whatever I say or do? Isn't that the tune I hum while chiseling away at the sculpture of "me" that I prepare to present to the world each day? I just want people to like me.

Do you, like me, earnestly try to be a person who is above ridicule or criticism? To be a person without a single kink in the armor, someone who cannot be assailed, someone who is above reproach? I want to be a "super nice and fun guy," and I want to make God happy. Growing up, I said, "What if I mastered academics, athletics, music, work, and so much more?" My inner likability was chained tightly to getting everything exactly right. It is pretty tiring trying to balance all the dominos, trying to juggle all the flaming torches, trying to keep the circus going for God, for myself, for the world.

Brené Brown calls such perfectionism the "20-ton shield." We carry this armor to avoid being blamed, criticized, and hurt. But it is a heavy burden, and what happens is that we avoid being seen. No one (even ourselves!) gets to see who we truly are—the image of God underneath the makeup and behind the curated social media posts.

We trip and we tear into ourselves, and this lack of grace for ourselves translates into a lack of inner grace for others. We become critical, mean spirited, derogatory, judgmental. We create an environment where others, too, must avoid tripping, must avoid being seen. They show us their own shiny armor instead of what is underneath. Over centuries, perfectionists like me have painted God with dark and dramatic brushstrokes. We have created a demanding, perfectionistic god, a god made in our own likeness.

About all these things, Jesus says this: "Come to me, all you who are weary, and I will give you rest." It's like life is a commotion of angry, violent noise and someone appears and speaks in hushed, calming tones. Jesus is the voice of rest. Jesus demonstrates a God who is not demanding; who is not harsh; who is tender and compassionate and requires nothing from us except our empty hands. Jesus wants us to be OK with ourselves, to say, "I am enough," to know that our worthiness is not at stake, no matter how poorly we perform.

Jesus wants us to look at our failed test, our lost game, our bad mistakes, the embarrassing moments in our day, our dearth of attention on social media, and the rest of the mediocrity in our lives and hear, over and over again, a God who sings over us with an effervescent and unstoppable river of love. He wants us to trust this sure and refreshing current, to release the oars from our tired hands, to freely fall overboard, to drift down the cold stream on our worn-down backs. He asks us to say, "I can lay down my heavy shield and rest. The real me that God made is someone likable."

We can tell ourselves whatever story we want, but until we release our self-punishment and harsh self-treatment, until we rest in God's grace, we will, even unwittingly, treat others the same. We can only extend grace to others to the extent that we have received God's grace for ourselves. Life is hard enough right now for everyone. Allow God and others to truly see you. The real, imperfect, goofy you. Your vulnerability will create a space for others to let their guard down too so they can breathe in the fresh air for which we all earnestly strain. Grace is so much better than the heavy shields we carry.

alone in my room

"Why do you call me good? No one is good but God alone."
—Luke 18:19

I was often alone during my first two years of college. I can remember sitting next to empty chairs at cafeteria tables, shoveling down meals before anyone noticed my solitude; Friday nights with nothing to do; and an oblong cycle of finding myself, once again, alone in my dorm.

I know that many of us these days are finding ourselves alone in our rooms, a rising and falling sun outside our window, an existential dissatisfaction with paper-thin people on our screens. The structure of modern society has a Jupiter-like gravitational pull away from physical human beings. We try to connect with two-dimensional faces in small squares. We fail to be truly seen and heard. If we are new to a place, creating new friendships can feel almost impossible.

How do we make friends in this modern world?

There is a superpower available to us. I didn't know I possessed it when I was eighteen, but now I know that I do, and you do too. Look at Jesus: he carried with him a strong sense of purpose and value. He knew who he was, what he had to offer, and why it was important for him to go out and meet people and interact with them. Jesus had important things to say, and he cultivated a strong capacity for embracing hurting people, sitting with them in their pain. Through these connections, he brought healing, liberation, transformation. But Jesus—the Messiah, the Son of God, the Savior of the world—he too was highly conscious of weakness and limitation. He often asked for help, resisted praise from people, wept in pain, and even experienced doubt from his cross.

Jesus was able to hold together these polarities within himself. Jesus was both strong and weak at the same time. Jesus had something to offer and something to receive in each moment of human connection. This was his superpower for making his own way in the world, for transforming it forever, and it is a superpower you and I can discover within ourselves as well.

Remember you are strong and say that you are weak.

First, remember that you are strong. The God of the universe created you, knit you together in your mother's womb with excellence and wisdom and love, and that God has called you by name. God does not make junk, so you have things within you that are inherently likable and valuable. When you choose to "be yourself," the good things God made in you will shine for others to enjoy. So always keep your chin up, your shoulders back, your chest out, and your smile on. You are awesome.

Second, say that you are weak. It is OK to admit, "Hey, I don't want to eat lunch alone tomorrow. Would you join me outside somewhere to hang out while we eat?" It is OK to say, "I'm going to be bored today after practice. Do you want to . . . ?" and you fill in the blank. It is OK to tell peers in your hall, class, team, etc., "I need you." The other side of this is that sometimes you must, like Jesus, reach out and associate with the weirdest, most awkward people. There is a temptation to think that being around cool people lifts our own social capital and that the converse is true as well. But this mindset is corrosive and leaves each of us more fractured and isolated than before. So be indiscriminate about the people to whom you reach out and say, "Let's hang out." Over time, more cohesive friendships will form while others fall away.

Remember that you are strong, and say that you are weak. This is a big part of the path to forming new and stronger friendships.

solicitors

The apostles said to the Lord, "Increase our [trust]!" —Luke 17:5

The year 2009 was rock bottom of the Great Recession, and it was also my gap year between college and divinity school. It was impossible to find a job I could only commit to for nine months, and in my desperation I ended up delivering Yellow Pages. (Ask your parents what those are.) The job was aggravating and boring and paid less than minimum wage. But my shiniest memory from those days was delivering a book to a rancher with a long driveway on Pine Ridge Road.

Pulling in, I drove past at least three signs with warnings like "No Soliciting," "No Trespassing," and "Watch Out for Dog." I had gotten out of my car to put the book on the front porch when a red-faced man in his sixties bolted out. "What are you doing? Get off my property! Get out of here!" I apologized profusely as my butt flew toward the driver's seat, and I tore out of there, the sound of vicious dogs snarling behind me. In my memory, there are bullets whizzing by my head (but maybe I made that part up).

I ask you, what would you expect of this man's relationships? Is he joyful, compassionate, and patient with his spouse, children, neighbors, and coworkers but the complete opposite with strangers at his door? I'm not sure I believe that. It is hard to believe he is happy. The trajectory of our lives can shrink over time. We can close door after door, letting trust in our family and friends split open, fray, rot. We can hunker down and armor up and callous over and become angry at dudes handing out collections of phone numbers.

There is a better way. The New Testament uses the Greek word *pistis* 248 times. That's a lot of times. It is often translated "faith," but many professor types agree that it could also be understood as "trust." Trust is when you assume another person is reliable and their intentions are good.

We are "saved by grace through trust" (Eph 2:8); "We walk by trust, not by sight" (2 Cor 5:7); "Love always trusts" (1 Cor 13:7); "Your trust has made you well" (Mark 5:34).

Trust is the lifeblood of strong relationships with God, spouse, family, friends, and neighbors. Trust is the bridge we stand on to finally be vulnerable, to be seen, to be known, to experience true connection in all of life. Trust is what makes our neighborhood safer, our democracy stronger, our economy richer. Trust is how the world pulls itself together to tackle global problems.

Jesus and the apostle Paul never wagged their fingers at anyone and told them, "You should trust people more." That's because trust is not something we can simply add on to our breastplates and say "Here it is." Trust is earned in drops and lost in buckets. Trust is like a tiny seed; it slowly grows in frail conditions. It becomes a life-giving mustard tree.

We grow trust in life by being trustworthy for others and by opening ourselves up to see the good intentions and reliability that others demonstrate. Jesus cultivated a high trust culture by forming what we call the church. This was not a weekly program people attended with weepy music and inspiring PowerPoint presentations. Church was a spiritual family that gathered together, sharing, caring, and laughing together, praying with, worshiping with, and serving those in need alongside one another. Together, they trusted God and built trust in one another. This had an overflowing effect of helping them become more generous and trusting with their neighbors and community—to see the image of God more clearly, to see the goodness inherent in their neighbors. Church was about cultivating more trust in others and in God.

When I'm an old man, I want to be expansive—extending peace, warmth, and gratitude to my wife and kids and neighbors, to the poorest of the poor, to the kid bagging my groceries at the checkout, and even to the desperate solicitor at my door. I want to receive God's good things from institutions—marriage, organized religion, education, health care—things built over time by bearers of the image of God. Trust is the sacred path for those transactions. "Lord, increase my trust!" Amen and amen.

pouring ointment

> *[Mary] came up to him with an alabaster flask of very expensive ointment, and she poured it on his head as he reclined at table. And when the disciples saw it, they were indignant, saying, "Why this waste? For this could have been sold for a large sum and given to the poor." But Jesus, aware of this, said to them, "Why do you trouble the woman? For she has done a beautiful thing to me. For you always have the poor with you, but you will not always have me. In pouring this ointment on my body, she has done it to prepare me for burial. Truly, I say to you, wherever this gospel is proclaimed in the whole world, what she has done will also be told in memory of her."* —Matthew 26:7-13

Granddaddy was dying in his home and I had come to say goodbye. By that point, he was sleeping around the clock. I sat in the room alone with him and held his hand. The air was thick and heavy. It was weighed down with lots of sad and important feelings. I sat with him for a long time. I had many things to say, but this time felt too sacred. Mumbled and imperfect words would probably break the fragile things I felt hanging in the air. I didn't even know if he could hear or understand me. So I sat with him, connected to him one last time.

At the best funerals, loved ones share funny memories and the legacies left behind. But sadly, it is not uncommon for us to wait until the funeral to say the important things. To finally tell someone exactly what they did that was so wonderful, helpful, important in our lives.

The disciples were angry that Mary sacrificed to show extraordinary love to her friend and teacher Jesus. They felt that her precious resources should be reserved for more pressing and wider work. The disciples did not understand. They thought they should anoint dead bodies, not living ones. They were a lot like us, two thousand years later. We buy lots of flowers and offer many kind words for the dead. Less so for the living.

In the words of Ronald Rolheiser, "The church is the place we go to help anoint each other for our impending deaths."[10] That is just it. This scene is what real church looks like—Mary, holding nothing back in anointing her friend and teacher with love during his life.

---

10. I credit Ronald Rolheiser for this reflection. Please read his excellent book *The Holy Longing: The Search for a Christian Spirituality* (New York: Image, 2014) for more gems like this quote (from pg. 131 of *Holy Longing*)

When I lived in Europe, I took every chance I had to visit historic cathedrals, some of them 500 years old. They were beautiful, ancient, incredible. But sometimes they were decorated with paintings or statues of skeletons and dead people. To me, this seemed ridiculous and creepy. But these Christians of long ago were less delusional than we are. Death comes quick, soon, and sometimes by surprise. It is not so far away. Anoint one another with love today.

Church is a spiritual collective, a family, and a kingdom. But here, things should be upside down. Here, we should anoint one another before funerals. We should say the good things, the important things, to one another today. We should buy the flowers today. Church looks like Mary pouring ointment. Church looks like encouraging, complimenting, lifting up, praying for, and giving thanks to one another every day, throughout the day. Every day we should shower people with love and affection and gratitude. We should tell people exactly what makes them so important and essential to us. Like Mary, we should do it with extravagance. We should overdo it. We should help anoint each other for our impending deaths.

Deathbeds and funerals are a time for weeping, laughing, and remembering. They are not a time to play catch up. Today, may you be like Mary. May you break the banks of time, energy, and money to show those around you just how important they are. For the Bible says that this kind of act, this kind of story, is so incredibly and indelibly important that it should be told every single time the gospel is told. May it be told in your story as well.

the performer

"The good person out of the good treasure of the heart produces good, and the troubled person out of the troubled treasure produces trouble; for it is out of the abundance of the heart that the mouth speaks."
—Luke 6:45

Growing up, I wanted to be a star, and not just at one thing—at most things. Music, sports, school, and eventually religion too. I wanted to stand in the middle of the circus ring with crowds all around, admiring and appreciating me. I needed to make no mistakes, fight my way to center stage, and dazzle the crowds. I found my strengths and built on them. I found my weaknesses and tried to fix them.

Performers like me excel, and that is a good thing. But in our race to center stage, we focus on external achievements while the things of our hearts get left behind. We don't pay attention to our hearts. We become popular and likable, but we struggle to be friends and to receive intimate friendship. We behave well for the church, but we struggle to connect authentically with the Spirit. Along the way of growing up, our hearts collect trouble: stress, insecurity, and lousy ways of coping with each little moment of pain and anxiety. Our hearts are troubled, but we have no idea because we don't pay attention to them. We don't pay attention because hearts don't perform in circuses, and things that don't perform in circuses seem irrelevant.

In a way, we are only following the inherited wisdom of our world. "Toughen up." "I'll give you something to cry about." "I don't care what you want." "People are too easily offended." These are the messages we hear that prey on our fears of looking within. Girls cannot be angry. Boys cannot be hurt. Emotions are weakness and affection is cheesy. And it goes on and on.

This is all radically opposed to the teachings of Jesus, who speaks clearly and directly on the subject and to the circus. If there is trouble in your heart, you are going to produce trouble in the world. Hurt people *hurt people*. When you don't heal your wounds, you bleed on people who didn't cut you. If you don't tend to your heart, "trouble" (also translated "bad" or "evil") will be the thing you produce, and you likely won't even see the pain and destruction you cause. Thus, the heart can't be an afterthought or something we tend to when we find the time. It must absolutely be our first priority, every single day of our lives.

How do we reverse course and fill our hearts with good things? How do we pull out the trouble inside and replace it with good? the heart (Greek *kardia*) is the seat of emotions and desires. Jesus says to remove the plank from your eye and focus inward (Luke 6:42). This journey begins with spiritual and emotional practices. Performers must do a 180-degree turn and finally prioritize practices of centering prayer and meditation, taught by a spiritual shepherd. Perhaps they should consider talk therapy from a licensed counselor. This inward journey is complicated, perilous, and long, and it is impossible to do it alone and without good guides. A worshiping community is important as well. In weekly worship, we tend to the heart and fill it up with good and sacred things. Our community of believers and all those who love us will lift us up, love us, and pour in goodness.

This journey will be expensive. Our circus may no longer be as entertaining. We will have to sacrifice many of our great performances to show up for the inward journey, the good treasure of the heart. Our world ignores the heart and applauds the circus: its intelligence, beauty, money, and success. Jesus does not. The heart is the doorway to connecting with God and others in authentic love. Its journey is the ultimate question of your life, and your circus, no matter how dazzling, is ultimately worth little more than peanuts in red-striped bags. Jesus invites us to pay the high price, to walk away from the performance, to write a much nobler story with our lives.

debts

> *Happy are those who find wisdom,*
> *and those who get understanding,*
> *for her income is better than silver,*
> *and her revenue better than gold.*
> *Her ways are ways of pleasantness,*
> *and all her paths are peace.*
> *She is a tree of life to those who lay hold of her;*
> *those who hold her fast are called happy.* —Proverbs 3:13-18

This morning my car battery died again, but that's the least of my automobile issues. My seventeen-year-old Honda doesn't have functioning air conditioning, stereo, or cruise control. The bumper (and I'm not joking) is zip-tied to the vehicle, and chipped paint and rust are sneaking around the car. But at my kitchen counter this week, in view of my thirty-fourth birthday, I wrote a big check to finish paying my student loans. Every month for twelve years, I have paid a bill for my education. Now it is finally done.

Today, at my computer, I can pull up talking heads on the news or social media, criticizing the value of college. College grads are unemployed, they say. Their salaries are often comparable to those of high school graduates, they say. Professors are blasted as liberal and irrelevant, and all while the price tag of tuition swells. So maybe I was wrong. Maybe all this time, I should have been paying off a loan on a cool car instead. To think—all this time I could have been driving a new truck with big tires and a comfortable interior.

But wisdom's income is better than silver and her revenue is better than gold.

Wisdom is not knowledge. It is not knowing lots of facts. Wisdom is not job training—a manual on how to do certain tasks so one can earn a salary. Wisdom is about having good judgment, creative thinking, good character, and the knowledge of what to do in complex crises. Wisdom is not shallow. It is deep, and it comes from years of being pulled along by teachers and mentors and coaches and books into wider territory, compelled to expand and explore, to do the scary thing of challenging previously held assumptions. It comes from years of experience, years of working, and years of struggle.

In school, I was forced to think about things I would have rather not thought about, forced to ask questions about things I was content to let sit in narrow assumptions. In seminary, I did not learn lots of "Bible facts" or how to successfully get kids to sign up for church camp. My teachers gave me job training, yes, but mostly they gave me wisdom. I was not taught what to think; I was taught how to think with depth and empathy and foresight.

Within my chest there is an expansive treasury of art, history, classical music, literature, and, above all, religion—good gifts my education gave me. No one will ever be able to take these things away from me. You can repossess my car or flood my house or steal my laptop. I will still be happy, because inside me are these precious gifts of wisdom, given to me by many faithful teachers and books along the way. Studies consistently show that expensive college degrees still pay off. That you will easily get back the money you borrowed over the course of your life because your income will be larger and more stable, and you will probably have more enjoyable jobs. But even if this were not so, it is worth it; I would keep paying that bill if I needed to. The Honda suits me just fine, because whatever path I drive, it will be for me a path of peace. This tree of life named wisdom is now something inside me, and life cannot easily cut it down. May it be so for you. May you embrace an education and discover for yourself wisdom, and may you be called happy.

scary things

When you lie down, you will not be afraid; yes, you will lie down and your sleep will be sweet. Do not be afraid of sudden fear, nor of trouble when it comes. —Proverbs 3:24-25

"Why are you afraid?" —Mark 4:40

For our anniversary one year, Ronella and I got a babysitter for our daughter and drove to an amusement park. It had been a long time since I had ridden roller coasters, so we decided we would work our way up, starting with the little rides up to the biggest one. "The Intimidator" would be the grand finale, a ride that started with a 300-foot drop. All day, I enjoyed the rides. But I would glance sideways and see that 300-foot drop and my stomach would turn knots. I was anxious. We finally got in line, and I felt short of breath. I knew it was perfectly safe—I wasn't going to get hurt. I just didn't know if I could handle the fear.

The Bible instructs us 365 times, "Do not be afraid." Every time I turn around, I hear someone else saying, "Faith over fear." And our former President Franklin Roosevelt famously said, "The only thing we have to fear is fear itself." The world can be scary, and there is no shortage of reminders to "not be afraid."

But think about this Jewish proverb: "Do not be afraid of sudden fear." Unlike FDR's saying, this ancient piece of wisdom says that we should not be afraid of fear itself. The proverb seems to assume that fear is a normal part of living life. The Bible was written in a time when people were immensely lucky to survive infancy and childhood. Women often died giving birth, men often died after simple cuts became infected, and even a simple cold could spell doom. Death was imminent at all times. The biblical proverb gives no "if" concerning trouble; it says "when trouble comes." So fear is important. When men and women feel afraid, they pay attention and find safety.

Our culture has a pathological relationship with fear, but the Bible does not. Two hundred times, the Bible instructs us to "fear God/the Lord." God represents the holy, the mysterious, the wild and dangerous thing that is always and ultimately just a little bit beyond us. Surely, there is some rightful fear involved here.

Fear should not control us ("do not be afraid"), but fear is also something important and sacred. It protects us from dangerous things and dangerous people. We cannot think of courage as an absence of fear; rather, courage is the willingness to work through and with our fear when it is necessary and right.

So listen to this wise teacher in Proverbs. When a certain individual is lurking around and you feel afraid, when you notice your seatbelt isn't on, when you see someone drink and get behind the wheel of a car, pay attention to your fear and hear the wisdom God might be offering you in it. Because maybe God is trying to protect someone's life.

Our culture keeps printing the words "faith over fear." But I wish they would say, "faith even in fear." I wish they would tell the story of Jesus walking on water in the storm, coming to his frightened disciples, and, instead of chiding their fear, asking them, "Why are you afraid?" The Bible does not condemn fear but asks us to listen to it with wisdom. We should fear touching hot stoves and recklessly driving a car. We should fear passing along a deadly virus to vulnerable people, we should fear men and women who do not respect our boundaries, and we should even fear coming in close contact with the wild furnace of Creator God. Those who are comfortable paying attention to their fear are the people whose sleep is secure and sweet.

Ronella and I crested the initial hill of the Intimidator and swooped down from the sky to the Earth. We were scared the whole time! But what fun we had. We got off, I looked at her, and I said, "Let's do it again." At the end of the day, we got in our car, worn out. We buckled our seatbelts and carefully drove home to our beloved daughter. That night we lay down, and our sleep was safe and sweet.

In the coming days, may God's gift of fear guide you to stay safe and protect others, and may God's gift of courage help you do the scary things you must do to love and serve others with your whole heart. Fear can be our friend. Let us not be afraid of it.

vulnerable Jesus

Taking the five loaves and the two fish and looking up to heaven, he gave thanks and broke the loaves. Then he gave them to the disciples, and the disciples gave them to the people. —Matthew 14:19

A natural-born introvert, I would rather fly solo and keep my mouth shut. One of my biggest spiritual struggles and journeys in life has been opening up the rusty lid to share what is going on inside my heart and my head. It's hard for me to trust others with the precious things I feel and think on the inside, and I would rather swallow the poison or gold than risk what someone might do with it in my open palm. I wonder, do you struggle to trust others as well?

We Christians have always believed that Jesus was God, and that is a weird thing to believe. God is supposed to be all powerful, all knowing, and beyond the reach of suffering. And yet Jesus wasn't any of those things. He didn't know what the future held. He sometimes struggled to heal people. He bled and died on a common cross. If Jesus was God, why would he need other people's help? Why would he lean on his disciples to distribute bread to the crowds or find him a donkey? Why would he beg them to pray alongside him before his arrest, torture, and death? Why didn't he fly solo, baptize himself, snap his fingers and heal Lazarus, wear body armor, or come down off of his cross? Heck, why didn't Jesus stay up there in air-conditioned heaven eating grapes?

Jesus chose to throw himself into a life of vulnerability and trust. He put himself out there. He trusted Peter to walk on water in the storm. He trusted his disciples to share the good news of his coming. He trusted John to baptize him and Mary to anoint him and Peter to be a son to his mother after he died. Jesus chose a life of vulnerability and trust.

"So God created humankind in his own image; in the image of God he created them" (Gen 1:27). That's what Jesus's Bible said on the very first page, and Jesus chose to trust that word: that God's goodness was sliding between dormant and vibrant in the disciples, in the crowds, in his enemies, and in us. Try to find a verse where Jesus sounds cynical. Jesus lived a life of vulnerability and trust. People were good, and he could take the risk to share his life with them.

Our trust in one another is at an all-time low. Surveys show that more than ever before, we distrust our government, our police, our professors, our journalists, our doctors, our neighbors, and even the people making our hamburgers in the drive thru. More than ever before, theories about conspiring powers overthrowing elections and spreading diseases, pedophiles in pizza parlors, and so on are blossoming. It's all a symptom of trust breaking down within and between us all. It's all a symptom of our deep fear of being as vulnerable as Jesus was. Jesus chose to live a life of vulnerability and trust in others.

One of those he trusted most, Judas, betrayed him, and Jesus died as a result. Sometimes our trust gets us crucified. We see that part all too easily. We understand that if we never trust anyone, we will never get pinned to anyone's cross. But it takes faith to believe that "those who lose their life will find it" (Matt 16:26). It takes faith to believe that the cross paves the way to salvation for ourselves and others. It takes faith to believe that on the other side of our cross, God offers resurrection.

And did you know that another word for "faith" is "trust"?

rest

> *"Come to me, all who are weary, and I will give you rest."*—Matthew 11:28

I remember one time during final exams, I did not sleep for over fifty hours. I just had way too much studying, writing, and working to do to find space for sleep. I have often felt this way as a father of two children, as a man working two different ministries, as an owner of a ninety-year-old, constantly crumbling house, and as one who finds the world too fun, too interesting, to ever stop playing and entertaining. No time for rest!

The first page of the Bible talks about how on the seventh day, God "stopped," or rested, on what would be called the day of the Sabbath. And if you pay attention, the rest of the Bible doesn't stop coming back to this idea. The Bible says many things but eventually comes back to Sabbath rest. There is a constant thread of God pulling all of history slowly toward an ultimate age of jubilee, of Sabbath, of rest. No more war, stress, or sleepless nights. Rest for our bodies and for our inner selves.

Rest is the thing that Jesus embodied in his life and is trying to give us in ours. Our lack of trust in God and in Jesus's teachings leaves us strung thin and burnt out. Do you want a litmus test for your spiritual walk? Here it is: We know we are authentically near to Jesus when we are free to make space for rest.

The God Jesus shows us is a God of grace, compassion, freedom, and a love that is expansive, warm, gentle, and unconditional. Daily trusting in that kind of God (rather than a demanding, threatening, harsh God) organically produces a more rested body and heart, a mind that is free to prioritize sleep, deep and relaxed breathing, centering prayer, and some playtime. When we remember that we are not in control of the universe, that we are small and the One Who is Big is gracious like this, we say to ourselves, "In the rhythms of today and this week, I can make space for Sabbath rest within and around myself."

To operate from a place of rest is to operate from a place of true, inner peace. We become buoyant, a life preserver for those around us struggling in the waves. We dress nicer, hold our chins higher, smile more, and are more empathetic and interested in those around us. In short, we embody the heart of God for our world and shine a bright light. Those around us feel more rested in our presence.

I keep coming across thesis studies that verify the ancient, biblical wisdom that getting enough sleep, deep breathing, healthy food, centering prayer, and quality playtime with loved ones is more helpful for our work than aggressive, overextended work hours. This week, may you come to Jesus. May you find and create spaces of rest for yourself, and may you be a warm light of rest for your world.

pale blue dot

What is your life? For you are a mist that appears for a little while and then vanishes. —James 4:14

Yesterday, I told my two-year-old son, "It's time to go to bed," and devastation ensued. It was like watching a dagger enter his side. His eyes clamped shut, his mouth gaped open in pain, and he began to cry in agony. He has done this every single day of his life—go to bed, wake up the next morning, do it all again. He will do it every single day for the rest of his life. But for him, that moment was everything. It was momentous and earth shattering. Playtime was over, and what a painful and surely irrevocable loss this was.

We all did this at age two, but most of us do it at twenty-two and some of us even do it at seventy-two. We are so convinced that this particular moment, this particular crisis, this particular decision is everything. This current disaster, breakup, failure, financial loss is the end. This is also often a power play. "This is the most important election in US history!" Or "Our opponents are not mediocre bad or good people with a few bad ideas; they are basically the spawn of Satan, intent on destroying everything you hold dear! They will end it all!" Now we are listening, aren't we?

"What is your life?" James asks. He invites us into a radical reframing of all these things. To say that our life is a mist that appears for a little while and then vanishes is true. Our life is a short blip in the span of trillions of years, and the three feet of carpet around our feet is but a fluff among the bustle of 7 billion other souls and the infinite horizon of outer space. Scripture is not simply minimizing our suffering. It's something quite different. The Bible is reframing our entire life—and our whole world. All of its highs and lows and mundane moments in between. It is all a mist. A beautiful autumn afternoon, a ripe peach, my cute toddler, a delicious meal, hugging my parents, or the "right" person being in the White House—all of these are like November wind between our fingers.

Seen from deep in outer space, our entire planet, with all 7 billion people and all their possessions, dramas, heartbreaks, and triumphs, is but a pale blue dot hanging inconsequentially in the universe. So it is with me. If I am blessed, my children will love me, and so will their children. But I will be lucky if my great-grandchildren will even know my first name. After that, I will certainly be forgotten forever. This is OK, the Bible says. All of our faults and fears and victories and accolades are just a mist. We are liberated by this truth to appreciate the present, fleeting moment and always do the right thing. Kingdoms will rise and fall. People will have fifteen minutes of fame. Setbacks and good days will find us. So may we all find deep, inner peace in our smallness and in the bigness and faithfulness of our great God, who holds the whole world with an eternal and compassionate hand.

November

thrones

*"He has brought down rulers from their thrones
but has lifted up the humble.
He has filled the hungry with good things
but has sent the rich away empty."* —Luke 1:52-53

"Might is right." For thousands of years, the world turned through force. The men with the biggest muscles and the lowest morals, or the men with the most money, or the kingdom with the most powerful army ruled over others. They always got their way, because if they didn't they just killed you. When the world is ruled by the strongest, wealthiest, most violent men, lots of people suffer.

If you read the story of Jesus, he had a radically different vision for humankind. He said, "Blessed are the poor, for the kingdom of God belongs to them" (Matt 5:3). That was a ridiculous thing to say. Since when do poor people get to be in charge?

In the great human experiment, nothing has come as close to Jesus's vision for humankind as democracy. A true democracy is where every man and woman, regardless of skin color, sex, status, or wealth, gets the same single vote as they elect their leaders to govern with justice and excellence. "Rulers" are brought down from their thrones as the humble are empowered to shape the world. The rich are sent away empty, unable to control the show, while the hungry influence elections to once again give them a shot at bread. Guns and armor and power are silenced by the power of truth and justice.

Our American democracy is far from perfect. But if you do not vote, if you do not actively participate in this democracy, this foretaste of God's kingdom of which Jesus and his mother spoke, then I would argue that you are rejecting part of Jesus's vision for our world. You are rejecting some good news of hope.

College students are poor, humble, and always hungry. If you're a college student, elections are your chance to bring rulers down from their thrones, send the rich away empty, and be blessed. Every election is an opportunity to shape your future instead of letting others shape your future for themselves. Do you believe in Jesus's vision for the world? Will you get informed and go out and vote?

stillness: part 1 of centering prayer

"But whenever you pray, go into your room and shut the door and pray to your Father who is in secret." —Matthew 6:6

Commune with your own heart upon your bed, and be still. Selah
—Psalm 4:4

I was sitting at the computer, but I couldn't maintain attention on the screen's blank page to write the paper. My brain was hopping all over the place. I wanted to focus on anything other than the blankness before me. We are all tethered to smartphones, constantly waiting for our next notification, flashing screens illuminating in every corner of our vision, Wi-Fi, 5G, and Bluetooth quite literally surging through our bones at every given moment. How can any of us focus on anything, much less find the inner voice within, the Holy Spirit, who tries to whisper guidance and direction to us?

Even before all these things—before the ubiquitous artificial noise and entertainment—men and women struggled to find the inner silence necessary for authentic spiritual connection. So Jesus taught a specific form of prayer. He said that sometimes you have to close yourself in and shut everything out. Since at least the fourth century, Christians in the East have followed this teaching by seeking union with God so deep that it goes beyond all images, concepts, and language. A prayer of stillness, of melding the head into the heart, of silencing the mind opens one up to union with God and clear thinking and listening. Saint Gregory wrote in the fourteenth century,

> It is not out of place to teach [seekers] to bring their intellect within themselves by means of their breathing . . . to recommend them to pay

attention to the exhalation and inhalation of their breath, so that while they are watching it the intellect, too, may be held in check.[11]

In my daily practice, I set a five-minute timer. This removes from my mind the voice nagging me about "losing" time. Then I get comfortable and close my eyes, and I focus on my breathing—the breath leaving me, the breath returning to me, the breath channeling down my body. Others might focus on just one word, such as "Jesus," "peace," or "compassion." But I just think about my breathing. And if something else floats into my head, I label it "thinking," and I let that thought float away as I return to my breath. I don't get mad at myself about it. I just gently let it go. Inevitably, my brain keeps going back to thinking about my last meal or a funny joke or wondering why men have nipples . . . or whatever. Again, I just label it "thinking," gently let it float away, and return to the breath. Over and over again, I still my mind. Doors keep opening and I keep gently closing them.

Beginning my daily prayer time with this five-minute practice, often called "stillness" or "breath meditation," helps connect me to God's Spirit and voice within. It is truly the only thing that silences the inner clamor, that closes the doors of intrusive thoughts. It calms my anxieties and makes me a gentler and more peaceful person, striving to live in the way of Jesus. I think it even makes me focus better on those blank screens. This daily prayer of stillness molds me into something better.

lamentation: part 2 of centering prayer

"My God, my God, why have you forsaken me?" —Matthew 27:46

I hate them with perfect hatred; I count them my enemies. Search me, O God, and know my heart; Try me, and know my anxieties. —Psalm 139:22-23

As a boy, to say out loud that I was afraid of something or that my feelings were hurt was tantamount to absolute, permanent, unfixable social suicide. What about anger? Anger was complicated. I saw it modeled in the men in my life and on the screen, in raised voices and in violence. W was I supposed to do with my anger? I wasn't allowed to yell. I wasn't allowed to

---

11. *St Gregory Palamas: In Defense of Those who Devoutly Practice a Life of Stillness*, orthodoxchurchfathers.com/fathers/philokalia/st-gregory-palamas-in-defense-of-those-who-devoutly-practice-a-life-of-stillness.html

be violent. Was I allowed to feel anything? "Feel happy and grateful," my church and my world told me.

What we find in the prayer book of Psalms and modeled in the life of Jesus is a safe harbor from these traps we have set for our boys and girls and men and women. Jesus and his prayer book show us a radically different path and practice to give space for the full range of emotions that God has given us. Early faith wasn't as cleaned up and mopped over as a lot of modern Christianity. The psalms are full of raw energy and passion. The psalmists use words like "hatred" and "the pit" and pray for the deaths of their enemies. Modern interpreters shudder and shrink back. But think about these prayers as a holding space for getting out their feelings. They trusted God with their deepest, darkest feelings and thoughts. Instead of leaving their shadow selves in a cobwebbed corner, far from the warm light of God's tender and compassionate love, instead of isolating that terrible and painful place within them, they connected to God through it. They brought the scariest and worst parts of themselves with full trust in our intimate, compassionate God.

I should also mention our struggle to sit in joy. We might think that if we enjoy happiness, the universe will surely tilt and take it away. Or that maybe we aren't important if we aren't working ourselves into the dirt. Or that joy is something we don't deserve because we aren't worthy of it. But this time of lamentation is also a time to say, "God, I am full of joy and my heart is glad today"—to claim this and own it and savor it.

In my prayer practice, after five minutes of "stillness," I am more aware of what's truly going on within me. I've been looking inward instead of outward. So now is a moment to search my heart and lay it all out on the table with God. I whisper all my prayers to focus my words. "God, today I'm feeling angry with him. I'm anxious about this. I'm bitter towards her." I also say things like, "I'm feeling joy because of my kids. I'm excited about what's coming tomorrow." I call all of this lamentation—the "wailing of the heart."

We can connect with God in a vulnerable act of trust, with our brightest and our darkest and most painful places. The alternative is for all these things to come out sideways and to hurt ourselves or others. Whatever is buzzing on the inside has to go somewhere. May you lay it all out on the table in lamentation, every day. In the way of Jesus, may you bring your whole self to the graceful God whom you can always trust.

confession: part 3 of centering prayer

> *"The Pharisee stood by himself and prayed: 'God, I thank you that I am not like other people—robbers, evildoers, adulterers—or even like this tax collector. I fast twice a week and give a tenth of all I get.' But the tax collector stood at a distance. He would not even look up to heaven, but beat his breast and said, 'God, have mercy on me, a sinner.' I tell you that this man, rather than the other, went home justified before God."* —Luke 18:11-14

It was like whirlpools of furious water were spinning in my head, and the words I needed to say were digging their claws into my throat, desperate to hang on and not come out. "I'm sorry I said what I said. I was wrong. I shouldn't have done that." Once those little monsters were released from my mouth for the first time, a baby inside of me took its first step. I focused a little less on what she did wrong and more on what I did. From then on, each time I practiced apologizing to my wife, my toddler legs got stronger.

All of us have a denial muscle and a confession muscle, located somewhere between our lowest rib and our skull. And we have to choose which muscle we're going to make strong. Jesus told a parable about a man who had a strong denial muscle and a man with a strong confession muscle. The first one, the Pharisee, threw his whole weight into setting himself apart. He said, "I am not like other people." That's a story we all tell ourselves. But this is the denial muscle at work. We are all the same underneath, separated by just a few degrees of circumstance.

Repeat these words in your head: "I am always responsible for my words, my thoughts, and my actions." Even when someone mistreats you, you're responsible for how you react. And if you do wrong, you are responsible to apologize, even if the other person won't. Do you, like the tax collector, exercise this confession muscle? Do you daily practice taking responsibility for your words, thoughts, and actions (or inactions)? The best way to create strong confession muscles is to practice confession in prayer every single day of your life.

In prayer, I stop blaming others for my circumstances, and I think about my sin. After a moment of lamentation and exploring the anxieties of my heart, I am more in tune with my moments of conflict, uncertainty, and pain. These are the times when we are most likely to react destructively and hurt others. So now I take a minute in prayer for confession. I remember my reactions. I remember the things I have said or left unsaid, done or left undone. Now is the time to confess to God and take responsibility for my wrongdoing. "Loving God, I lashed out at Mom because I felt criticized. I receive your mercy. It's hard, but I'll call her and make it right."

The purpose of confession in prayer is not to feel ashamed, like a filthy rag in light of a burning hot, angry God. The purpose of confession is to become more connected to God and others and to finally begin taking responsibility for our lives. Prayer is the perfect weight room to work on that muscle because we can trust that God is safe, compassionate, and merciful. God won't shame us or run off and betray us if we confess. Our confession muscles become strong and we can apologize to our loved ones and others. We can empathize with others because we see our own moral brokenness within. Pharisees are set apart and isolated in life. They feel strong, but underneath they are lonely and anxious. In confession, we are broken open. Love and trust flood in. We are drawn closer to God and to others.

gratitude: part 4 of centering prayer

[Jesus] took bread and gave thanks. —Luke 24:30

The LORD has done great things for us, and we are filled with joy. —Psalm 126:3

This cool-looking dude piled into his Subaru with his beautiful wife and kids, and they trekked across Utah, taking in amazing National Parks, camping out, the whole family smiling and laughing as they eagerly explored a world that was theirs for the taking. Mesmerized for the entire thirty-second commercial, I found an empty hole growing inside me. I realized how happy I would be if I owned a new Subaru and if I had the chance to cart my beautiful wife and kids around Utah—only to realize that, sigh, I couldn't afford a brand-new Subaru or even a family trip out West. So I was sad.

Consciously or unconsciously, American religion preaches that happiness comes to us after we have provided happiness a comfortable fortress—built with lots of money and good-looking people. But the real truth is this: not just happiness but also joy come up from within us. They spring up inside us when we actively practice daily gratitude wherever we are and whatever our circumstances may be. If we want joy, we need to think about gratitude instead.

I recently read an article where a researcher talked about interviewing thousands of people and finding that, in every single case, when someone said that their life was joy-filled, they also shared that they had some sort of regular practice of gratitude. There was not a single exception. If someone had joy in their life, they had an intentional, regular practice of gratitude. It is not experiencing joy that makes us feel grateful. It is practicing gratitude that makes us feel joy.

Do you want to live a happy, joyous life? Practice daily prayers of gratitude. This is very different from saying, "Every time something bad happens, just be grateful it isn't worse." Instead, this is about a daily practice of centering prayer.

After prayers of stillness, lamentation, and confession, I am ready to say thank you. Since I have just confessed the pain and sin within my own life, I begin with this prayer: "Thank you, God, for loving me. Thank you, God, for loving me. Thank you, God, for loving me." The best kind of gratitude is the kind that can hold the bad with the good and still give thanks. I may thank God for other angles of God's character: "Thank you, God, for your nearness. Thank you, God, for your Son, Jesus." But I find it important to give thanks for specific good things in my life and, more important, for specific people and specific things they have done or been. "Thank you for the rain today. Thank you for my friend who brightened my day."

Studies show that daily practicing gratitude has a significant impact on how happy and joyous we feel, whether we are highly functioning or clinically depressed, and regardless of how much money we have. Daily practicing gratitude has even been shown to boost one's immune system, improve sleep, and decrease the risk of disease. It is the easiest and cheapest way to elevate our entire lives and the world around us.

A daily practice of gratitude prayer will likely have a profound transformative effect on our brains. We will start telling others "thank you" more. We will become people contagiously overflowing with effervescent gratitude, making those around us feel truly appreciated, seen, and loved. Daily pausing for prayers of gratitude transforms us into people who give thanks to God without ceasing throughout the day. We will pray prayers of gratitude in the car and in the classroom, and we will stop to say grace before our meals. This ceaseless gratitude will make us more present and mindful to each fleeting moment of our lives and will inflate our hearts with joy. What better witness to the power of our faith in Jesus could there be?

trust: part 5 of centering prayer

"I'm praying for them. I'm not praying for the world but for those you gave me, because they are yours." —John 17:9

How would you feel and what would you do if you knew a close friend was about to drag you off to be tortured to death? That's a dramatic example and maybe not something you'll experience this afternoon. But how would you feel and what would you do if you were waiting for a doctor to call and talk with you about a mass they had found in your mother's body? How would you feel and what would you do if you were waiting for a boss to come and talk to you about a disappointing thing you did? How would you feel and what would you do if you felt alone, unloved, and disconnected, like no one was by your side?

Read the end of the Gospel of John. There's a long stretch of Jesus talking and praying between his last supper and a close friend hauling him off to be tortured to death. As you read the story, you hear Jesus saying these great and inspiring things, and you know that meanwhile, a terrible fate prowls in the back of his mind. How does he keep standing and giving in the shadow of his forthcoming cross?

In the hours preceding his arrest, torture, and death, Jesus centered himself through prayers of trust in the garden. Observe his composure on the cross, his faith and care for others, all the way to the bitter end. How did he do that? He settled down and quieted himself, and he prayed prayers of trust for the people in his life. Look at his language; he recognizes that these people belong to both him and to God at the same time. Both a gift and a "trust," owned rightly by God.

To pray for the people in your life is to trust them unto God. It is to say, "God, I hope that in your power you can do this or that for them. But I trust you with them, no matter what happens, because they are yours and you are good."

In my daily centering prayers, I pray prayers of stillness, lamentation, confession, and gratitude, and then I am ready for prayers of trust. I pray for my children, my wife, and the people whom I shepherd. I pray for special cases of illness, injury, and tragedy. As an example, I might pray, "God, thank you for my daughter. Keep her safe and healthy. Draw her toward your light and rest. And help me be the best daddy I can possibly be for her." I suppose that last sentence is the most important one.

In our anxiety and pain, we sometimes forget about others. We become self-absorbed. And in that inflated space, we scramble God's wiring within ourselves, lose balance, topple, and lash out instead of maintaining God's peace within. But Jesus shows us that on our most anxious days (on every day), we will find our ground and our center by remembering the vulnerability and the suffering and the hopes of those whom God has given us and who also belong to God. Will you be like Jesus and daily pause to trust your loved ones unto God? Will you center yourself in daily prayers of trust?

surrender: part 6 of centering prayer

"Yet not my will, but yours be done." —Luke 22:42

"Thy kingdom come, thy will be done, on earth as it is in heaven."
—Matthew 6:10

It was an early spring day. I was eighteen years old, and I was driving my bright blue Ford Ranger past a soggy cow pasture near my home in Dandridge, Tennessee. Spiritual and religious experiences from preceding weeks weighed heavily upon me, and the air in the cab of my truck became thick—a weight upon my chest. I finally said "yes" to the call to ministry I had long heard but rationalized away. I remember weeping with a sense of release. A dam had broken. Every moment since then has strengthened my sense of call to ministry. It has not ever diminished.

Many people will go through life having never experienced a moment of surrender to the Almighty, to the Divine, the Mystery of the Universe, the Great Creator, the God Who Is Love. They will never have a moment of recognizing that they are not the center of the universe; Someone Else is.

An un-surrendered life is a bit like a solar system with no sun at its center. Eventually, everything spins out into oblivion, losing its center, its balance, its rhythm and order. I have an enormous amount of respect for my atheist friends, for their strong sense of morality and integrity and intellectual rigor. But Jesus demonstrated a fundamentally different life. A life that chose to believe. A life that said, "Do not call me good. Because no one is good but God." A life that was even willing to receive the cross if that is what God called for.

But we should not wait for gilded moments at church camp, feverish religious services, brilliant sunsets, or exhilarating mountaintops. Surrender is a daily spiritual practice in the midst of dirty dishes, interactions with family, and paying our bills. It may not always be quite as emotional as the special transfiguration scenes, but it is the way of Jesus. It is an act of daily centering prayer.

After praying in stillness, lamentation, confession, gratitude, and trust, I am ready to close my time of centering prayer. Maybe this part is the most important. I surrender everything and all I am to God. I might pray something like, "God, I give my whole life to you and to the doing of your will. I put myself in second place." Many poets and songwriters have found ways to say this much better than I ever could.

I think a life void of daily surrender to God is a little bit less happy, a little lonelier, a little more upside down. It's not the way it's supposed to be. It's like trying to dance with two left feet. Today and every day, may you surrender your whole life—every breath you breathe, every dollar in your hand, every possession you possess, every second of your fleeting life. Surrender all of it to our very good and faithful God, to whom Jesus did the same. In this kind of dying, we find a new and resurrected life.

save thanksgiving

Above all, love each other deeply, because love covers over a multitude of sins. —1 Peter 4:8

Many of us are eager to drive home this Thanksgiving and finally be back with the family we have missed. You may have little kids to love on or siblings to catch up with or great traditions to enjoy. Oh, and the food—all the wonderful food!

On the other hand, some may be returning to more complicated homes.

Your time away has shown you just how messed up things were at home. You'll have to endure someone's opinions on things, or bear the pain of a disinterested parent, or come home to a family that will be celebrating their first Thanksgiving without a loved one who passed away.

Perhaps you can't even go home at all. They say that "Jesus saves." I wonder, does Jesus save us from hard Thanksgivings?

One of Jesus's closest students, Peter, said this: "Above all, love each other deeply, because love covers over a multitude of sins." As we head home for Thanksgiving, so many things may wait to assail us. The temptation might be to descend into the chaos, to fight back, to shame back, to prove yourself right, to teach someone a lesson, to ignore your pain or the pain of the other, to enter the argument and not let them get away with saying that."

But this Thanksgiving, you will not be able to tie down all the craziness or wipe away the pain of the whole family. You will not undo any bad things that happened this year. Even so, you always have a choice to rise above it and choose to love your family deeply and enjoy the time you have with them.

Maybe that means remaining silent on certain things or apologizing about certain things or refusing to argue about certain things. Maybe it means finally speaking up and asserting your actual feelings with love. Maybe loving deeply means focusing on all the things for which you can be grateful this year. Maybe love means thanking God for the positives, even in light of a lot of negatives. Try to hold hands at the table, close your eyes, and give thanks for all the good stuff. Every family is a bit bonkers, but there is almost always so much for which to give thanks.

Choose to love deeply above all. It will cover over a multitude of sins, and who knows? It might even save Thanksgiving.

boring

"A certain man was preparing a great banquet and invited many guests. At the time of the banquet he sent his servant to tell those who had been invited, 'Come, for everything is now ready.' But they all alike began to make excuses.... The servant came back and reported this to his master. Then the owner of the house became angry and ordered his servant, 'Go out quickly into the streets and alleys of the town and bring in the poor, the crippled, the blind and the lame.' 'Sir,' the servant said, 'what you ordered has been done, but there is still room.' Then the master told his servant, 'Go out to the roads and country lanes and compel them to come in, so that my house will be full.'" —Luke 14:16-18, 21-23

College is a time ripe for gossip. College students are in a state of flux—learning, growing, and reinventing themselves along the way. They are figuring out important romances and friendships, and they are forming cultural and political tribes. This is all good and right, but in that zone of constant disequilibrium, we are exposed to all kinds of public embarrassments and mistakes, stupid decisions, heartbreaks, and dramatic rises and falls of personalities. It's juicy gossip galore.

But gossip—sharing unverified reports about someone else's behavior—is terribly harmful. When we talk about others rather than talking to them, people and relationships get damaged, sometimes beyond repair.

We even gossip about the news. We share unverified information, especially on social media, before fact-checking with third-party outlets. We find that real news is pretty boring. As it turns out, our opponents are not all that evil or smart. But out there on the internet are millions of voices with electrifying things to say about events in the world: mass government coverups, plots to control the world, mind-reading microchips in our hamburgers, and billionaires who are quite literally controlling the news media. Very exciting stuff.

As an example, after the 2016 election, MIT and Twitter did a study and found that completely fabricated stories were shared six times as fast as actual news stories. In all cases, the fake stories made certain political personalities or organizations look way more evil than they were in reality. The gossipers responded dutifully. But as with common gossip, passing along fake news truly does hurt actual, living, innocent human beings. It is wrong.

Jesus lived in a boring world. Things were quiet and uneventful all day, every day, from cradle to grave. But not once did Jesus pass along juicy stories about the king in Jerusalem or the young woman in the neighborhood. He was sober minded. He didn't need gripping gossip and conspiracy theories in his life.

Beware of the latest gossip about "what she did at the party" or conspiracy theories about a covert but influential organization responsible for something huge going on in the news. People are vying for your heart by appealing to your soul's craving for exhilaration. They are offering you cheap thrills that hurt innocent people. Jesus was able to find the spark of life by turning common water into wine, tables into parties, and the bedridden into clapping and dancing friends. This common carpenter forged a path to get his heart racing in his day-to-day life. His motive wasn't to get lost in the lives of celebrities or uncover secret political movements or share how drunk someone got last weekend. The real spark for Jesus came from lifting up those around him, from accepting absolutely no excuses because he was hosting a party for everyone to eat and laugh together face to face. And people wanted to hear his earned wisdom about real, everyday life. "Look at the birds," he said (Matt 6:26). "Where your treasure is, there your heart is also" (Matt 6:21). That's what came out of Jesus's mouth. What are you saying, texting, or posting about?

Jesus made life invigorating. So may you take the water right in front of you and turn it into wine. May you host the party with your life. May your house be full and your laughs be deep. May you be and make all the zest our world is craving.

And may you remember that when you are trying to decide what is true in this crazy world, the truth is almost always the most boring possible option.

red pills

The tempter came to him and said, "Since you are God's Son, command these stones to become bread." Jesus replied, "It is written, 'People won't live only by bread, but by every word spoken by God.'"
—Matthew 4:4

Neo was just a normal guy living a normal life when he begins to learn that he has been someone important all along. He follows a rabbit trail of clues until he finally meets a cool guy in shades and leather named Morpheus, who offers him a red pill.

If he will swallow this red pill, Neo's matrix-infused blindness will finally begin to unwind, and he will see "just how deep the rabbit hole goes." After taking that infamous pill, Neo learns two essential truths: 1) that everything everyone sees in the world is a masquerade for the real truth, which is that evil robots are ruling the world, and 2) Neo is the One. He is the one the world has been waiting on and upon whom everyone depends to save them from the fleece over their eyes.

The *Matrix* trilogy was hugely successful. But how could it not be? Neo is a seductive character. A totally average guy and all he does is discover a secret, and he becomes the center of everything. His peripheral life rockets into eternal importance. The movie writers understood something profound about human nature: our souls crave to be important because our life needs meaning. It's why so many kids want to become famous athletes, musicians, and actors. It's why so many adults hurt their families or their own health to climb corporate or political ladders. And its why conspiracy theories are so alluring to every single one of us. Let me explain.

A conspiracy theory is a belief that some covert but influential organization is responsible for a circumstance or an event—exactly like the plot of *The Matrix*. Sinister ideas about UFOs, QAnon, the Deep State, or some international foundation . . . are never made up without some facts at the base, and they are followed by very intelligent, moral, and normal people.

But consider what it would feel like to take a red pill and know that everyone around you was still asleep? Still in a matrix! Would your life feel more special if you could see what no one else could? That it was upon you to wake everyone up to see the matrix blinding their eyes? Yes! This is why *The Matrix* made three billion dollars and it's why millions of people bite into conspiracy bait.

The devil knows the same trick the writers of *The Matrix* did. Jesus was lonely and bored in the wilderness for forty days, and the devil saw his chance. He quoted isolated Scriptures and theological truth to spin lies that appealed to Jesus's ego. "Since you're God's son . . . It is written in Scripture. . . . ." "Prove you're the son of God to everyone. I'll give you all the kingdoms of the world." If the devil quoted something true like Scripture, how could Jesus argue with facts? With truth? But Jesus saw the spiritual game being played. He saw all the facts being left out of the conversation and he saw it was all an ego stroke. It was a red pill to turn an average, hungry, human, into someone special. Jesus was unpersuaded. He kept God at the very center of things and started his humble ministry.

It turns out, Morpheus and the devil are offering the same thing—the chance to be the star of the show. In Hollywood, that's a good thing. In the gospel, not so much. Biblically speaking, everything becomes a wreck if we ever become "the one." We may think it is harmless to entertain and pass along curious possibilities, but if Jesus would have taken the devil's pill, everything would have been lost. It is true for you and I as well.

Christian theology dictates that Jesus was the Son of God . . . that he was The One. But his very purpose on Earth was to give all that away. To become a humble, insignificant carpenter in an insignificant village in the middle of nowhere. Jesus demonstrated purpose in the irrelevancy of his own neighborhood. We all should do the same. There are very real and serious problems in our world. May we, like Jesus, give ourselves to that important work before us.

good people

Early on the first day of the week, while it was still dark, Mary Magdalene came to the tomb and saw that the stone had been removed from the tomb. So she ran and went to Simon Peter and the other disciple, the one whom Jesus loved, and said to them, "They have taken the Lord

> *out of the tomb, and we do not know where they have laid him." Then Peter and the other disciple set out and went toward the tomb . . . the other disciple outran Peter and reached the tomb first . . . but he did not go in. Then Simon Peter came, following him, and went into the tomb. He saw the linen wrappings lying there, and the cloth that had been on Jesus's head, not lying with the linen wrappings but rolled up in a place by itself. Then the other disciple, who reached the tomb first, also went in, and he saw and believed.* —John 20:1-8

It was that first Easter Sunday of 2020, when everyone was in lockdown. For those in ministry, it was a hard and stressful day, and after we led our virtual service, I was wiped out. It had been a long, difficult week. After lunch, it was time for my Sunday afternoon coma. I settled into my couch. I closed my eyes. I breathed deep and felt my body give way to the soft cushions beneath.

But my wife Ronella had other plans for me.

She and our five-year-old daughter had packed treat bags for friends in our church family, mostly folks who lived alone and were probably feeling a little more isolated and lonesome this Easter. She made me get up, drink a little coffee, and get the kids in the car. I gave her a little grief for it but obeyed. We drove around town. We knocked on doors and set down candy bags, and stood six feet away in the yard and chatted. Our daughter played with our two-year-old son in the grass. We shared some great conversation and smiles and laughs with people we hadn't seen in a while. We had tons of fun.

The truth is, visiting with folks who lived alone made them feel great on the inside, and it made us feel great on the inside. We got home that evening and my heart was full—much fuller than it was during my post-lunch coma or even during worship that morning. A lot of people's hearts were resurrected that Easter afternoon.

On the first Easter Sunday, Mary found the stone rolled away. She couldn't bring herself to look inside and ran off. But she got Peter and the Beloved Disciple. The Beloved Disciple arrived first, but he couldn't bring himself to enter. Peter came last and had the guts to enter the tomb. But it was the Beloved Disciple, the Bible says, who finally looked in and "saw, and believed." Resurrection was possible. Resurrection had happened.

Mary, Peter, and the Beloved Disciple tugged on one another until, finally, one of them got close enough to Jesus to truly encounter and receive the resurrection. None of them would have seen and believed alone.

One of the most important decisions you will ever make is to choose and create relationships with people who have strong, shared values. This is the best dating advice I can give you. Look for a spouse who has strong, shared values. Friends? Make friends with people who have strong, shared values. Role models? Find mentors who have strong, shared values. Community? Get involved with a local church that has strong, shared values. Employment? Find a company with strong, shared values.

Our values are is everything. Our character is everything. It carries us through the hardest situations and inspires us to become more life-giving people in the world. It's great neat to have relationships that connect through mutual recreational interests. And it's great for me to look at my wife every day and say, "Wow, how beautiful!" But our marriage is best when we are making one another better, lifting up one another, like iron sharpening iron, faith giving way to more faith, love making space for more love. This is true for all our relationships. And this is precisely what happened that first Easter morning. This is how we all tug and pull one another into encountering God's resurrection in our lives.

Do you want dead things within you and around you to come back to life? Get your Mary and your Peter and your Beloved Disciple. Strong, shared values. Seek those, build those. Tombs are supposed to be full of dead things. But maybe it doesn't have to be that way if we surround ourselves with good people.

how to get to heaven

> *How does God's love abide in anyone who has the world's goods and sees a brother or sister in need and yet refuses help? Little children, let us love, not in word or speech, but in truth and action.* —1 John 3:17-18

> *"Sell what you own, and give the money to the poor, and you will have treasure in heaven."* —Mark 10:21

It is easy for me to throw a pity party, to complain about how "little" money I make, the cheap groceries I eat, and the restaurants I avoid. It is easy to feel disappointed when I see the paint chipping on my old car, my old house in disrepair, or the vacations that others are enjoying.

Then I remember when I was a missionary in the poorest neighborhood of Bucharest, Romania. The families were stacked together in small concrete apartments, landscaped with garbage instead of grass or flowers or trees. The children slept on the concrete floors at night, rats scampering around, often with ten people in one- or two-room apartments. They went hungry. They couldn't afford to wash their (very few) clothes or their hair. They couldn't afford health care or dental care. They couldn't afford to go to school.

Really, I am not struggling or missing out, and I am certainly not poor. And yet I cling so tightly to my possessions and material dreams and somehow believe the lie that what I have is "not enough."

John was sensitive to this. It does something bad to our hearts to see someone in need and build a wall around us so we can keep our fun stuff. What we want to do is look the other direction. We want to look at the people who have more than us and say, "I don't have as much as them." But Jesus grabs our chins and turns our faces towards the poorest neighborhood of Bucharest. "Let us love in action."

Consider this a call to simplicity. "Sell everything you have and give to the poor," Jesus says. If we all lived more simply, we could focus more on the wisdom of savings and, even better, of making a huge difference in the lives of innocent people. It is nice to drive a cool car. It is nicer to change people's lives. The reality of my Romanian friends would be dramatically changed if those with greater wealth more generously invested in thoughtful missions that holistically ministered to poor communities.

Do you want eternity in your heart? All the infinity and joy and peace and fiery goodness of God's love blazing inside of you? You must rearrange your life priorities. You must sell everything you have. As Jesus said, you must give to the poor to inherit eternal life.

Eternal life living of inside us looks like living simply and giving generously and, finally, having treasure in heaven—a reality that comes to us now and endures beyond every grave and material possession.

deep

> *Tired as he was from the journey, he sat down by the well. . . .* "*Sir,*" *the woman said, "... the well is deep."* —John 4:6, 11

We go to class and to work and we try to crank out papers and cram in some study time. We try to squeeze in some fun, to be human, to laugh and play, but even that can be difficult and exhausting. The imperfect people around us stretch our limits. There always seems to be some drama, and sometimes we simply can't find sufficient time to sleep and sit and be at peace. We get tired on our journey.

Jesus offers the Samaritan woman "living" water (v. 10). She is perplexed because he has nothing with which to draw out the water, and the well they stand beside is deep. But a deep well is precisely Jesus's point. Jesus is the source of living water. Jesus is the well, and the well is deep indeed. Sometimes I just need strength from somewhere else because the caffeine from my coffee cup after the restless nights just isn't enough to meet the incredible demands of the day.

Energy. Life. When I have days like this, tired from the journey, I look to Jesus, who is the inspiration for my life. I pray. I remember the presence of his spirit. Jesus offers us a form a caffeine that nothing and no one can offer quite as well—Jesus offers us purpose for our day. Purpose is a deep well. It is the deepest well. We can take on whatever challenge comes our way today if we have a reason for what we do. In all the normal, mundane things of life, we can see an opportunity to be the light and love of God to others, to build God's kingdom on Earth, and to offer our minutes up to God as an act of worship.

Are you tired? Stressed? Jesus has a purpose for your life today. Perhaps you too will find Jesus to be a deep well of living water for your life. Pause, pray, look, contemplate, trust, and worship. Remember that you are not alone. As Jesus told the woman, "If you knew the gift of God you would have asked him and he would have given you living water" (v. 10).

people

Jesus was standing by the lake, with the people crowding around him and listening.... He got into one of the boats... and asked to be put out a little from shore. Then he sat down and taught the people from the boat. —Luke 5:1, 3

The word is out, and most folks agree: people can be annoying. And it seems like the more you have to be around people, the more annoying they can become. Roommates and teammates and boyfriends/girlfriends and ex-boyfriends/girlfriends and loud and gross and mean and unreliable people.

In the midst of our frustrations with people whom we cannot control, who do not act according to our desires and needs, things come out sideways—harsh words and bitter feelings and behind-the-back kind of talk.

For his entire three years of ministry, Jesus was constantly pressed in by a desperate and huge crowd of people. The Gospels indicate that at times it induced stress and exhaustion for him. It was too much. He couldn't breathe, couldn't accomplish what he needed to accomplish.

So sometimes he set boundaries.

Luke records two steps Jesus took in a moment of too many people. First, Jesus stepped away from the crowd at the shore and got into a boat. He put up a definite boundary between himself and the people he loved—not out of anger or hatred but out of love for them. Second, he sat down, faced them, and continued teaching. Despite the little distance he had established, Jesus did not turn his back on them. Jesus still sat down with them. Jesus still spoke with them.

Sometimes, like Jesus, we need to set up definite boundaries with the people we love the most (or the least). But also like Jesus, we are called to continue loving them and finding ways to connect with them. At times, we are wounded by people we love or we feel suffocated by people or sense an unhealthy level of time spent with certain people. It's OK to step into the boat and put a little water between you and others. Just remember to sit down, face them, and continue to love them.

loneliness

"Don't you know me, Philip, even after I have been with you such a long time?" —John 14:9

To be known—it's something we want so much. I think it's written deep in the fabric of our souls. There is a permanent craving to be intimately connected to, and known by, someone else. Even if we struggle with trust and fear and relationships, deep down underneath it all we desire to be fully known and accepted.

So it is hard to feel lonely. To have no close friendships. To have no one to be in love with or be married to. To sit in your room and watch your screen all alone. To feel so unsure of where to sit in the cafeteria or what to do with yourself on a Friday night. And it can be equally frustrating when, as with Jesus, some of our closest peers don't truly know us. They seem content with the shallow projection of ourselves we have posted online or around others.

It is helpful to remember that Jesus spent much of his life feeling misunderstood. He was never married, never had children. One of his best friends betrayed him by kissing him on the cheek, while his other best friends ran away during his darkest trial. Jesus, just like you, was lonely and, in a very real way, unknown by his closest friends. The 139th Psalm, with which Jesus was undoubtedly familiar, sings about God with powerful words; I imagine Jesus singing them often in times of loneliness:

> O LORD, you have searched me and known me.
> You know when I sit down and when I rise up;
> you discern my thoughts from far away.
> You search out my path and my lying down,
> and are acquainted with all my ways.
> Even before a word is on my tongue,
> O LORD, you know it completely.
> You hem me in, behind and before,
> and lay your hand upon me.
> Such knowledge is too wonderful for me;
> it is so high that I cannot attain it.
> If I take the wings of the morning
> and settle at the farthest limits of the sea,
> even there your hand shall lead me,
> and your right hand shall hold me fast.
> If I say, "Surely the darkness shall cover me,
> and the light around me become night,"
> even the darkness is not dark to you;
> the night is as bright as the day,
> for darkness is as light to you. (vv. 1-6, 9-12)]

Maybe we are not as alone as we feel. Maybe we are known by God like the psalmist sang. Our solidarity with Jesus and our relationship with God can help carry us through times of loneliness.

December

home and family

"Foxes have dens, and the birds in the sky have nests, but the Son of Man has no place to lay his head." —Matthew 8:20

"Whoever does the will of my Father who is in heaven is my brother, sister, and mother." —Matthew 12:50

I grew up in the South, with big houses and open fields, Southern drawls, and three siblings running around antagonizing me. Our family spent weekends together at the lake, and our extended family in another town was a huge part of our lives. But at twenty-seven years old, I found myself living as a missionary in a tiny apartment in the poorest neighborhood of Bucharest, Romania—one of the densest cities in one of the poorest countries of Europe. Living abroad was exciting in many ways, but to be honest I found it to be very hard. No one understood my jokes or listened to my banjo music or knew what chicken and dumplings were. I was far from my beloved family and what I thought was home.

Family and home mean everything to us. But the meandering paths of life have a way of calling them both into question. They are made complicated if we move away or grow up and learn more about ourselves, or maybe home and family have always been a hard source of pain for us.

Jesus was born in Bethlehem, was a refugee in Egypt, moved back to Nazareth, and then at age thirty became a traveling healer and teacher. Ultimately, he died in a city not his own. We never hear about his dad after he is twelve years old; it seems like Joseph is dead when Jesus is an adult. Jesus never got married, never had kids, never even had a pet dog.

Our modern culture touts a nuclear family with a big house, a mom, a dad, 2.5 kids, and a dog named Spot. Jesus absolutely does not do that. Jesus does not say things about home and family looking a particular way.

For Jesus, home and family take many different shapes over the course of one's lifetime. Everyone's family is going to look different. There will be things like death and divorce and migration and more, all of which will disrupt someone's fantasy that we could or should all live in one place forever, with a perfectly assembled nuclear family unit.

Jesus never let go of the "Nazareth" part of his identity, and he loved his mother until the end. But what is undeniable for Jesus, what is nonnegotiable for him, is that home and family must be more expansive, diverse, and spiritual than in our wider culture.

The great vision of Christianity and "church" is what the Reverend Dr. King called the "beloved community," a spiritual home and family. It is a place where you know and are known by others, a place where you care for and are cared for by others, most especially by our "heavenly Father," who is God. Some people are understood, respected, and loved better by their church than by their own family of origin.

Ironically, this alternative way of living helps us love those original families even better. It helps us have an extra sense of rootedness and love, so when our own families let us down or loved ones pass away, we have something else in which to rest. And if there are toxic systems in families, we are less prone to getting pulled into them ourselves. Finally, we are more equipped to enjoy our families and current homes when they don't fit the perfect mold that our culture celebrates. We are freer to just be what we are in all the strangeness or brokenness of our messy family stories. As I write this, my foster daughter is smiling at me over breakfast cereal. She looks nothing like me. Jesus says, "Who cares?" We are a beloved community, a spiritual family, and we are building a spiritual home.

This Christmas, may you give thanks for what your family and home are by remembering the beloved community, the extra home and extra family, that Jesus has so graciously and generously given to you and to anyone who will open their hearts to receive it.

free time

> *"'Lord, when was it that we saw you hungry and gave you food, or thirsty and gave you something to drink? And when was it that we saw you a stranger and welcomed you, or naked and gave you clothing? And when was it that we saw you sick or in prison and visited you?' And the king will answer them, 'Truly I tell you, just as you did it to*

one of the least of these who are members of my family, you did it to me.'" —Matthew 25:37-40

In all four Gospels (Matthew, Mark, Luke, John), there are only two passages in which Jesus tells people how they can inherit eternal life after they die. In our typical, modern vernacular, we would describe this as "getting saved" or "going to heaven." If you doubt that Jesus talked so little about how to go to heaven after you die, look it up yourself!

Even more surprising is that Jesus does not refer to a laundry list of beliefs for life after death: "you must believe this, you cannot believe that." Here and in Luke 18, Jesus simply refers to what you do for "the least of these"—the poor, the imprisoned, the sick, and the "stranger" (meaning immigrants, refugees, and those who are different from you).

Jesus is less interested in after death. He is more interested in before death.

Jesus is less interested in where you will go. He is more interested in where you are.

Jesus is less interested in what you believe. He is more interested in what you do about your beliefs.

Many of us are about to have nearly four weeks of break time, and I want you to simply listen to Jesus's words. With the spare time you have, will you commit to spending time in local nursing homes? Visiting your aging grandparents? Serving at a local homeless shelter? Helping kids with homework? How can you take the time you have to give food to the hungry, give water to the thirsty, and offer welcome to immigrants and refugees in your community? How can you visit the sick and imprisoned in a way that obeys Jesus's incredible words? What will you do in this life and in this place? What will you do about your beliefs? You have four whole weeks of opportunities to serve Jesus!

To forsake people in need is to forsake Jesus; those were Jesus's own words on the matter. Surely you can do something. Maybe you can do a lot. What better way to celebrate the birth of Jesus than to "do unto him" by doing unto the least of these in your midst?

expensive blenders

"Do not store up for yourselves treasures on earth... for where your treasure is, there your heart will also be." —Matt 6:19-21

Right after my wife and I got married, we felt absolutely certain that we had to buy a very specific, very expensive blender. It was right during the "Great Recession," and I could not find a job in my transitional season. But sure enough, I found a way to purchase a blender that needed almost three full days of working for minimum wage to afford.

I told everyone about our blender. Friends would come over; I would show it to them. I would say, "Hey, let me show you my blender." Everyone politely nodded, but no one ever cared about the blender.

Our culture has perfected the science of making *stuff* cheap. (In other places and times, *stuff* is expensive, while things like health care or education are more affordable.) So we have an endless game to play in our world: see the next thing you want to buy, drool until you own it, then decide on the next thing, and on and on it goes.

This shallow focus on toys and fashion diverts our gaze from the wounds within ourselves that need to be healed and all the immature ways we navigate conflict and crisis in our lives. In other words, our materialism papers over the hard things within; it distracts us from what is most important.

Like the Trinity, in whose image we were created, God created our hearts for relationship with God and others: to live lives of deep intimacy and presence to one another and to the Holy Spirit, to share generously with the poor, to talk for hours around fires at night, to go on walks with loved ones, to stay a moment before leaving the car to breathe slow and pray deep.

Notice how the verb tense shifts in Jesus's words: "where your treasure is" versus "your heart will be." In other words, today, we buy something, believing we have become its owners. Soon, though, and without realizing it, our something will own us. One follows the other.

Jesus's invitation to you today is to aggressively push back against the pressures of the culture in your own life. Limit media exposure and limit shopping outings when you can. Hold fast to the truth that truly, things cannot produce joy in human life; relationships do. Learn to treasure prayer and eating food with people and serving those in need and chatting with gray-haired friends after church on a Sunday. If that is where your treasure and heart is, you will discover life much more abundant, right here and now and on into the rest of your days.

the origins of peace

> *"A farmer went out to sow his seed. As he was scattering the seed, some fell along the path, and the birds came and ate it up. Some fell on rocky places, where it did not have much soil. It sprang up quickly, because the soil was shallow. But when the sun came up, the plants were scorched, and they withered because they had no root. Other seed fell among thorns, which grew up and choked the plants. Still other seed fell on good soil, where it produced a crop—a hundred, sixty or thirty times what was sown."* —Matthew 13:3-8

The weather outside is frightening. If you look around enough, you'll some rough things happening in our world. There are storms. There is bad weather.

Bad weather is not good for crops and gardens. They need a good a balance of rain and nutrients and temperatures. But for the most part, bad weather is something every farmer and gardener knows is a possibility and tries to plan for. One of Jesus's most famous parables is often titled "the parable of the sower" by those who edit modern Bible translations. That is an interesting choice because the farmer himself demonstrates very little choice or agency or particular talent in his "seed scattering." It is also not a parable about seed because there is no distinction between different kinds of seeds. And it's not a parable about weather. There is no comment about different seeds getting different kinds of weather.

This is a parable about soil. Jesus is telling us that the circumstances of life land on different kinds of soil, and the soil—beneath the surface of things, deep in the darkness, inside the earth, where water and bugs and all kinds of hidden things are—is where seeds will wither or do something truly miraculous.

This cold Advent season, do you want to embody peace? Do you want to be at peace?

You will not find peace in the circumstances and the stories around you. You will not find it in good health and friendly people and nicer stuff and pleasant weather. The only thing you can do is go deep into yourself beneath the surface of things. You have to learn the spiritual path. You have to learn how to pause in your days. To quietly listen to your breathing and pay attention. To pray. To share with God the things disappointing you, hurting you, angering you. To share with God the sins and mistakes you are making. To give thanks to God for every good thing you enjoy. To trust God with the burdens making you anxious. To surrender your whole self to doing God's will.

In the spiritual reflections of worship and Scripture, we cultivate soil within us that is neither rocky nor shallow nor thorned. Jesus offers us a different path in life, a way of cultivating soil within us that is deep, dark, rich, and at peace, no matter how frightening the weather is outside.

Today, even if the weather is ugly, God is scattering good seeds your way. May you give your full self to cultivating rich soil so you can grow Christ's peace for our world. The world desperately needs that.

boat ride

> *[The king] sent and had John beheaded in prison . . . . Then [John's] disciples . . . went and told Jesus. When Jesus heard it, he withdrew from there by boat to a solitary place by himself. But when the multitudes heard it, they followed him on foot from the cities. And when Jesus went out he saw a great multitude; and he was moved with compassion for them, and healed their sick.* —Matthew 14:10, 12-14

The morning my grandfather died, my wife and I got in a silly fight. I overreacted to something trivial. Have you ever caught yourself overreacting to things? Or being weirdly frustrated and defeated by what should be tiny nuisances along the way?

Jesus, on the other hand, is always overflowing with energy, power, and compassion for the masses. The Gospels record him running around fixing everything and changing the world—even when his beloved cousin, John the Baptist, was unjustly killed. They had known each other since before they were born. Surely, Jesus and his entire family was in disarray. But Jesus just pops over, is "moved with compassion," and heals all who are sick in the crowd. Jesus, it seems, is like a superman of patience and compassion.

But let's look again. "When Jesus heard it, he withdrew from there by boat to a solitary place by himself." Listen to Matthew's vocabulary: "withdrew," "solitary place," "by himself." How many words of solitude can Matthew squeeze into the same sentence when Jesus hears the tragic news? When a loved one dies, it is natural to express grief this way, by withdrawing from the crowd. This might concern friends and family, but usually it shouldn't. Like many people, Jesus did what he had to do to mourn and grieve this cousin he had so dearly loved for his whole life.

What was the result? The world pressed in on Jesus yet again, and he could overflow with compassion and healing for them. He took some time to sit in his boat. After that, he was ready. This year, you may have endured some losses. You may have lost a loved one. But you likely lost other things, like closeness with a friend, an old naiveté about something, or something that led to heartbreak or disappointment. We tend to pay less attention to those small losses. We tend to buck up and say, "It's nothing compared to what others have lost." But maybe even little losses deserve short boat rides and brief pity parties. Whatever you have lost, give it some time and space for grief. Write down, say out loud, or say in prayer whatever it is. "Hurt people *hurt people*," they say, because if we don't take our own boat rides and get away to grieve, these painful things end up coming out sideways. We overreact to little things and unfairly treat the ones we love. When we are connected to our own pain, we can connect with the pain of others. That is where healing happens.

As this year, which was probably a good one but also probably marked with some losses, nears its end and everyone is happy about Christmas, may you be like Jesus. May you find a little time to sit in your boat and attend to your heart and do what you must—feel sad, feel disappointed, feel betrayed, feel angry if need be. Your family and the world will be calling for you, and their needs for you are great. May honoring your loss make you a warm and steady source of God's compassion for our world.

soccer games

> *By common confession, great is the mystery of godliness:*
> *He who was revealed in the flesh,*
> *Was vindicated by the Spirit,*
> *Seen by angels,*
> *Proclaimed among the nations,*
> *Believed on in the world,*
> *Taken up in glory.* —1 Timothy 3:16

I remember playing one game of intramural soccer in college. There was a group of cute girls watching us that night. On the other team? A guy whose musical talent made me immensely jealous. I remember three things from that game: the musical prodigy also being way better than me at soccer, the cute girls cheering for someone else on my team, and myself almost scoring a cool goal but barely missing it and contributing basically nothing to my team, which lost the game badly. I felt beat down and small after that soccer game.

Have you ever felt like you were inferior to others? Or unloved? Have you ever walked across the grass on a cool spring night and wondered if you had a place in this world? I'm remembering this ancient Christian creed regarding the resurrection of Jesus—something the very first Christians said together in worship when they remembered his resurrection: "Jesus was vindicated by the Spirit."

Crucifying someone was a common practice in Jesus's world. It was reserved for slaves and political traitors. And the mob mentality, the "right equals might" spirit of that age, meant that anyone crucified was roundly considered unloved and unlovable, someone totally and indisputably without honor in this world.

So to believe that God had resurrected Jesus from the grave and that Jesus had triumphed over that cross meant a vindication of his belovedness, a restoration of the real truth of the matter. The resurrection of Jesus meant that he had been released from claims that he should be ashamed and rejected and unlovable. That is what the word "vindication" means. That is what resurrection is.

Together, the early worshiping Christians would say this creed, believing that resurrection was available to them as well, that God was offering to them and to you and to me a vindication of our belovedness, a restoration of the truth that we are worthy of love and belonging, that we have a place in this world, that God has a plan for our lives, that we each have something unique and important to give. God is offering us a different story to believe about ourselves.

This is resurrection life. This is what is offered to us today, because all our crosses have been turned upside down and our graves have been robbed. Every story of shame and rejection that you or anyone else tells you is a lie. Will you open your empty hands and receive this resurrection story? Will you receive the vindication and restoration of your belonging and belovedness? You are beloved not because of the great things you have done and the praise you have earned and the soccer games you have or haven't won but simply because God has thrown down your cross and stomped God's foot and said it is so because God meant it. Together, with our sometimes frail and unsure voices, we can recite that creed again. We can proclaim that message of resurrection again to the nations.

plosions

"You are to name him Jesus, for he will save his people from their sins."
—Matthew 1:21

Coming home for Christmas or visiting family can spark a lot of "plosions." We can explode on the nagging mom, the brother who doesn't know how to keep his mouth shut, or the dad who is too old-fashioned. Or we can implode with the boredom of four weeks off, the shaming voice of a parent, or the lack of connection in our family. We withdraw, isolate, stare at screens, and distract ourselves. All of these "plosions" are ways we try to navigate complicated and difficult people, relationships, and the shifting tides of life. They can make us feel better, put someone in their place, or distract us for a moment, but ultimately they always do more harm than good.

Jesus had his own word for the tragic ways we cope with our discomforts, insecurities, and scars. He called it sin. Sin means "missing the mark." It means we could have dealt with a hard situation by hitting the bullseye, but we chose the easier path and missed it. The bullseye of handling a hard moment or relationship perfectly is admittedly a small and hard one to hit. Nevertheless, the word *sin* illuminates the miss and says, "There is hope to do better next time."

Jesus taught us a better way to deal with the complications of family life, romance, friendship, and the hard and often lonely path of growing up and changing. He modeled a life that would save us from our sin—those explosions and implosions that make things worse. He taught us how to make hard relationships and hard situations better through how we respond instead of worse by how we react. Over time, as we continue to study and follow Jesus, we are slowly saved more and more from the messes we used to create, the ways we used to make bad situations worse. Slowly (more quickly, I wish!), we become the ones who make bad situations better. Jesus's example that he lived out day to day, from his vulnerable infancy to his life of healing and teaching to his offer of forgiveness at his crucifixion to his resurrection, shows us a better way. We are saved by grace through the faithfulness Jesus offered us.

This is good news for Christmas. It is the message that you have the power to carve a better path and make a better life for yourself. That next year can be better than this one. When we put Jesus in the driver's seat and say, "Show me the way," Jesus saves us from our sin. Jesus saves us from ourselves. Jesus doesn't change the people around us. He doesn't give us great parking spots or perfect health, and he doesn't snap his finger and make tuition, phone bills, or pizza free of charge. Jesus doesn't save us from the normal challenges of life. Jesus saves us from ourselves. Jesus saves us from our sin. That, in the end, changes everything. That is a revolutionary offer of hope.

van rides to Disney

> *"The coming of the kingdom of God is not something that can be observed, nor will people say, 'Here it is' or 'There it is,' because the kingdom of God is in your midst."* —Luke 17:20-21

If you're not tired or stressed or depressed or anxious today, chances are that someone around you is. There's a good chance that every day, you work with or drive by someone who is going through a tough time right now. This world is a tough place.

We religious folks often set up a deal with people: "Look, I know it's tough, but believe x, y, and z, and after you're dead, everything will be great because you'll go to heaven!" Salvation is something that is somewhere else for a later time. The result is that we spend a great deal of time making sure you get the transaction just right. You say the right words, clock in to church enough, and stop cussing when you smash your finger.

But think about what Jesus said: "The kingdom of God is in your midst."

Today, this very instant, the kingdom of God is among you, right now and right here. Salvation is something you experience today in your actual life. God's kingdom is not Disney World. It's not a vacation spot for which you save all your money to fuss with the family on a long van ride through central Florida with no air conditioning until you finally stand in long lines to see the big castle and hear the song "It's a Small World" sung by creepy animatronics.

God's kingdom is back at home where your family and your job and your church and the traffic are. God's kingdom is where you find unconditional love, peace, and laughter in God's Spirit.

In his letter to the Roman church, the Apostle Paul said that the kingdom of God is not eating and drinking; it is justice, peace, and joy in God's Spirit (Rom 14:17).

The destination of Disney World is far away and a long time off, but the kingdom of God is not. Today, may you choose to receive God's kingdom and God's salvation. Don't wait until you die. Don't wait until you graduate or have X amount of dollars or move out of your deadbeat town. Justice, peace, and joy—receive them right where you are. Live into them. Let God's kingdom life of justice, peace, and joy eclipse your exhaustion, your stress, your negativity, your anxiety. Let it transform the darkness of this world we drive by and work in every day. Let God's kingdom of justice, peace, and joy sustain you, transform you, and save you in the normal, mundane life you live with the people you love and struggle to love.

judgment

"And this is the judgment, that the light has come into the world, and people loved darkness rather than light because their deeds were evil."
—John 3:19

One night last week, I was walking my dog when to my horror she started going #2 in someone's yard and I realized I had no bag for it. Far from my house, I slipped away under the cover of darkness, hoping no one would see our stinky deed. The truth is, when we prefer darkness, anonymity, and secrecy, it's because what we are doing is wrong—like leaving dog poo in some kid's front yard.

It is unfortunate, then, that modern technologies have made it easier to keep us hidden in that darkness. Think about it: you can be so hyperselective in what you reveal (if you reveal anything at all) through digital interfaces—interacting with social media, commenting on articles and videos, and viewing pornography. Even text messages hide a huge part of ourselves, reducing the way we assert our human experience to someone else through that small amount of text from their far-off screen. In this virtual world, we are all less real and less connected, so we are less exposed than we would be in real life.

So here's the question: if we are drawn to these platforms, what's behind that draw?

Jesus has some feelings about this. When we avoid the light, when we don't want the full picture of our whole selves to be exposed, when we prefer anonymity or a filtered version of ourselves, Jesus says we face a moment of judgment. It is revealing something about the state of our spiritual health when we are drawn to these platforms, away from face-to-face conversation with our family, friends, and neighbors.

Jesus invites us to close our laptops, delete social media from our phones, and just put our phones down altogether. Talk to people incarnate—in the flesh. Physical human relationships are scarier, harder, and sometimes more boring than online ones. But all of those things conspire together to shape our spiritual character and our social skills into something much stronger. Incarnation—in the flesh—is what Jesus lived and wants you to live. Jesus wants you to live in the light, where people see your flaws and choose to love you anyway. Today, may you come into the brave light where things can feel hard and scary but where God and God's salvation are always ready for you.

heartbreak

> *He had no beauty . . . to attract us to him,*
> *nothing in his appearance that we should desire him.*
> *He was despised and rejected by mankind,*
> *a man of suffering, and familiar with pain.* —Isaiah 53:2-3

Until I fell in love with woman who is now my wife, heartbreak was my least favorite part of adolescence and young adulthood. It stinks getting rejected by someone. It's almost as miserable as turning someone else down.

I read somewhere that rejection is one of the most painful experiences a human can live through—that it destabilizes the sense of belonging we need for survival, that it temporarily lowers our IQ, and that it is even the greatest catalyst for human violence and aggression. Rejection hurts. You'd have to be crazy not to go crazy if you felt rejected by someone you cared about.

Jesus was rejected by nearly all his best friends and followers when he was betrayed to the cross, "rejected by mankind." That is helpful for normal people like you and me because in that painful experience, Jesus meets us right where we are. Jesus heals our pain by touching it and shows us a better way.

Jesus didn't lash out. He didn't rebuild his ego by slandering people or deal with the hurt with alcohol or promiscuity or whatever else. He didn't pretend like it didn't hurt. Instead, Jesus chose forgiveness, at one point crying out from the cross, "Father, forgive them, because they don't understand what they're doing" (Luke 23:34).

If she turned you down, if he broke your heart, if you weren't invited to the party . . . Jesus knows exactly how you feel. He meets you in your pain, touches it, and heals it. And Jesus, who hung on the cross and endured the crowd's insults, shows you that in your rejection, the path ahead is to admit the truth of how bad it hurts to someone you trust and to offer a forgiving heart to anyone whom you feel has hurt you.

the first Christmas

When Herod realized that he had been outwitted by the magi, he was furious, and he gave orders to kill all the boys in Bethlehem and its vicinity who were two years old and under, in accordance with the time he had learned from the magi. —Matthew 2:16

The first Christmas ever was marked by the violent murder of all the baby boys in a village. Can you imagine how terrible that was? I'd rather not think about it myself. Still, I think it helps to envision two pictures, side by side: one is Herod's village-wide infanticide, and the other is what we usually see of the first Nativity—a glowing, peaceful mother, a humbled husband, bowing shepherds, a happy baby boy ("no crying he makes"). The two images could not be any more different. The fact is that Christmas has always existed in a world of both brilliant joy and also the worst possible pain.

The remarkable thing about the first Christmas was not how pleasant and cute the barnyard animals were or how beautiful the angels in the sky were—the things that make for great children's pageants every December. What was remarkable was the Divine revelation that God, to all our surprise and wonder, is not only above us but right alongside us in all the splendor and mess of human life. God is truly with us. If God is with us, surely there is hope despite whatever is happening to us or around us. Jesus, the Son of God, took on human flesh, experienced being a frightened baby, an insecure thirteen-year-old boy, and a man working hard as a carpenter. Finally, the Son of God was brutally murdered by violent people. God is with us even during violence and death. There is hope. Even when things are tough. Even when tragedy strikes.

There is still hope if our ideal Christmas image is disrupted this year by a stomach bug, a family fight, financial worries, a painful breakup or, yes, even the loss of someone we love. Tragedy and trial are an integral part of the DNA of Christmas. If our holiday is a comparatively painless one, that can free us up to think about loving others in need—visiting homebound and nursing home-bound folks or taking care of some overdue chores at a local nonprofit or church. Like God in a manger, we can become incarnate—in the flesh, part of the suffering world around us.

gifts

"Lazarus is dead.... Father, I thank you." —John 11:14, 41

I know that for many people, Christmas is like the commercials: it's good to get together and laugh with family, eat a roasted duck on a candlelit table, open up a thousand dollars' worth of presents from under a perfectly lit tree while the snow falls gently outside.

But for most, it's not quite like this.

Maybe you have rejoined a complicated family. Or a sibling screwed things up this year. Or your family lost a loved one. Maybe your family has hit hard times financially, or maybe you have grown and changed so much this year that it is strange to return home.

I think of a time when Jesus experienced loss and anxiety and difficulty. His friend Lazarus died. Jesus's friends and family were devastated and sad and even angry. Some even blamed Jesus: "If you had come earlier, my brother would not have died!" (v. 21, 32) and "Could you not have kept this man from dying?" (v. 37).

The story talks about Jesus groaning within himself and even weeping.

This is my first gift of advice for an anxious Christmas: imitate Jesus, and feel the feelings. If someone is stressing you out, say it out loud to yourself or someone you trust. If someone you love is disappointing you, if things are hard, if you're mad at God for the way things are going, say it out loud! Don't deny or minimize what's going on inside.

Second, Jesus prayed, "Father, I thank you that you have heard me." Jesus leveraged this great practice called "prayer" in a time of difficulty. Right there, he recognized God's presence with him in the storm. Prayer is an amazing tool each of us has in our tool belts that we often ignore. What's going on? Talk to God about the things that weigh down your heart. Like Jesus, remember in prayer God's presence, faithfulness, and goodness. When times are dark, we are saved by remembering the brightness of God's enduring presence and brilliant love.

This Christmas, you will be a light to your family when you rise above the chaos instead of falling victim to it. May you navigate the complex dynamics of family and life in the way of Jesus. May you confess what is going on inside your head and your chest. May you pray without ceasing.

And even if your family isn't laughing and you eat boxed macaroni and cheese instead of roasted duck and the tree tips over and the cold rain falls instead of snow, may you create a very merry Christmas and a happy New Year.

how to be happy

"Do you want to get well?" —John 5:6

My back was aching and my legs were tired and my eyes were bleary, and still I scrubbed the skillet and loaded the dishwasher. I had to get done as soon as possible so I could get to bed as soon as possible so I could fall asleep as soon as possible, because in just a couple of hours our baby would wake us up again to be fed. Early the next morning I would get up and go to work again. This was my life: go to work and care for our babies and take care of our house all while hoping that nothing else would break in my car, saying "no" to every desire to spend money on anything fun in order to make ends meet.

Every day I would get in the car and listen to a bluegrass song, "Where's a Train When You Need One?" The song lamented a world without trains to hop on and run away from life and its worries.

Have you ever felt like happiness was hard to come by?

Jesus met a man who felt sorry for himself. For thirty-eight years he was stuck on the ground with no working legs and no friends to carry him. He said that every once in a while, something healing would happen in the water nearby, just out of his reach. He could never get up and walk, and as a result his life never changed.

Until Jesus entered into his life. Jesus did not grab his hand and pick him up. He did not take him to any kind of magical waters to fix his legs. He did not pronounce a magical prayer or perform some kind sign. He never even touched the man. All Jesus did was ask him if he wanted to get well and then tell him to get up and walk.

Do you want to get well? Get up and walk. Whatever life is hammering you with right now, you have to ask yourself the question, do I want to get well? Or do I prefer the comfort and ease of feeling sorry for myself on the ground? Is it easier to lie down than to fight for my joy and happiness?

If you want to get well, you must get up and walk. No more excuses or waiting for miracles. Get up and walk. Choose to live every moment with gratitude and positivity and goodness and faith. Shower kindness and joy on everyone you meet. Say lots of good prayers. Be better than your circumstances.

Eventually, I decided I had to fight for my life. I had to fight for joy. I had to fight for my relationships. I decided I was not going to be defeated by life. I was going to be happy in the joyous way of Jesus. We have to remember that around us and within us, laughter is contagious. Joy, gratitude, peace, compassion, and faith spread wide. We just have to choose these on the front end and get the heavy rock rolling. Martin Copenhaver says that Jesus was inviting this man to be a part of the healing partnership.[12] No one can love you or fix you or help you without you choosing to get up and walk because you have finally decided that, truly, you want to get well.

the observer

> *Now there was a Pharisee, a man named Nicodemus who was a member of the Jewish ruling council. He came to Jesus at night and said, "Rabbi, we know that you are a teacher who has come from God. For no one could perform the signs you are doing if God were not with him." Jesus replied, "Very truly I tell you, no one can see the kingdom of God unless they are born again."* —John 3:1-3

The hours leading to the birth of my first child were fraught with dire warnings of catastrophe, a room full of trembling doctors and nurses and worried parents. But our daughter came into this world whole and safe. She was frail and vulnerable, totally naked, and all at once both ugly and the most beautiful human I had ever seen. Crying, she was carried around the room, the air thick with awe and wonder at God's miracle of new life.

In my life, I have been an observer, one to stay safe in a womb where I drink in pretty words and key-turning data points and watch others do the talking and stumbling. I am addicted to inhaling information all day, every day. I love school and books, and in meetings and gatherings I often defer from speaking until called upon.

---

12. Martin Copenhaver, *Jesus Is the Question* (Nashville: Abingdon, 2017), 71.

I sometimes wonder if Nicodemus was like this. He was an educated, philosophically oriented individual. He was an indisputably open and curious thinker. He wanted to know more about Jesus. But like me, his curious mind was a way of staying safe. There is danger in acting but not in thinking. Coming by night and shrouded by the ruse of "I'm still thinking it over," Nicodemus stayed safe from the burn of daylight on his skin, from a bad choice hurting his career, from a fake messiah holding his heart.

This observer thing I have translates poorly into my most precious relationships. I keep my mouth shut and my brain running. I listen and analyze. The sour parts fester into bitterness, judgment, resentment. I leave conversations, and maybe I yell and shout on the inside, letting the bullets bounce around inside my own skull. Even in the secrecy of prayer, I struggle to tell God the ugly things I feel and desire, preferring flowered praises and intercession. I am so grateful for this curious Nicodemus in me, but this observer, safely hidden in the dark, is a curse too.

Things never quite worked out between Jesus and Nicodemus. He faithfully anointed Jesus's dead body for burial, but he never showed up in the vulnerable, bright light of day. John's Gospel ends and we don't know where Nicodemus stands on the Jesus question.

Indeed, to tell a person "you must be born again" is a tough sell, for birth is a moment of utter and perfect weakness. And not just weakness, but utter and perfect dependence on the hands and breasts that hold and nourish you. You cannot be born again without being seen and known in your entirety. Cuss words, hurt feelings, warts and all. There are lots of clothes and shields and hats and makeup and titles and accolades that must be shed.

Saying out loud that you are angry, afraid, hurt, incapable makes you feel totally naked and vulnerable and dependent. But this is being born again. Whom could you trust to hold and nourish you, even when you look like that? Rebirth means telling the truth about yourself and the relationship instead of lying to maintain pleasantries. It's sharing your truth instead of lying to God, to yourself, to your family. These are all the ways we stop looking like Nicodemus, sliding along in the dark, and start looking like my daughter in the birthing room. These are the ways we find the kingdom of God thick in the air we breathe.

If we want this new, incredible, life-saving kind of kingdom in the life we build for ourselves, we cannot remain hidden in the dark, collecting information, only to muse and fume. Heaven, like a marriage or parenthood, like sonship, daughtership, siblingship, or whatever else, is not a thing you can study your way into. You must be born all over again. You must be known and seen in all your places and moments that are messy and frail. And this is the good news of the gospel—that you can trust God and the ones God has placed near to you in your most vulnerable moments.

habits

As his custom was, he went into the synagogue on the Sabbath day.
—Luke 4:16

"If you fail to plan, you are planning to fail." That's what Benjamin Franklin said. So now you have a short time until a new year arrives. A new year offers a new beginning, a fresh opportunity to take charge of our lives and write a great and redemptive story. Next year will consist of 365.25 days, each of which will consist of approximately 16 waking hours, each of which will consist of you choosing how to engage, respond, speak, think, and act. The world around you is going to make its own choices about what it will offer and do to you. But ultimately, you will create your year. You will write your story.

Still, our habits—the routines we choose to create—will pave many of the pathways for the hard choices we need to make. Habits make hard choices much easier. "If you fail to plan, you are planning to fail." Luke says that Jesus went to the synagogue every Sabbath day. He never had to think about it. It wasn't a choice. He didn't have to agonize about sleeping in versus going. His custom, his habit, was to go to synagogue if it was the Sabbath Day. Ultimately, his commitment to synagogue shaped him into the incredible spiritual leader he became in history.

Next year, I want to challenge you to establish habits of prayer, habits of exercise, habits of study/reading, habits of faith-based relationships and community. Maybe you have other habits you know you need to establish. These are things from which we so easily backslide. They require effort to choose to do. So we have to make a plan. "Every day I'm taking the first five minutes at my desk for prayers." "Every night I'm reading for ten minutes before lights out." "Every weekday morning I'm getting up at 6 a.m. to go for a jog." Remove the choice element, the daily "oh yeah, I should read more often, but TV sounds easier tonight." Late December is the perfect time to plan out the habits that will shape your life in the new year.

Good things are not just going to come your way. Jesus did not save the world because one day great opportunities were just handed to him on a platter. And for you, your ability to serve others, help others, take responsibility for others, make the world a better place… it depends so greatly on you being your very best self… the self God intended on you becoming. What are the hard choices you routinely failed to make this year, and how can routines and habits, help make them a bit easier in the next? Jesus had his habits. What are yours?

Plan diligently now for what kind of story you are going to write this next year; for what kind of story you are going to write with your life.

Scripture Index

Genesis
1:27   190
4:10   157
32:31   45

Ecclesiastes
3:1-8   138

Song of Solomon
8:6-7   26

Job
1:8-11   102

Psalm
4:4   196
56:8   66
126:3   200
139:1-6, 9-12   214
139:22-23   197

Proverbs
3:13-18   186
3:24-25   188
31:4   5

Isaiah
40:31   75
53:2-3   226

Matthew
1:21   223
2:16   227
3:16-17   125
4:1-2   38
4:4   207
4:10-11   119
4:21-22   133
5:3   195
5:13   105
5:14a, 16   7, 14
5:21-22, 24   101
5:27-29   115
5:28-29   56
5:37   14
5:44   12, 28
6:6   196
6:10   203
6:19-21   218
6:21   110, 206
6:26   14, 109, 132, 206
6:27   151
6:28   68
6:34   144
7:1-2   145
7:7   148
8:20   215
9:36   17
10:13   163
10:29, 31   169

10:30	8, 14	10:47-49, 52	42
11:28-29	9, 140, 178, 191	10:50	66
12:36-37	80, 81	12:38-40	40
12:50	215	14:26	97
13:3-8	219	14:34	24
14:10-14	20	15:32	58
14:19	189	15:34	53
14:23	10		
16:26	191	**Luke**	
18:25-28	137	1:52-53	195
21:7-9	18	2:46	141
22:9	74	3:23	100
22:35-40	90	4:16-21	13, 141, 32
25:31-46	47, 113, 217	4:42	128
26:7-13	183	5:1, 3	212
26:36, 39	61	5:15-16	69
27:46	197	5:29-30	168
28:27-28	5	5:30-31	11
		6:17	48
Mark		6:42	185
1:11	88, 111	6:45	184
1:17	145	6:47-48	29
1:35	89	8:9-13	165
1:45	67	9:52b-56	22
4:40	188	10:33	76
5:34	182	10:40-41	39
6:56	16	13:11, 16	60
7:34-35	153	14:16-18, 21-23	205
8:17-18	99	15:2	127
8:23-25	96	15:18-20	121
8:31	41	16:5	84
9:24	45	17:5	181
9:50	94	17:14	93
10:6-8	19	17:20-21	224
10:17, 21	46, 210	18:1-5	135
10:18	63, 78	18:9-14	106, 199
10:21-22	166	18:19	179
10:30	65	19:37, 39-40	50
10:31	65	22:42-44	120, 203

23:34	49, 53, 163, 226	13:15	41
23:43	53	14:9	213
23:46	53	14:16, 18	177
24:3	55	14:26-27	3, 81, 163
24:30	200	16:21-22	27
24:31-32	94	17:9	202
		17:11	161

John

1:1	15	17:21-22	44, 78
1:14	4, 15	18:36	118
1:38-39	43, 85	19:26-30	53
2:3-10	112	20:1-8	209
3:1-3	152, 230	20:9	159
3:8	70	20:11	123
3:14-15	156	20:22	175
3:19	225	20:24-26	59
4:6, 11	211	20:25	176
4:10	212	20:27	125
4:14	134	20:29	104
5:6	83, 229	21:3-6	108
6:3-4, 10-11	173	21:15-17	61
6:12	175		
8:4, 7	30		

Acts

8:32-33, 35	25

8:32	165		
8:39	73		

Romans

9:3	79	5:3-4	139, 176
9:41	129	8:37	87
11:14	32, 33, 228	12:2	132
11:41	228	12:21	163
11:15	33	14:17	24
11:21	228		

1 Corinthians

13:7	182

11:25	34	
11:32	228	
11:35	32	

2 Corinthians

5:7	182

11:37	228	
11:43	35	
11:44	37	

Galatians

3:7	73

12:24	21	
13:3-5	51	

5:13   155
6:2   142

Ephesians
2:8   182

1 Timothy
3:16   221

James
4:14   192
5:16   157

1 Peter
4:8   204

1 John
3:14   161
3:17-18   117, 210

Revelation
3:8   31

Topic Index

addiction	38, 66
alcohol	143
anger	39
anxiety	3, 13, 39, 50, 128, 144, 151, 162, 168, 202
beauty	68
blame	30, 102, 106
boredom	94, 216
born again	151, 230
boundaries	212
calling/vocation	99, 133
celebrities	40
change and transition	3, 31, 138, 161, 186, 215
character	110, 139, 208
church	3, 44, 46, 63, 66, 74, 90, 121, 132, 153, 154, 160, 232
college	141, 186
community	11, 40, 44, 212
compassion	9, 17, 28, 60, 137, 140, 153, 220
confession	199
confidence	125
conspiracy theory	165, 166, 168, 205, 207
creation care	42, 131
cross, the	10, 21, 120, 155, 221
crucifixion	58, 61
cynicism	53, 168
daily habits	232
democracy and elections	18, 63, 85, 163, 165, 192, 195
demons	28
desiring fame	184

despair	13, 53, 97
doubt	45, 104
Enneagram	10, 51, 178, 230
evangelism	74
faith	21, 45, 104, 181
family	39, 73, 90, 118, 154, 204, 215
fasting	38, 119
fear	13, 188
forgiveness	49, 137, 163, 226
freedom	119, 154
friendship	11, 29, 121, 127, 132, 147, 179, 208, 226
God's plan	84
good news	25
gossip	80, 205
grace	62, 88, 104, 111, 137, 178
gratitude	94, 200
grief and sadness	73, 183, 220
health and exercise	16, 232
Holy Spirit	70, 81, 174, 177, 211
home	215
hope	7, 24, 25, 33, 34, 37, 53, 58, 61, 65, 75, 76, 79, 87, 95, 97, 107, 123, 139, 148, 159, 168, 173, 223, 227
identity	58, 65
immigration	113
introverts	169, 230
joy	12, 78, 94, 134, 153, 200, 229
judging	85, 145
justice	25, 46, 83, 135
leadership	5, 43, 63
loneliness and being single	19, 44, 160, 179, 181, 226
love	8, 12, 42, 53, 63, 76, 90, 96, 101, 105, 107, 111, 117, 118, 120, 127, 140, 143, 145, 161, 163, 183, 204, 221
lust	56, 115
marriage	19, 26, 44, 90, 208, 226
meditation	89, 109, 151, 174, 196
money	134, 110, 218

TOPIC INDEX

parents	133, 155
patience	96
peace	3, 69, 75, 81, 118, 144, 151, 211
pornography	56, 115
poverty	13, 15, 16, 17, 18, 105, 210
prayer	10, 69, 81, 89, 95, 109, 144, 148, 151, 153, 174, 177, 196, 197, 199, 200, 202, 203, 211, 219, 232
presence	50, 68, 84, 196
pride and humility	11, 48
purpose	84
racism	22, 58, 113, 135, 157, 168
redemption	142, 175
relationships	19, 39, 44, 120, 163, 169, 208, 212
resilience	32, 33, 34, 37
responsibility	30, 33, 62, 99, 100, 102, 106, 117, 143, 157, 159
rest	10, 128, 191
resurrection	24, 55, 58, 83, 120, 123, 124, 155, 159, 208, 221
sacrifice	10, 120
salvation	210, 216, 223, 224
self-hatred	9, 28, 65, 112, 117, 140, 178
serving others	5, 11, 29, 41, 51, 216
sex	26, 56, 115
silence	67, 69, 89, 196
sin	106, 199, 132, 223
social media and technology	67, 179
stress	3, 65, 69, 75, 211, 229
trusting God	45, 81, 104, 144, 169, 173, 177, 181, 189, 197, 202
vulnerability	4, 62, 66, 88, 124, 155, 169, 189, 230
wisdom	165, 186
worship	97, 151, 219

www.ingramcontent.com/pod-product-compliance
Lightning Source LLC
Chambersburg PA
CBHW071707160426
43195CB00012B/1605